TEACHING SPANISH

TEACHING SPANISH

A Linguistic Orientation

ROBERT L. POLITZER
Stanford University

CHARLES N. STAUBACH
University of Arizona

BLAISDELL PUBLISHING COMPANY

A Division of Ginn and Company

WALTHAM, MASSACHUSETTS · TORONTO · LONDON

Preface
TO THE REVISED EDITION

Our aim in publishing this volume remains the same as that stated in the *Foreword* to the first edition. We wish to express our thanks to scores of our students and to a number of our colleagues whose suggestions have been responsible for many of the clarifications in this revision. In particular, Mr. James A. Parr, of the University of Toledo, and Professor Lawrence Poston, Jr., of the University of Oklahoma, have been helpful. In spite of our best efforts, errors and infelicities surely remain, and for them the authors are, of course, responsible.

RLP

CNS

Stanford, California and
Albuquerque, New Mexico

Foreword

This book is a companion volume to *Teaching French: An Introduction to Applied Linguistics* (Blaisdell Publishing Company, 1965) by Robert L. Politzer. It deals with the teaching of Spanish—primarily the imparting of the basic skills at the high school or college level. It is a textbook on the application of linguistics, with heavy emphasis on application. We feel that the language teacher, primarily concerned with concrete problems facing him in his language classes, is not likely to pursue in detail the study of the rather refined and exacting science of language, unless he is first made aware of the possible contribution of this study to the solution of teaching problems. The first part of this book is, therefore, devoted essentially to general methodological considerations. In the second part, linguistic concepts are introduced, but the emphasis remains on the teaching of Spanish rather than its scientific analysis. It is our hope that many teachers will want to pursue the science of language more deeply and in greater detail than it has been dealt with in this book. The connections between language teaching and linguistics are varied and subtle; further study of linguistics will prove for language teachers a rewarding experience in terms of their teaching skills and competency.

The aim of this book is not to teach Spanish, but to show how to teach it on the basis of linguistic knowledge; the reader is presumed to have a mastery of the Spanish language, and the book aims to develop in the reader an awareness of the pattern conflicts between Spanish and English and the remedies which a "linguistic" teaching method can offer. We fervently hope that we have avoided the pitfall of describing the already familiar facts of the Spanish language under the guise of a new and different terminology. We also feel that this book supplements rather than duplicates various other pedagogical and linguistic works which have either appeared recently or are about to appear in the near future (general works on applied linguistics, laboratory methodology, or an exhaustive Spanish–English contrast analysis).

The authors accept joint responsibility for the whole of this volume. The basic plan and the general foundation laid down in the first five chapters are the work of Mr. Politzer, except as revised for specific application to Spanish by Mr. Staubach. The Spanish materials which are the subject of Chapters VI–VIII and some retouchings of Chapters IX and X have been provided by Mr. Staubach, whose contribution has in turn been checked and revised by Mr. Politzer.

RLP
CNS

Ann Arbor
May, 1961

Contents

PART ONE

CHAPTER I

The Meaning of "Applied Linguistics"

There is, or at least there ought to be, a very intimate relationship between linguistics, the scientific study of languages, and language teaching. Yet the exact nature of this relationship seems to be disputed; some language teachers, especially those coming from the linguistic camp, see in linguistics and its application to language teaching the answer to all the problems that have ever confronted the language teacher. Others feel that linguistics contributes nothing except a new jargon that can change little in the language teaching situation. For others, holding less extreme points of view, the application of linguistics to language teaching means an emphasis on an audio-lingual (aural–oral) approach, or the use of the language laboratory, or classes taught by native informants, or the "Mim-mem" method, which consists primarily of the student's mimicking sentences uttered by the instructor.

Perhaps some of the confusion concerning applied linguistics is due to the fact that so far comparatively little work has been done in showing the application of linguistics to the teaching of any one particular foreign language. The primary reason for this textbook is, then, to show how linguistics can contribute to the teaching of one particular language Spanish—to native speakers of American English. Yet before undertaking the demonstration of applied linguistics, the authors would like to summarize very briefly the most important contributions of linguistics to language teaching. These contributions concern two phases of language instruction: the preparation of teaching materials and the actual presentation and drill of teaching materials in the class-room and the laboratory.

1

(A) THE PREPARATION OF TEACHING MATERIALS

(1)   By comparing the linguistic analysis of the native language of the learner—in our case English—with that of the language to be studied—in our case Spanish—we highlight the major difficulties encountered by the learner. This comparison enables us to construct teaching and testing materials quite systematically and to give due emphasis to the points of real difficulty.

(2)   Linguistic analysis may enable us to describe the language to be learned more simply or economically than is done in conventional grammars. This simplification will, in turn, facilitate the task of the learner.

(3)   Linguists are primarily interested in **spoken language** and see in written forms only a secondary representation of the spoken word. Linguistic analysis will furnish rules of the spoken language which are often simpler than (or at any rate different from) the rules of the written language, which are given in many traditional grammars. There are various advantages for the teacher in being able to formulate rules concerning the spoken language; obviously, these are the only rules that can properly be used in the planning of the purely audio-lingual phase of any course, and even if writing and orthography go hand in hand with speaking, students should be aware of their behavior in speech as well as in writing.

(B) CLASSROOM PRACTICE

(1)   Linguists emphasize that **language is behavior** and that behavior can be learned only by inducing the student to "behave"; in other words, to perform in the language. Thus, linguists distinguish rather unanimously the learning of language (performing in the language) from the learning of rules and grammatical terminology. This does not necessarily imply that rules and grammatical terminology are superfluous and can be dispensed with altogether; but description and prescription cannot take the place of language learning itself.

(2)   Linguistic analysis gives an excellent clue as to what **units of behavior** should be taught in individual exercises. Linguistic analysis is basically a way of decomposing utterances of a language into their component elements until the linguist obtains the inventory of building

stones which the speaker of the language has at his disposal in order to construct those utterances. Language learning as viewed by the linguist is in a sense the direct application of this process of analysis. The learner gets to know slowly, systematically, and one by one each one of those building stones that has been identified and analyzed by the linguist, and how they fit together into structures.

Applied linguistics is, then, that part of linguistic science which has a direct bearing on the planning and presentation of teaching material. This means that applied linguistics is primarily connected with that branch of linguistic science which deals with the description and analysis of current contemporary languages: **synchronic** or descriptive linguistics. This does not mean that the other main branch of linguistics, historical or **diachronic** linguistics, is completely unrelated to language teaching. Historical linguistics is important insofar as it helps in understanding the present state of affairs. Only historical linguistics can provide a meaningful answer to the question why, which is so often asked by our students: Why are certain verbs irregular? Why are there two sets of pronouns in Spanish? and so on. The answers can only be given in terms of the history of the language. This means that the teacher should have a grasp of the essentials of that history. At the same time, historical linguistics does not have the same immediate bearing on teaching that descriptive linguistics has. Too much historical explanation or the confusion of historical statements with those describing the present state of affairs will only bewilder and confuse the student.

One point should be made clear from the very outset: linguistics or applied linguistics as such has no answer to many of the problems which are still confronting the language teacher; in other words, applied linguistics will not help us in designing the one method with which we can achieve fluency in a langauge after two years of high-school work. Applied linguistics does not tell us how to teach effectively in overcrowded classrooms, nor will it lead to the preparation of teaching materials which can be used efficiently on students of widely varying intelligence and ability in the same classroom. Linguistic science as such has no direct answer when it comes to some of the purely psychological factors in language learning, such as motivation and attitudes on the part of the student; nor should it be expected that in a language as well known and studied as Spanish, the application of linguistics will lead to major new discoveries concerning the basic facts of the language. Linguistic analysis of current Spanish speech may bring our ideas on Spanish somewhat more up-to-date or may lead to a more accurate description of such elusive features as intonation and stress. This is, however, not the major contribution of linguistics to teaching.

The major contribution of this science lies in the systematic comparison of English and Spanish and the application of a teaching methodology which, through systematic drills, attempts to build up the student's knowledge of the structure of the foreign language, while at the same time eliminating those errors which are caused by the patterns of the student's native English. It is primarily to the demonstration of these aspects of applied linguistics that this book will be devoted.

CHAPTER II

A Linguistic Teaching Method?

Our views concerning language teaching have been largely dominated by our concepts of language. The belief in universal grammar was the basis of the traditional grammar–translation approach. Semanticists interested in the meaning of language rather than the linguistic system itself elaborate teaching methods concerned with the relation of language to specific "sense" situations. Linguists interested in the linguistic systems emphasize in their approach the analysis and manipulation of structure. Our language-teaching methodology tends to reflect our views concerning the subject to be taught rather than a knowledge of the psychological processes involved in its acquisition.

Some linguists have taken the point of view that there is no such thing as a linguistic teaching method; linguistics as the study of language deals with the subject matter to be taught in a language course, not with the teaching method to be employed. Strictly speaking, this is true; yet the basic facts concerning the very nature of language seem to endorse some and contradict others of the currently employed methods of teaching.

How, first, do linguists see language?

A language may be defined as **the system of arbitrary vocal symbols by which the members of a speech community communicate with each other.** The word arbitrary in the above definition is in need of some further explanation. It implies that normally there is no intrinsic and necessary connection between the symbols and the concepts for which they are used. Exceptions to this normal state of affairs are, for instance, the onomatopoetic words, i.e., calling a dog a "bow-wow" in imitation of

5

the noise made by the animal. But usually the reason for any symbol or construction in language lies not in what is to be expressed but in (1) the history of the language and (2) the system of the language itself. In other words, a Spaniard calls a cat *gato* not because *gato* seems to be the sequence of sounds particularly suited to refer to a cat but because (1) the word evolved from a late Latin word *cattus*, which is the ancestor —the reason—for modern Spanish *gato*, and (2) if a Spaniard changed all or only one of the sounds of the word *gato* (let us say to *rato*), he would no longer be understood as referring to a cat: *gato* is what is required by the system of the Spanish language.

The fact that language is a system in which every particle receives its value from the total complex in which it functions is all-important. Perhaps an analogy may help to elucidate this point. Let us think of a linguistic system as a set of building stones that are available, again and again, to every speaker of the language, in order to build the bridge of communication between himself and others. A speaker of Spanish is asked: *¿Dónde está su libro?* Quickly he turns to the set available to him and answers:

A speaker of English in the same situation might have answered:

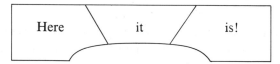

To pursue our analogy: the Spanish and the English bridges are the same insofar as they fulfill the same purpose. The Spanish and English utterances have the same meaning, but the individual building stones of Spanish have absolutely no relation to those of English—their shape, the very possibility of fitting them into this particular bridge was determined entirely by the Spanish set from which they were taken, and the same was true, in turn, about the English building stones.

A great many, perhaps most, of the mistakes made by a learner of a foreign language are the result of one simple and comprehensible failure: the learner mistakenly equates building stones of the foreign system with individual building stones of his system. He wants to use the foreign building stones as if they had been taken from his own set.

It is perfectly true that there are many constructions in which two languages parallel each other. These constructions are responsible for many of the errors of the students. They are a blessing in one way because they are easy in themselves; they are a curse because they establish that mistaken identification of building stones of different systems. Certainly

corresponds very nicely to

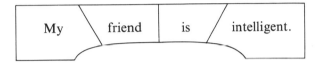

But it is also that type of construction which is indirectly responsible for such an impossible construction ("fractured Spanish") as, let us say:

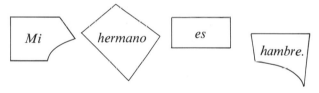

The fundamental lesson that every language student has to learn is simply that elements of one language cannot be equated with those of another language. Dictionaries are a necessary evil, of course, and good dictionaries try to remedy the evil as much as possible by supplementing the correspondences of isolated words with sample sentences demonstrating how the foreign word, or the foreign building stone, actually fits into a construction. But the simple fact that building stones of language systems do not correspond to each other discredits any teaching method which attempts to present the foreign language precisely in terms of such correspondences. A student should never learn isolated words, isolated building blocks. He must learn complete constructions; he must learn how the individual building stones fit together. Only that will enable him to avoid the production of fractured Spanish.

Contrasts are more fundamental than parallels in the comparison of two languages.

In connection with this, a word concerning linguistics and the "grammar–translation" method: many teachers have said with some concern that they felt that some of the new so-called linguistic methods seem to neglect the teaching of grammar. We, however, have never seen how an approach rooted in linguistics could possibly dispense with an explicit or at least implicit grammatical analysis on the part of the student. The student must not only learn a construction; he must also realize how this construction is made up, how it comes apart, how some building stones can be replaced by others. From the linguistic point of view, the legitimate objections are not to the appropriate use of analysis or description, but rather to the substitution of the learning of grammatical terminology and rules for the learning of the constructions themselves, which is a misuse of grammar; and to the idea that the grammatical analysis of a construction in the native language, in our case English, should be the basis for translation into the foreign language.

The latter idea can be best demonstrated at its probable source, the traditional process of translating English into Greek or Latin. Take an English sentence like

The father sees the boy.

Conventional grammatical analysis applied to this sentence shows that it is composed of a subject, verb, and direct object:

subject	verb	direct object

The subject, father, is identified as the nominative of a noun, the verb as a third person singular present, the direct object as the accusative of a noun:

nominative	third person sing. verb	accusative

With this information the student is now able to put the English sentence into Latin:

Pater	*videt*	*puerum.*

There are various theoretical and practical objections to this teaching approach. On the theoretical side, this approach presupposes the idea of some sort of universal grammar: the English sentence is analyzed and transformed into a sort of disembodied ghost construction—subject + verb + object—which is given a concrete body again in another language. The underlying grammatical analysis is presumably equally valid for both languages. But in our sample sentence the analysis was possible only because we analyzed the English sentence in terms of a grammar which was imported from Latin in the first place. Nominative and accusative, terms which refer to a declensional system of nouns with specific declensional endings, make good sense in Latin, but they do not mean much for a language like English, in which nouns are no longer inflected. Note, incidentally that the process of going from English to Latin in terms of a common grammar not only require a latinized grammatical analysis of English, but also that the translation we obtained, *Pater videt puerum*, presented a slight anglicization of Latin, for the word order, subject + verb + object, is highly unusual in Latin. *Pater puerum videt* would have been a better answer. The process of going through the medium of a presumably universal grammar somewhat obscured the specific characters of either language; in this case, the fact that in English the subject–object relationship is expressed by word order, while in Latin it is signaled by case endings.

In the case of Spanish the lack of a universal grammar is perhaps less of an obstacle to the translation approach than it is in the case of Latin. In many ways English and Spanish resemble each other more than English and Latin. Neither English nor Spanish have declensional endings, and while Spanish has more of a conjugational system than English (the -s of the third person singular is practically all that is left of the English conjugational endings), both languages rely largely on similar mechanisms to express grammatical relationships: A doctor built this house. *Un médico construyó esta casa.* The house was built by a doctor. *La casa fué construida por un médico.* To evolve a nonuniversal grammatical system which would fit both languages in a majority of cases does not seem too difficult. But we think that in the beginning Spanish class the objection to the grammar translation method is not so much to the underlying theory, but rather to its practical results: It forces the student to analyze and identify individual building stones in his own language first, which means that instead of learning complete constructions in Spanish, he must arrive at the Spanish constructions by learning sets of correspondences between English and Spanish; the constant cross-association between English and Spanish leads—just because English and Spanish are parallel in so many cases—to the assumption on the part of the student that they are parallel in many other cases, in which they are not; and finally all the cases in which English and Spanish are not parallel must be presented as special problems or "exceptions" or "idioms."

In a linguistic teaching approach **the construction in the foreign language is the starting point of instruction.** The student learns how the construction is made up by exercises in which one building stone is replaced by another. This shows him how the construction fits together and what the value of each building stone is. In a sentence like:

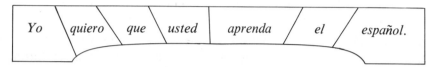

we show the student how *español* can be replaced by *francés* or *latín*; *aprenda* by *estudie, sepa, comprenda*; and *quiero* by *deseo, espero,* and so on. This teaches the student not only the fact that the building stones *aprenda, sepa,* or *quiero, deseo,* belong to the same category since they can fit into the same slot of the construction, but it teaches also the construction, the pattern itself. For while we are replacing the individual elements of the construction by others, the pattern remains constant.

Another approach to the teaching of the use of a building stone is the comparison of two patterns which differ from each other only through the building stone or stones the student is supposed to learn. The comparison shows exactly how the new building stone fits into the pattern:

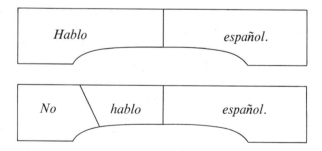

Again the student sees how the building stones fit into the pattern, and he learns the value of the building stones by fitting them into a series of identical patterns:

>   *Busco el libro.*   >   *No busco el libro.*
>   *Hallo el lápiz.*   >   *No hallo el lápiz.*

The learning of constructions or patterns and the study of the value of building stones, through the processes of transformation and substitution, are probably the cornerstones of the linguistic teaching approach. Most of the other linguistic teaching techniques to be discussed and illustrated later are basically adaptations of these two principles.

The advantages of these methods are that the student learns the constructions of the foreign language by processes which work from within the foreign language, not through translation from his native language, and that he learns them by observation and by speaking the foreign language, not by speaking about it. This does not mean that he should not learn rules, but that rules are primarily summaries of what the student is observing or doing. They are descriptive statements about the language, and they are, therefore, the description of the student's own performance. **Rules ought to be summaries of behavior.** They function only secondarily as predictors.

In conjunction with a drill in which, let us say, the student substitutes *extraño, temo, celebro* into a construction like *siento que usted se vaya*, it is certainly necessary to discuss the verbs which require the subjunctive and to point out the rules governing its use. But a rule like "The subjunctive is used in a subordinate clause after verbs of emotion"—even if it is a reasonably accurate predictor—will not by itself establish a behavior pattern that will lead the student to use the subjunctive correctly. The behavior is formed by actual performance in the language. The rule can reinforce the student's behavior, but it cannot establish it. We all know from our experience and that of our students how we can make certain mistakes in a foreign language again and again, even though we know perfectly well the rules governing the particular point in question.

The objection is sometimes raised that the linguistics-based teaching approach with its emphasis on the learning of complete patterns and oral performance contributes but little to the teaching methodology of a course in which reading knowledge is the primary goal. But here again several points can be made in favor of the learning of complete patterns and a certain amount of oral performance regardless of the ultimate objective. On the side of oral performance, it seems fairly clear that we make some sort of oral response—at least a silent one in form of lip movement—whenever we read. As long as there is a response, we might as well make sure that it is a reasonably correct one. But perhaps the major argument in favor of the linguistic approach is the case for pattern learning. Unless the student learns to recognize complete patterns, his "reading" in the foreign language will in fact be a complicated, drawn-out, and often erroneous process of deciphering. The identification of isolated building stones of the foreign languages with those of the native language is just as detrimental to effective reading as it is to effective speaking. Only after the major patterns, especially those in which Spanish and English are at variance, have been learned through drill and pattern practice should the student be made to read extensively on his own. The dictionary should then serve the purpose of filling in gaps in a pattern already recognized by the student, but, just as in the process of learning to speak, it should not be used by the student to identify the individual elements in an attempt to assemble them into a meaningful whole. For example, a student faces a sentence like

Le quiero ocultar la verdad.

and with the help of a dictionary comes up with the translation

* I want him to hide the truth.[1]

This student should have received extensive drills in this particular pattern:

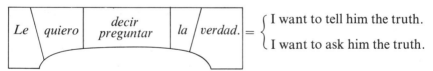

| Le | quiero | decir preguntar | la | verdad. | = | { I want to tell him the truth.
I want to ask him the truth. |

Such drills should include further items, parallel in Spanish, but corresponding to a non-parallel structure in English.

| Le | quiero | explicar ocultar | la | verdad. | = | { I want to explain the truth to him.
I want to hide the truth from him. |

All these parallel structures in Spanish should be contrasted with the standard alternative,

$$Quiero \begin{cases} decirle \\ preguntarle \\ explicarle \\ ocultarle \end{cases} la\ verdad.$$

---

[1] An asterisk (*) preceding a word or structure indicates a merely hypothetical or (as above) erroneous form.

A further contrast with the Spanish subjunctive structure, and a corresponding contrast in English, would establish a basis in which understanding and skill, or habit, would go hand in hand.

$$\textit{Quiero que el} \left\{ \begin{array}{l} \textit{diga} \\ \textit{pregunte} \\ \textit{explique} \\ \textit{oculte} \end{array} \right\} \textit{la verdad.} = \text{I want him} \left\{ \begin{array}{l} \text{to tell} \\ \text{to ask} \\ \text{to explain} \\ \text{to hide} \end{array} \right\} \text{the truth.}$$

not

$$\text{*I want} \left\{ \begin{array}{l} \text{to tell him . . .} \\ \text{to ask him . . .} \\ \text{to explain . . . to him.} \\ \text{to hide . . . from him.} \end{array} \right.$$

Pattern practice with drills based on a sound contrastive analysis of potential conflict points can indeed help avoid fractured translations as well as fractured spoken Spanish; it thus seems valid for the development of reading knowledge, as well as for the teaching of production. Depending on the primary aim, the exact application will, of course, be different. In pattern practice for **production** the student must be induced to produce the pattern actively, first through repetition and then in response to varied stimuli. Pattern practice for **reading** is practice in **instantaneous recognition of meaning**; it takes a slightly different form. First of all, the continuous successive repetition of the same pattern seems less appropriate than in practice for speaking. Continuous repetition increases facility in production but may distract the learner's attention from the meaning of the pattern. In preparation for reading, a spaced-out repetition which provides for **re-occurrence of the same pattern** appears to be more effective.

For example, we may be involved with the three different structures:

1. *Necesito un secretario que sepa castellano*
   (subjunctive in adjective clause)
2. *Es preciso que tenga mucho tiempo disponible.*
   (subjunctive in noun clause)
3. *Si tuviera tiempo lo buscaría yo mismo.*
   ("unreal condition")

When our concern is for teaching active production, we will build separate pattern drills for each of these constructions, as for example:

1(a) Substitute *hombre, ayudante*, et cetera

1(b) Substitute *Busco, ¿Conoce Vd . . . , No tengo . . .* ,

1(c) Substitute *hable, estudie, escriba*, et cetera

If our interest is to prepare for reading—that is for instant recognition of the meaning of each structure—it will be more effective to arrange the structures in meaningful sequences, using a technique of rotation:

Sequence 1: 1, 2, 3, as above.

Sequence 2: 1(a) *Busco un médico que sepa castellano.*

2(a) *Es necesario que me vea por la mañana.*

3(a) *Si estuviera en Nueva York, conocería uno.*

Sequence 3: 1(b) *¿Conoce Vd. un estudiante que necesite trabajo?*

2(b) *Es importante que sea joven.*

3(b) *Si tuviera un automóvil, sería mejor.*

Pattern practice for recognition must be an exercise which continually centers attention on the meaning of the pattern as it is encountered by the student. Thus, in pattern practice for recognition, the patterns, in other words the grammatically essential elements, must be presented to the student in their entirety. The student's attention may be directed to them by asking him to provide substitution words within the pattern. The substitution words would, of course, have to be words which do not affect the grammatical meaning of the pattern as such; those whose meaning could probably be guessed from the context or looked up in the dictionary. A reading pattern exercise may thus take the form of a substitution exercise in which the student is asked to provide any meaningful replacement in sentences like: *No creo que _____ nos diga la _____. No quiero que _____ nos acompañe a _____,* et cetera. A somewhat similar approach, focusing on structure rather than on vocabulary, is taken by an apparently rather successful method which permits interlinear translation for vocabulary items, while at the same time it withholds such translation for the elements essential for the recognition of grammatical relationships.

We have tried to show the difference between a linguistic approach and the so-called grammar–translation method. Another question which is often asked by language teachers is: What about linguistics and the direct method? The answer is that the—or a—direct method is not necessarily in contradiction to a linguistic approach to teaching, though in fact it is incompatible with it in many cases. Linguistics as such cannot contribute significantly to the pedagogical decision of how the meaning of structures is to be supplied to the student.

Let us take the constructions:

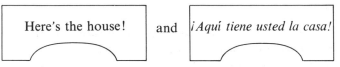

Here's the house! and *¡Aquí tiene usted la casa!*

We can say that they mean the same thing because these are the constructions that a Spanish speaker and an Englishman would use in an actual situation, pointing at a house. These sentences refer to the same thing, i.e., they have the same **reference.** We can simply explain this to the student, ask him to accept the total meaning of the total English sentence as the equivalent of the meaning of the Spanish sentence and then drill the Spanish construction by substituting other nouns for *casa*, or we can actually produce the reference of the sentence in the classroom—point to a house or at least the picture of a house and say, *Aquí tiene usted la casa*, and then go on to other objects or pictures and say (making the student repeat), *aquí tiene usted el caballo, aquí tiene usted el cuadro*, and so on. We believe that the important phase of this operation lies in the drill and not in the way in which the meaning of the sentence was supplied in the first place. Even if the explanation in English were avoided, there is, of course, a good chance that some students at least may have interpolated an English response between the picture and the *Aquí tiene usted la casa* of the teacher and may have translated the teacher's sentence. At the same time, it is likely that the avoidance of English will diminish the chance of students' distorting Spanish by trying to establish the equation of Spanish words with English words. Moreover, the approach through the object or the picture rather than through supplying the English equivalent may be important for sustaining the student's interest, especially, perhaps, at the elementary or junior high school level. In other words, if the linguistic approach can be preserved and made compatible with the direct method, the latter seems to have an advantage over the explanation in English.

At the same time the very nature of the direct method makes it often very difficult to proceed according to a strictly linguistic organization of teaching materials. The linguist would like to organize his course and the presentation of the language according to the system, the structure of the language. He would like to add one by one the building stones of Spanish, always going in minimal steps from one known construction to the next. The direct method channels a course into an organization which follows the patterns of the reality around us, the sequence of events, rather than the structure of the language.

A typical early lesson in a direct methods course is apt to sound somewhat like this:

> *Llamo a la puerta. La abro. Entro en la clase. Me siento a mi pupitre* (or: *Tomo mi asiento.*) *Escribo unas notas en mi cuaderno. Me levanto. Empiezo a hacer preguntas a los alumnos.*

It is quite obvious that this "simple" lesson contains a variety of rather complex structures, some of them easy (*Escribo en mi cuaderno*), and others of particular difficulty for the speakers of English (*Empiezo a hacer preguntas a los alumnos:* I begin to ask the students questions). Strict adherence to the direct method makes it difficult to single out these difficult constructions for special drill, and it makes it almost impossible to give grammatical explanations in the initial phases of the course. However, if the sentences used in the direct method lesson were based upon minimal structural steps, this problem would be eliminated, and the two methods made compatible.

This desirable fusion of methodologies appears to pose serious problems to writers of text books. Most of the "new key" courses so far published revolve around dialogues to be memorized. These dialogues introduce extensive vocabulary and constructions of a variety and complexity far beyond the level to be drilled or analyzed in the remainder of each corresponding unit. Any clear-cut application of linguistic principles, as outlined above, is obscured where content becomes an overriding concern.

These, then, would seem the features that a teaching methodology has to follow in order to qualify as linguistically oriented:

(1) The starting point of any grammatical exercise is a complete construction in the foreign language.

(2) Special emphasis must be put on those elements of the foreign language which are made especially difficult by interference coming from the native language.

(3) The actual learning of the foreign language takes place primarily by performance and habit-formation on the part of the student.

(4) Rules and grammatical explanation serve the purpose of describing to the student what he is doing and not of prescribing what he ought to do; constructions in the foreign language must be learned as a

whole rather than assembled. However, there is no stand at all in a linguistic orientation either for or against teaching grammatical structure as such.

(5) The presentation of teaching materials and the sequence of presentation is the one that is dictated by linguistic structure—and new building stones of the foreign language are learned one by one.

CHAPTER III

Some Psychological Aspects of Language Learning

The analyses and teaching procedures discussed in the following chapters are, to a large extent, the application of linguistic rather than psychological principles to the language learning area; but they are more than that, for linguistics does make certain psychological assumptions about languages, which in turn lead to psychological principles of language learning. Some of the more recent experiments and studies in the area of learning in general, and in language learning in particular, do seem to bear out the validity of the principles of pattern drill, repetitions, and so forth, involved in the linguistic teaching approach. In this chapter, then, we shall explain very briefly just what psychological assumptions, problems, and principles are involved in the linguistic approach to language teaching and its most important methodological adjunct—the language laboratory.

A complete review of learning theory and principle would go far beyond the scope of this text and it would not be very useful for our purpose. Much of modern psychology of learning is in itself controversial and debatable. Few of its principles, some derived from the observation of animals rather than humans, have been tested in their concrete application to language learning, although a number of promising studies have been undertaken in the last few years.

As a general framework for our psychological discussion it will be sufficient to keep in mind a few generally accepted principles: by **learning** in the psychological sense we understand an **observable change in performance on the part of an individual.** Whether this change in performance is for the better or worse is not involved in the definition; one can "learn"

18

arithmetic or French as much as one can "learn" bad table manners. The acquisition of the new habits of performance can be brought about in two distinct ways; either of the two involves the mechanisms of **stimulus** and **response.**

The first type of learning, called **classical conditioning**, involves an associational shift. This process may be described, in a very oversimplified form, somewhat as follows:

A piece of candy placed in the mouth serves as a stimulus (**S**) which produces salivation and a sense of pleasure as a reaction (**R**):

candy	>	pleasure
(physical stimulus)	>	(reaction)
S	>	**R**.

The candy is now called by a name, "gumdrop," which is repeated each time a piece of candy is presented. "Gumdrop," a linguistic abstraction or symbol, is now associated with the physical object, candy, and becomes a participating or alternate factor with the original stimulus; we can denote this factor as **A**, and summarize the new situation thus:

candy	+	"gumdrop"	>	pleasure
(physical stimulus)	+	(name)	>	(reaction)
S	+	**A**	>	**R**.

As a result of this association, we soon find that the word "gumdrop" alone, in the absence of any actual candy, will produce salivation and what we might popularly describe as an echo of sweetness and pleasure:

"gumdrop"	>	pleasure
(name)	>	(reaction)
A	>	**R**.

By the association of stimulus (**S**) with a substitute or alternate (**A**) we have **conditioned** the response mechanism or reaction (**R**), so that it will function even when the associational shift from **S** > **R** to **A** > **R** has been completed: the organism has been conditioned to react to a symbol even when the physical stimulus is not present.

In the learning of the mother tongue, **S** corresponds to the complex of stimuli created by a situation, and **A** represents the linguistic symbols —words, forms, and structures—with which the stimuli are constantly associated. So persistent is this process of association that the linguistic symbol, **A**, a substitute for reality, **S**, comes to evoke whole complexes of responses or reactions, **R**, and so **to have meaning**.

When the learning of a second language is undertaken, the process of associational shift cannot be repeated in this simple form. We do not refer here, however, to the simultaneous learning of two languages by a very young child in a bilingual environment, but to the acquisition of a new or foreign language by one who is already a speaker of a native tongue.

Much traditional methodology has focused the learner's attention on the association of elements of the new language, which we can designate as A^1, with those of the native speech, A. This gives us an additional substitution between S, the situation or external reality, and R, the response or meaning. Our formula would now be

$$S + A + A^1 > R.$$

The meaning (R) of the foreign language (A^1) is thus not one derived directly from the situational association. It is also identified with the meaning of the symbols of the native language. Our formulation, therefore, may become increasingly complex. For example,

$$S + \begin{array}{c} A \searrow \\ \updownarrow \quad R, \\ A^1 \nearrow \end{array} \quad \text{or} \quad S + A > R \searrow \atop \nwarrow A^1 \swarrow .$$

It must be recognized that some association, such as $A \leftrightarrow A^1$, appears to be inevitable. The learner (at least the learner who is past the age of puberty) invariably seeks the meaning of the foreign language by relating it to his own. This natural process leads, however, to serious interference in second-language learning. The first and more obvious form of interference is the painful necessity of translating to get at meaning, a slow and frustrating obstacle to communication, since it involves the interposition of an extra associational shift between stimulus and response. The more insidious form of interference is the intrusion of sounds, constructions, and meanings of the native language, all of which are matters of habit, into the patterns of the language being learned. This interference is the more difficult to combat because so little attention has been given heretofore to constrastive studies of pairs of languages.

"Mother tongue interference" is perhaps the most important psychological as well as linguistic consideration affecting our examination of methodologies. This concept will be constantly present in the rest of this book.

The second basic type of learning is called **instrumental**; in addition to an association of stimulus and response, it involves also the idea of the **reward** or **satisfaction** which the individual receives as the result of his performance. As we watch an infant or a small puppy beginning to react to sounds and sights in the environment, it is quite obvious that response may at first be almost completely random; but very few of the responses result in the satisfaction of some desire or the lessening of an anxiety. This satisfaction or reward becomes associated with the specific response after a number of chance occurrences. It thus serves to **reinforce** the learning of a particular response in answer to a particular stimulus.

In first-language learning, the child produces sounds at random, but certain configurations of sounds will win the approval of his parents or bring about certain results. The child is, then, communicating, and the reward will be his parents' attention. The response which brings reward will be learned. It is generally believed today that this process of chance + reinforcement is more fundamental in the very beginnings of the infant's learning than is direct imitation of sounds and words modeled by the eager parent.

In second-language learning, of course, conscious imitation of sounds produced by the teacher becomes an important and obvious basis for identifying bits of new behavior to be learned. Nevertheless, the value of reward or reinforcement of correct responses to speed real control seems beyond the need for argument. Our problem will be to determine what teaching or learning devices are best calculated to provide for such reinforcement by reward or approval. We must observe carefully the way we use the term "reward." A student may be anxious to get his homework done and be worried about not finishing it in time so that he can get to the baseball game. The response he produces in Spanish, no matter how wrong, will find an immediate reward by his lessening of tension ("Thank God I'm done with the homework"), and will thus be reinforced and learned. Our goal must be to control the learning of the student in such a way that reward of any kind be reserved only for correct responses.

Varying theories concerning the nature of learning lie behind the concepts of classical conditioning and instrumental learning, as well as other concepts we have not yet dealt with. The two most diametrically opposed views are those associated with behaviorism and those held by the "gestalt" psychologists.

In the behaviorist view, all learning results mechanically and automatically from stimuli and responses which are associated in the learning organism, and all learning is basically of this mechanical habit–formation type. Classical conditioning and reinforcement are the central mechanisms of all learning, according to this view.

The other view, which is more flattering to our self-esteem and more popular with non-psychologists, admits the role of habit formation but sees learning as more than that: the learner brings to the learning process his own creative ability to perceive and detect relationships, to appreciate patterns and configurations, to recognize analogies and contrasts. However much he may indeed be a mechanism shaped through stimuli or impressions received from the outside, he is at the same time an interacting organism, influencing the environment, and conscious of at least a part of the processes in which he participates.

The linguist–pedagogue is forced to make a choice in the face of such conflicting views. For us, these views need not be mutually exclusive. Both kinds of learning seem to be involved as we analyze different parts of the complex processes of acquiring a foreign language. It will be seen in what follows that we recognize the importance of awareness and of the ability to abstract; the essential role of intellect is not at all denied, contrary to the erroneous interpretations of some defenders of older ideas. A natural concern for understanding must not blind us to the inevitable role of habit.

Our appraisal of second-language learning must take into account three important facts which inevitably determine much of the learning process:

(1)   Language is an elaborate system, full of analogical forms and patterns.
(2)   Language is habit, or a complex of habits.
(3)   The native language (an established complex of habits) interferes with the acquisition of the habits of new language.

The concept of system and analogies leads us to consider the role of transfer in the language learning process.

We can communicate in our native language without apparent awareness of the nature of these patterns, without the slightest notion of what the structure of our native language is like. We manipulate the structures mechanically and automatically. Having mastered the formula "was . . . ing" in phrases such as I was walking, I was singing, the child is soon observed to extend the analogy—**transferring** his learned behavior—to enormous numbers of other verbs previously learned in other structures: I was eating, I was running, et cetera. The mere fact that children will transfer "wrongly" or negatively while learning their native language (singed for sang, runned for ran) testifies that some sort or some level of awareness of pattern is implicit, and that transfer is an important factor in learning.

The goal of all language instruction is to achieve precisely the same kind of automatic control in the foreign language. But the fact remains that we learn our first language through a staggering number of stimuli and responses. In addition, there is no danger of the patterns being interfered with by other established patterns.

So when we acquire a second language, we can hope for an approximation of this type of learning process only if we have a very large amount of time to learn the language, we start the language at an age when our brain is still plastic enough to acquire new responses without much interference from others, and if we create a large number of situations in which the use of the second language is absolutely necessary. It is very unlikely that any of these conditions will be fulfilled in a school or classroom. Even in the programs of teaching language in elementary schools the first condition we mentioned is normally not met.

All this points to the fact that in most second-language learning situations the stimuli and responses should be arranged in such a way that they make the patterns of language clearly apparent to the student. This does not mean that the student needs to be able to verbalize about the patterns, to tell us what the nouns or objects are; what he does need is a perception of the analogies involved, of the structural differences, and of the similarities between sentences. It is at this point that language learning becomes the perception of a pattern or configurations of patterns. Without necessarily mastering grammatical terminology, the learner must be able to see that certain expressions follow definite patterns. For example, if in *Voy a la universidad* the phrase *a la universidad* is replaced by *allá*, hence *Voy allá*, then similarly the phrase *a la escuela* in *Voy a la escuela* may also be replaced by *allá*, hence *Voy allá* once more. Likewise, if *Le hablo a un amigo* can be shifted to the perfect tense *Le he hablado a un amigo*, then *Le hallo a un amigo* may be shifted to the the the hablado in this untenet,

The ability to see such relations is partly a function of scholastic aptitude or intelligence as measured in most of the conventional I. Q. or scholastic or verbal aptitude examinations. It seems thus inevitable that we should find some correlation between a student's general intelligence and his ability to control the pattern mechanism of a foreign language.

Experimentation and research on language aptitude have shown that the ability to recognize the function of words and to infer the rules and patterns inductively are essential for success in language learning; this appears to be true regardless of what particular teaching method is used. While transformation and substitution exercises operate on a stimulus–response basis, the very fact that we arrange them according to patterns indicates an appeal to the student's ability to perceive these patterns. Thus, the pattern practice approach is essentially a middle-of-the-road approach. It is an attempt to establish responses while at the same time showing the student the pattern involved in the responses. It combines a purely mechanical stimulus–response approach with a utilization of the student's intelligence. It undertakes to teach the student a method by which he can transfer linguistic patterns to new situations through a transformation or substitution procedure.

Our second concept was that language is habit, a complex of habits. No matter how large or small the area we choose to leave to transfer (awareness of pattern and carryover of analogies) a certain number of correct responses must be learned in any case, even if only as the anchor or point of reference for transfer. Responses, automatic and appropriate, must be taught by producing the desired reactions to external stimuli.

It should be kept in mind that (1) a response can be learned only if it is performed; (2) a response is learned if it is rewarded; (3) rewarding of desired responses is by far more effective than the punishing of wrong ones; and (4) the rewarding of desired responses is usually effective only if the reward is immediate rather than delayed.

The application of the above principles to teaching methodology is obvious. The important point is not to have the student "construct" correct or half-correct sentences. He must be made to produce a correct utterance. This may first take the form of repetition, but the correct utterance must be produced preferably in a situation in which it represents a response to a given stimulus and thus satisfies the student's desire. This satisfaction may be the lessening of tension resulting from the student's answering the teacher's question, or it may be the satisfaction of pleasing the teacher or his own ego. Once the right response occurs, the teacher must let the student know immediately that the response was correct, so that the reinforcing effect of reward is exploited to the fullest degree.

It has long been a well-recognized principle among language-teaching methodologists or educational psychologists that the real skill of the teacher lies not in correcting and punishing wrong responses but in creating situations in which the student is induced to respond correctly. Linguistic teaching methodology is basically just such a way of bringing the student into a situation in which wrong responses are impossible. In substitution and transformation exercises, the possibility of error is small. Dealing with only one new element at a time also narrows down the possibility of gross errors.

Our third point has to do with interference of the native language habits with those of the language to be learned. A new linguistic system must be created in the brain and neural system of a learner who is already conditioned to one set of language habits and who reacts to one set of patterns and analogies.

The problem may perhaps be illustrated in the following way: A speaker of English is to learn the responses *Pablo es listo*; *Pablo es tonto*; *Pablo tiene calor*; *Pablo tiene frío*—all in the appropriate situations. One way of approaching the problem would be to teach all of the items involved separately as responses to specific stimuli (such as English sentences or pictures). This learning process would be the safest, and also the most time-consuming. The other way would be to teach only *Pablo es listo* and *Pablo tiene calor*. This approach would be more economical: only two responses have to be drilled instead of four. For *Pablo es tonto* and *Pablo tiene frío* we could rely on the student's ability to transfer, to react to analogy; but it is obvious from the example that the reliance on **positive transfer** (*Pablo es tonto* from *Pablo es listo*) also invites the possibility of **negative transfer** or **interference** (**Pablo "es" frío* rather than *Pablo tiene frío*). Much of the discussion and confusion about teaching methodology, best age for learning, and so on, simply stem from the fact that in language learning one can put the emphasis either on maximizing the learning by direct stimulus and response reaction, and narrowing the area left to transfer, or on relying upon the individual's ability to transfer. It does not appear that one can decide in absolute terms which approach to language learning is best: both have advantages and disadvantages. The first (minimizing the area left to transfer) implies by definition that more time must be spent on practice of individual examples of patterns, that a large number of stimulus and response reactions must be provided for. The obvious advantage is that by narrowing the area left for transfer, we also cut down on the possibility of negative transfer or interference: the more practice, the fewer the mistakes. Reliance on transfer is more economical but with transfer may also come negative transfer, so economy or efficiency on the one hand may, on the other, be exchanged for errors.

The curious fact about second-language learning is that its two major psychological aspects, namely, pattern perception and habit-formation, are in potential conflict with each other; for the temptation is very strong to substitute the perception of the existence of a pattern for its actual acquisition as a part of one's habitual, automatic performance. The student who has either learned or perceived that "expressions like *a la escuela* or *a la universidad* can be replaced by *allá*" is often unwilling to go through exercises in which this realization is to be transformed into an automatic habit. As a matter of fact, he may be so happy with his discovery of this relationship that he is unwilling to have the actual operation of using *allá* in response to *a la escuela, a la universidad*, or *a la iglesia* become part of his subconscious, rather than conscious, behavior and reaction. The failure of some highly intelligent students to become really proficient in a foreign language is undoubtedly often due to their unwillingness to perform automatically and their insistence on complete, intellectual realization of all the details involved in their various performances.

An analogy may perhaps elucidate the point made above. If we teach someone to drive a car using a manual shift, we have to point out to him how to shift gears. The pattern involved in the process has to become clear. We show how to depress the clutch pedal while releasing the accelerator, and shifting the gear while retaining the control of the car, which involves using both feet and both hands. This explanation of the pattern is necessary, but no one will ever maintain that the explanation alone will teach the student how to shift gears; the only thing that will teach it is the student's performing the act of shifting, correctly and repeatedly. No driving teacher will take it for granted that his student has mastered the skill because he can describe the pattern involved in the act, or even because he has shifted gears a few times correctly. Again, the actual realization of the pattern must be put out of the realm of consciousness if the student is ever to learn to drive a car. We cannot indeed conceive of any driver who, every time he shifts gears, says to himself in his mind, "I am now putting the left foot on the clutch, I am depressing it while the other foot is off the accelerator, and my right hand is shifting the gear while the other is steering the car," et cetera, et cetera. Some driving this would be! Perhaps the driver may pass his test, though it is very doubtful. In the same way, the student who says, upon answering a question, "The noun stays at the head of the sentence, then comes the pronoun, then the verb," may perhaps pass his Spanish examination, especially if it is a written examination that allows lots of time for his responses; but he cannot speak Spanish any more than our driver can drive a car in the street.

The potential conflict between the perception and the intellectual awareness of a pattern on the one hand and its automatic performance on the other could conceivably be corrected and perhaps even eliminated if our teaching relied solely on the stimulus > response type of approach. In terms of our comparison, we never explain to our student the complete pattern involved in shifting gears, but we make him put his foot on the clutch pedal, and after he has done this and practiced this, we teach him to depress it. After that we make him associate this act with the handling of the gas pedal. In other words, instead of presenting a complete pattern, we divide the problem into a small number of stimulus > response situations, reward and reinforce each response, and build up habitual performance without teaching at first the total pattern as a unit. The same approach can be tried in language instruction. The result could be the practical elimination of the type of intellectual interference that comes from wanting to think about what one is doing when shifting gears.

This approach would drive the principle of minimal step-by-step learning to an unworkable extreme. A pattern drill in which we shift singulars to plurals (like *El profesor es inteligente > Los profesores son inteligentes, Mi profesor es inteligente > Mis profesores son inteligentes*) would have to be broken down into its component parts in such a way that only absolutely minimal automatic responses are at first made. Thus, the student being drilled on the singular plural contrast would first be taught to respond to *el* with *los*; then to *mi* with *mis*; to *la* with *las*, and then, one at a time, he would learn the responses *tus, sus, nuestros, estos, esos*, for *tu, su, nuestro, este, ese*. The next step involves changing *es* to *son*; then *profesor* to *profesores*; *inteligente* to *inteligentes*.

Only after all of these responses have been practiced separately and become automatic would the complete pattern drill be undertaken. The possibility of error is practically eliminated by the absolutely minimal nature of the individual learning steps. This kind of teaching, which stresses habit-formation almost exclusively, relies heavily on the language laboratory. It has not been shown to be practicable in so extreme a form as that just described.

While it is possible to decompose utterances analytically into small units, it is also true that the components function only because they are in relation to each other, because they form complete patterns. Perception or awareness of the complete pattern underlying any utterance is likely to take place sooner or later; if this awareness is allowed to become the student's major concern, the danger inherent in his rationalizing and thinking about the pattern will again come into being. We also must keep in mind that the reaction produced in response to the original stimulus must eventually be transferred to other stimuli. In terms of our previous example, plurals are usually *not* produced in response to singulars. The transfer of the response to a different situation, making it independent of the original stimulus, involves precisely the use of the awareness of the total pattern and those intellectual processes which the method is designed to circumvent in the first place.

There is probably no general cure against the type of interference that comes from stopping at intellectual understanding and resisting the development of automatic responses. It is up to the individual language teacher to recognize this problem and deal with it according to circumstances. This transition from the realization of the existence of pattern to its automatization can be accomplished in several ways: in some cases the language teacher may simply have to convince the student that he needs further drill and participation in class and laboratory exercises even though he has understood what it is all about. In other cases, the teacher will run into individuals who are perfectly capable of perceiving a pattern but who practically refuse to take part in the drill exercises and automatization of the pattern unless they receive some sort of intellectual explanation. In many cases in which this kind of explanation is asked for, the experienced teacher will give a minimal explanation which, as such, may not contribute significantly to the performance of the student but will relieve his anxiety so that he can then proceed with the real business at hand, the drill of the grammatical pattern. To give an example, a grammar book may contain a series of sample sentences, or the teacher may give them on the board, such as: (1) *¿Usted le da a Juan este libro?—Sí, se lo doy;* (2)*¿Usted le manda a María el paquete? —Sí, se lo mando;* (3)*¿Usted le escribe a mi hermano la carta?—Sí, se la escribo.* The student who has perceived that *le* . . . (*a Juan*), *le* . . . (*a María*), are replaced by *se* when a direct object noun is replaced by *lo* or *la* has understood the grammatical point these sentences are meant to illustrate. Whether he can state the rule in question, whether he can identify the *se* as a substitute indirect object pronoun, is of secondary importance. A statement like "the substitute form *se* replaces the indirect object pronouns *le-les* before a direct object pronoun of the third person" contributes little to the student's awareness of the pattern, but it may relieve his intellectual anxiety and allow him to proceed in his actual learning process. A further statement, such as "So Spanish avoids (for whatever reason) the pronoun combinations *le lo, *les la, that is, the placing of two *l* pronouns together," may help to focus the attention of some students on the contrasts they are actually to learn through repetitive pattern drill, but it is still the drill which actually teaches.

Another trick to get the student to perform automatically is to divert his attention from the complexity of the pattern itself. This approach should be stressed especially in connection with patterns which are so complicated that intellectual assembly and synthesis is necessarily doomed to failure. A sequence like *No se lo he dado nunca*, assembled by intellectual processes, cannot be made automatic if the student insists that he first has to think out what he is doing. Usually a student can be made to produce such a sentence automatically by having his attention diverted from the complicated structure to another point of the utterance. For example, we ask the student to go through a substitution exercise in which apparently the replacement of *nunca* by *hoy, jamás, esta mañana, muchas veces*, is the main focus of the drill.

Perhaps the best way of overcoming the student's concern with the pattern itself, rather than with its automatic use, is to give him the opportunity to use the pattern in context, to make him talk about something that interests him more than the pattern itself. Of course, this approach should not be confused with making the student talk before he has learned the pattern at all. This will only force him into making mistakes. But to combine pattern drill with a meaningful context which, in fact, disguises the drill is a quite different matter. For example, we can tell a story about a man *"que dá dinero a los pobres, que escribe cartas al periódico; que manda regalos a sus amigos; que dice chistes a todo el mundo."* We can then ask him questions about this man: *"¿Dá dinero a los pobres? ¿Escribe cartas a los periódicos? ¿Manda regalos a sus amigos?"* All these questions amount to a pattern drill in which the student answers, *"Sí, se lo dá. Sí, se las escribe. Sí, se los manda."* The meaningful context diverts the student's conscious attention from the analysis of the pattern and contributes to the process of automatization.

The attack on the other psychological conflict, the interference coming from the native language, depends upon applying special emphasis and automatization drills just at those points of interference. As we shall stress again later, the complete avoidance of English (as in the direct method) is by itself no guarantee that interference will not take place. On the other hand, it seems only logical to assume that the continuous juxtaposition of English and Spanish in the classroom will encourage interference. As we shall point out in the next chapter, there seem to be certain reasons for a justifiable use of English. Nevertheless, as much as possible and in as long stretches as possible, the Spanish class should be conducted in Spanish. It is extremely important to create a situation and environment which the student associates with Spanish, in which he expects Spanish stimuli and responses, in which—to use the psychological technical term—his entire mental set is keyed to the Spanish language.

There seem to be two more possible ways of attacking interference. The first is to start the student's learning process at an age when interference is still slight or at least readily overcome. Depending on the individual, this might be up to the age of ten or eleven. The other possibility, a rather startling one, but one that has been proved feasible by some experimentation, is to eliminate meaning almost totally from the initial phases of language instruction. It seems entirely possible to teach the major patterns of a foreign language without letting the student know what he is saying. For instance, the class could learn to shift statements like *ellos buscan los libros, ellos hallan los libros, ellos escogen los libros* to *nosotros buscamos los libros, nosotros hallamos los libros, nosotros escogemos los libros.* Or the students could be taught to respond automatically to ¿*Buscan ustedes el libro?* with *Nosotros buscamos el libro*, and on that model they could respond to ¿*Hallan ustedes el libro?* with *Nosotros hallamos el libro.* They could be conditioned to make these, and many other patterned responses, even if they did not know what they were saying. As far as they are concerned, they would simply hear a stimulus, *ellos . . .-n*, to which they are trained to respond automatically, *nosotros . . .-mos*, or a stimulus, *. . .-n ustedes*, to which they are trained to respond, *Nosotros . . .-mos.* The point could also be illustrated with "nonce" words, equipped with grammatical inflections arranged to behave in the same pattern as real words would do: **Ellos fripan el plurdo* > *nosotros fripamos el plurdo;* *ellos londan > *nosotros londamos.*

The patterns of grammar would be acquired by such procedures, and the next step might be to tell the students the grammatical meaning of the patterns. For one group of examples the explanation might be, "I am making a statement about a group of people, and you are changing it to a statement about yourselves as a group." For a second group of examples one might say, "I am asking a question and you are answering it," or "I am asking a question of you as a group and you are answering it for yourselves as a group." Only after the student has gained complete and automatic mastery over a grammatical pattern would he be acquainted with the full meaning—the lexical meaning or content—of what he has learned. This means that the temptation to construct Spanish in terms of English (using *por* before the object of *buscar* or *esperar*, for example) could be practically eliminated. At least, by the time it is introduced the student would be well fortified against it.

This proposal to teach grammar patterns independently and before the introduction of the meaning of words is one of the new frontiers of language teaching which have been opened up as a result of linguistic analysis and which have been stimulated by the increasing availability of language laboratories. Detailed programs of courses putting this kind of teaching into operation remain to be worked out; just how much native language interference could reappear in such courses, after meaning has been introduced, remains to be seen. It also remains to be seen whether undesirable side effects, such as sometimes reduce the value of new drugs, will prevent useful development of this interesting idea.

Perhaps the most promising way of combatting interference or negative transfer would be to start the student's learning process at an age when negative transfer seems slight, or at least readily overcome; depending on the individual, perhaps before age ten or eleven. At the same time, those who advocate the early start should be aware of the fact that their case seems to rest primarily on avoidance of interference or negative transfer rather than on maximization of positive transfer. In other words, we have no definite proof at this point that the child's resistance to interference may not be in part the result of a less developed ability to transfer under any circumstance, positive or negative. If this is so, early language training may appear uneconomical in some respects and would in any case have to be fairly intensive.

Perhaps the best way of avoiding negative transfer in any learning situation may be to concentrate on stimulus > response learning—in other words, intensive practice—in the areas in which interference is likely to occur. Transfer can do the job in areas where it is likely to be positive, but we must rely on practice where transfer is likely to be negative. In terms of our initial example, *Pablo es listo*, it is not necessary to drill *Pablo es bueno, Pablo es malo*; whereas the structures *Pablo tiene frío, tiene calor, tiene miedo*, et cetera, must be the object of extensive practice.

For example, a problem which the type of course mentioned above shares to some extent with any other course in which automatization of response through drill is part and parcel of the teaching method, is how to keep the student's motivation and attention alive during the drill period. This is obviously a problem even in a course in which meaning on all levels is introduced from the very beginning. The teacher, as well as the student, must be convinced of the necessity of pattern drills. The student must realize that the pattern drill is not an end in itself, but that it gives him the command of the mechanics of the language, which can be applied in a practical situation. In the chapter on course outline and programs we shall suggest that pattern drill alternate with dialogues and situations in which the patterns find a practical application. This could not be possible during the initial phase of a course which is devoted entirely to the teaching of grammatical patterns. This type of course consists necessarily of several months of uninterrupted pattern drills and mechanical stimulus > response manipulations. During this phase the students must remain motivated in terms of the overall reward they may expect as the result of staying with the course. While some experimentation with this type of course has been undertaken, its general applicability at various levels of teaching remains to be studied.

For the time being, intensive drill at the points of interference remains our most practical tool in overcoming the obstacles created by the native language habits of the mature student.

CHAPTER IV

Linguistic and Non-Linguistic Teaching Procedures

Having in mind the general specifications of a linguistic method as discussed in the previous chapters, we can now take a look in more detail at the way in which a linguistic methodology affects the language classroom. In connection with this, we shall examine some of the facets of teaching procedures which seem of greatest interest to every language teacher: the place of English in the classroom; the types of exercises to be used in language drill; the organization of the individual lessons; and the use of visual aids.

(A) THE USE OF ENGLISH IN THE SPANISH CLASS

Some of what can be stated here has been implied in our discussion of the direct method. Since in a linguistic approach we want to concentrate as much as possible on specific drills dealing with specific problems, we can use English for the purpose of economy. A brief explanation or an "attention-pointer" given in English may save time. At certain stages of the course it may be possible to give explanations in Spanish, and such explanations will afford a certain amount of language practice to the student. But he will be listening to a great variety of structures, some of which may still be unfamiliar to him. He may not, as a result, understand the teacher; he may become bewildered, and his mind may wander from the particular problem; it is not part of the overall learning scheme of the course. Thus, a brief explanation in English may save time for more concentrated learning and avoid disorganization and confusion.

33

Translation or explanation in English may also be the most economical way of supplying the meaning of structure, and especially of vocabulary items. Here again the arbitrary avoidance of English makes it not only difficult to arrange the material according to linguistic patterns, it may —especially in the case of fairly obvious vocabulary items—lead to rather involved and unnecessarily lengthy explanation. It is perfectly true that building stones of different languages should not be equated. But the danger involved in marking these equations is especially great with words like for, about, when, will, shall, by. Those little words which determine the overall shape of construction have been compared by some linguists to the mortar rather than to the stones themselves. No English explanation or translation should even be attempted for these words, which have the primary purpose of denoting grammatical relationships and which we shall call the construction or **function words** of the language. But with words which denote obvious concepts and, above all, easily identifiable physical objects, the danger involved in giving Spanish–English equations may not be very great. Even if the equation is not given by the teacher, it may be supplied by the student anyway. Thus, if a student meets a sentence like *yo quisiera que usted mandara este paquete ahora mismo*, and he is in doubt as to the meaning of *paquete*, it is probably better to explain that *paquete* means package rather than to attempt to define the word in Spanish, a procedure which will take the student's mind off the construction which he is studying and which is the real problem of the above sentence.

Other reasons for the possible use of English in a Spanish class go beyond the realm of economy, but have an independent linguistic and pedagogical justification of their own. Difficulties usually revolve around contrasts between English and Spanish. The use of English makes it possible to focus attention on those contrasts and drive them home to the learner. The most obvious example of the principle involved here comes from the realm of phonology, and will be discussed with more examples and in greater detail at a later point in this book: a speaker of English will have difficulty in the pronunciation of certain Spanish sounds because he will tend to substitute English sounds for those of Spanish. Thus, for the vowel of Spanish *le* he might substitute the diphthong of English lay. One way of combatting this mistake is to contrast the English and Spanish sounds for the student, make him conscious of the difference, and teach him to identify the Spanish and the English sounds.

This principle of overtly contrasting English and Spanish can also be applied in the realm of constructions. Thus, a drill in which the student substitutes different nouns in a construction like *Quiero que usted aprenda la lección* can be preceded by an overt comparison of that construction with the English I want you to study the lesson. Moreover, the contrast between English and Spanish itself can be made part of the pattern drill in which the teacher asks the student to "translate" sentences like I want you to study the lesson, I want you to study the book, I want you to study the rule, and the student goes, in fact, through a pattern drill exercise which impresses a structural difference between English and Spanish upon his memory.

From the linguistic point of view, it is difficult to decide whether this kind of pattern drill, which consists of an overt comparison of English and Spanish, is more useful than the exercises in which the Spanish structure is drilled in Spanish alone without comparison with English. The answer depends, no doubt, on psychological factors involving the student, his age, aptitude, et cetera. One thing can be pointed out, however, from the linguistic point of view, namely, that this kind of drill should be performed orally. There are at least two reasons for this. Using the native language as an oral stimulus minimizes the danger of the student's using the English sentence as a basis for word-for-word translation. Seeing English sentences written out gives the student time to figure out correspondences between English and Spanish building stones, the activity which we have characterized as the arch-enemy of successful language learning. Once the overt comparison between English and Spanish has been made, English should not be used as a basis for word-by-word translation, but only as a stimulus to provoke a Spanish construction already known *in toto* by the student. The response triggered by the English I want you to study that idea must be an automatic *Quiero que usted estudie esa idea*, and not a slow *Quiero . . . Yo quiero usted . . . .* It is only through oral practice that we can make sure of that particular nature of the response.

The other reason for insisting on limiting oneself to the use of oral English as the stimulus for Spanish is the simple fact that in some cases only oral English allows us to make an accurate comparison. Thus, the difference between *no me gusta* and *a mi no me gusta* is expressed in English by a difference in stress: I don't <u>like</u> it versus <u>I</u> don't like it. In English different parts of the sentence may be stressed with a resultant difference in meaning. <u>John</u> wants that book (stress on <u>John</u>) means that John, and not someone else, wants the book; John wants <u>that</u> book (stress on <u>that</u>) means that John wants that particular book, and not a different one; John wants that <u>book</u> (stress on <u>book</u>) means that John wants the book and no other object. In Spanish such differences of meaning are often conveyed by differences in structure rather than by stress alone. Thus, the students whom we want to put through a pattern exercise drilling the Spanish emphasis construction (for example, the subject pronoun expressed) should be made aware that the Spanish construction corresponds to the English use of emphatic stress, and their Spanish responses may then be triggered by English sentences like I did it, I saw it, I read it (all with heaviest stress on I), in contrast with I did it, I saw it, I read it.

The positive advantage of the deliberate, but limited, use of English lies thus in showing and drilling the **differences** between English and Spanish. This very advantage is lost in many textbooks by the practice of adapting English to Spanish structure to as great an extent as possible. The reason for it is evident if English is used as the basis for translation into Spanish: this manipulation of English will lead the student to avoid a translation mistake in the specific sentence on which he happens to be operating. For example, if the student is asked to render into Spanish a sentence such as It is probable that he will not come, he may translate quite neatly, *Es probable que no venga*; but wanting to express He probably won't come, he will almost certainly say *Probablemente no vendrá*, instead of the much more likely *Es probable que no venga*. The same may apply to the beginner who says or writes *El hombre a quien hablé* in response to the English The man to whom I spoke but who may be at a loss to render The man I spoke to, and who may say— as more than one learner has done—*El hombre yo ví* for The man I saw. If the student is led to use a given Spanish construction only in response to an English phrasing he would most likely never use, he will almost certainly "create" pseudo-Spanish structures parallel to the ones he does, in fact, use in English.

Pedagogically, a similar circumstance affects the student whose response *Se habla inglés* has always been triggered by the formal, although not exactly parallel, One speaks English and never by They speak English or English is spoken. We have known students who could translate One tells me that you are right quite beautifully into *Se me dice que usted tiene razón* but who in free composition or conversation came up with such strange expressions as * *Soy dicho* or * *He sido dicho*.

Even if there is a choice between two equally good English constructions, one paralleling the Spanish and the other not, we should suggest that the construction clashing with Spanish be made the stimulus of the pattern drill. Of course, the construction of I give the book to John prepares the ground very neatly for *Le doy el libro a Juan*, but why should a student be allowed to go wrong whenever he happens to be influenced by I give Charles the book? Certainly the translation of *Hubiera podido ir* by He would have been able to go may at times save the teacher and student some trouble, since in the English as well as in the Spanish construction, to go, and *ir* appear in the present infinitive; but the consistent use of He would have been able will not teach the student to cope with the problem created by the interference coming from the more usual English He could have gone (= *Hubiera podido ir*).

What we have said really adds up to one fundamental point: the English with which Spanish is to be contrasted must be normal English as spoken by the student. It is the student's actual behavior in English that creates the problem. For this reason, the accurate and truthful description of the English spoken by our student must be the basis of our comparison and contrast with Spanish, since it is the way the student speaks English that creates the problem, not the way he ought to speak. To manipulate the English or to be prescriptive about it may only obscure the real point of difficulty and create unnecessary confusion. Many Spanish grammars go into long explanations about the Spanish equivalents of I should give (*Daría* versus *Debería dar*) trying to solve a problem created by the assumption that the student uses, or at least ought to use, should as the first person corresponding to He would. The fact is that most students never use should as a conditional anyway and understand *daría* perfectly well as I would give (I'd give) and *Debería dar* as I ought to (or should) give.

Of course, the main abuse of English in the Spanish class lies simply in using it too much. After all, Spanish can only be practiced by speaking Spanish. English explanations, no matter how accurate or elegant, will never take the place of practice. Even the suggested use of English in pattern drills should be put into practice judiciously and sparingly because **the use of English as stimulus for Spanish does not correspond to a normal speaking situation,** nor does it give the student the same practice in auditory comprehension that is afforded by a Spanish stimulus. We defend English in the Spanish class primarily as an economy measure to free class time for more practice in speaking Spanish patterns. The excessive use of English and the constant switching from English to Spanish defeats its own purpose and cannot be justified by any possible pedagogical, linguistic, or psychological argument.

(B) TYPES OF DRILLS AND EXERCISES

Let us first look at **substitution exercises**. The mainstay of the linguistically oriented drill is stimulus in Spanish. We have already characterized substitution and transformation as the main features of linguistic drill. We shall now take a closer look at them and contrast them with other types of teaching devices.

In a sentence like *Quisiera que usted escuchara mis preguntas*, we are dealing with a rather complex Spanish structure which offers several difficulties to a speaker of English. It clashes with the English pattern expressed by I'd like you to listen to my questions, or I want you to listen to my questions. The Spanish construction requires the use of a subjunctive in the subordinate clause; listen requires the preposition to; *escuchar* requires the direct object. Thus, whether or not we point out these difficulties to the student, the construction must be made the object of a special drill; perhaps the initial step in such a drill may be the repetition of the sentence itself. But a single sentence by itself does not teach a pattern. We shall, therefore, ask our student to substitute *mis palabras, mi canción, mis órdenes*, et cetera, in the original sentence. The substitution of these items will not cause any great difficulty to the student. They change nothing in the structure as such; they do not require the formulation of new subjunctives, nor changes in person or tense. Thus, substitution is basically a way of making the student repeat the pattern, making it a matter of habit. After these sentences have been drilled this way, we may ask the student to substitute *oyera*; then, with *órdenes* as the last word, he may substitute *obedeciera, siguiera*, then *Desearía, Me gustaría*, and so on, so that the final response of the student might be a sentence such as *Me gustaría que usted siguiera mis órdenes*.

In the last response the overall pattern which has remained constant during the exercise is the same as it was in the first line, but except for the small function words involved (*que . . . usted . . . mis . . .*) the vocabulary items have changed. In spite of this there is still a certain identity of meaning that was also kept constant during the exercise, namely, I, would like, you to do something. This part of the meaning of the sentence is not identical with the sum of the **lexical meanings** of the vocabulary items involved, but it is the **structural meaning** of the pattern itself. A structure or pattern may therefore be identified as the **common element of different sentences or phrases which have the same**

structural meaning. Strictly speaking, a single sentence can thus be only an example of a pattern; by itself it can neither be a pattern nor can it teach one. The pattern is the grammatical relationship itself and the structural meaning expressed by the sentence.

The pattern of:

Quisiera	que	usted	escuchara	mis	preguntas

may thus be thought of as a structure or frame in which only the function words and endings indicating grammatical relationships remain constant. The lexical items can be exchanged with others, and the "meaning" of the sentence thus changed; but the purpose of the exercise is to teach the pattern itself and its constant structural meaning.

The **transformation exercise** has a similar purpose. While the substitution exercise keeps the structural meaning, or pattern, constant, the transformation exercise takes different examples of a given pattern and, by repetition of a specific operation, transforms each of them into a new pattern or construction. It thus emphasizes contrast, the relation between an element in the cue and one in the transformed response.

El profesor enseña el español.   >   *¿Enseña el español el profesor?*
El muchacho busca el libro.   >   *¿Busca el libro el muchacho?*
La madre prepara la comida.   >   *¿Prepara la comida la madre?*

All the sentences in each of the two columns above follow identical patterns, and the element differentiating them is represented by the change in word order (plus a change in intonation).

That all other types of pattern practice are basically related to substitution or transformation will be seen quite easily:

Expansion involves enlarging a frame by adding a new element. It is therefore a type of transformation. The sentence, *He visto al profesor*, may be expanded by the addition of the element *muchas veces*:

He visto muchas veces al profesor.

And likewise:

He encontrado al profesor.
He encontrado muchas veces al profesor.

Replacement (of nouns by pronouns, for instance) involves a regular change of one frame to another, and it is again a type of transformation.

He hallado el libro.   >   Lo he hallado.
He visto el coche.   >   Lo he visto.
He buscado el lápiz.   >   Lo he buscado.

Transformation in echelon is a special type of transformation exercise which starts by changing one element of the frame and then introduces gradually other simultaneous transformation operations.

(a) ¿Busca usted el libro?   >   Sí, busco el libro.
¿Halla usted el libro?   >   Sí, hallo el libro.
(b) ¿Busca usted el libro?   >   Sí, lo busco.
¿Halla usted el libro?   >   Sí, lo hallo.
(c) ¿Busca usted el libro?   >   No, no lo busco.
¿Halla usted el libro?   >   No, no lo hallo.

Transformation and substitution are often combined in the same exercise. For example, a substitution of a different subject will necessitate a transformation of the verb form:

Yo busco el libro.   >   Nosotros buscamos el libro.
Yo hallo el libro.   >   Nosotros hallamos el libro.
Yo miro el libro.   >   Nosotros miramos el libro.

Restatement exercises are basically rather complicated forms of transformations involving several simultaneous operations:

Dígale a Carlos que él estudia el español.   >   Tú estudias el español.
Dígale a Roberto que él mira el cuadro.   >   Tú miras el cuadro.
Dígale a Concha que ella busca el lápiz.   >   Tú buscas el lápiz.

In all types of pattern practice exercises, especially in those based on transformation, it is advisable to keep in mind that simple transformation involving only a minimal operation should be drilled before the student is asked to go through complex operations. In many transformation or expansion exercises, the completely automatic response will also have to be replaced eventually by a response involving a choice on the part of the student. This involves all the cases in which Spanish makes exceptions to its own patterns. In such cases the pattern and the exception must be drilled thoroughly and independently before the exercise involving choice between two patterns is presented to the student. The response, let us say, in such a group as:

Obedezco a María.   >   La obedezco.
Enseño a María.   >   La enseño.
Espero a María.   >   La espero.

and in the group:

> *Hablo a María.*   >   *Le hablo.*
> *Escribo a María.*   >   *Le escribo.*

and that in the structure:

> *Me acerco a María.*   >   *Me acerco a ella.*

must be separately and firmly established before the student is confronted with an exercise in which the several patterns are mixed, such as:

> *Obedezco a Dolores.*   >   *La obedezco.*
> *Escribo a Juana.*   >   *Le escribo.*
> *Me acerco a Elisa.*   >   *Me acerco a ella.*
> *Espero a Elena.*   >   *La espero.*
> *Hablo a María.*   >   *Le hablo.*

It may appear that students are likely to find pattern practice of the types just described somewhat tedious or boring. No doubt it can be for some. The points to be made here are simply that (1) repetition is not supposed to replace the analytical understanding of the construction, but (2) it alone can assure **automatic response**, and (3) it leads to successful manipulation of language skills on the part of many students who would be unable to construct a sentence by a purely analytical approach.

Of course, pattern practice is not meant to be the only type of exercise or practice to be used in a language class. **Pattern practice is a means to an end.** The end to be achieved is the ability to use the language freely, as in exercises of the more traditional type in which students ask or are asked questions about a story or are engaged in conversation on a specific topic. The point is that the question-and-answer type of exercise or the free conversation are usually a test of whether or not the patterns have been learned, rather than a way of practicing the patterns. The pattern practice may be compared to the exercise and drills that a football or basketball player must undergo in order to be ready and fit for a game: Certainly the game as such is the interesting part and the culmination of the effort. To do nothing but pattern practice would be very much like putting someone through football practice without ever giving him a chance to play. No coach would do this, but neither would he put anyone on the team who had not gone through a rigorous training in all the little detailed operations which make up the skill of the football players.

What we have said about questions and answers and conversation applies also to many of the other traditional kinds of exercises. Most of them are really tests of whether or not learning has taken place rather than teaching procedures themselves. It is, of course, true that a test given over and over again can become a teaching instrument, but teaching through testing, teaching through letting the student make mistakes, is not a very efficient procedure.

Perhaps the old-fashioned type of translation exercise in which examples of different patterns are scrambled up in, let us say, ten or twenty sentences to be put into Spanish is the best example of what a teaching device should not be like.

Suppose we give the student a lesson about the present subjunctive, explain its formation, then tell him that the present subjunctive is used after verbs of emotion, verbs of thinking in the negative, verbs expressing doubt, verbs expressing volition and impersonal expressions (except those denoting certainty), and so on. Each one of these rules may be illustrated by one or more examples. Then we ask the student to translate sentences like:

> Do you think that he is right?
> We doubt that he will arrive tomorrow.
> I hope they won't be afraid.
> It is not necessary for you to read these papers.
> I expect all of you to do your duty.

The above sentences translated into Spanish are examples of many different patterns; practically the only feature they have in common is that in each of these patterns one of the building stones used is an ending which we can identify as the present subjunctive. But this is not enough to establish any identity or even great similarity between the patterns themselves. Actually, this "exercise" does not teach the pattern. It tests whether or not the student—from the rules and the few examples alone—has already been able to recognize the underlying patterns. Every language teacher knows that only the most intelligent and analytically minded students are able to do this, and even those students are not able to give anything like an automatic or spontaneous response.

Another favorite type of traditional exercise consists of Spanish sentences, parts of which are either left blank or replaced by English expressions. A variation of this type of exercise is the Spanish sentence for which the verb is supplied in the infinitive and is to be put into the real form required by the sentence:

A. *Quiero que usted* (leave:) *en seguida.*
B. *Quiero que usted* (*salir*:   ) *en seguida.*

As far as type *A* is concerned, we must first of all protest against the hybrid English–Spanish sentence which gives the impression that English building stones or their "equivalents" can be made to fit into a Spanish construction. As far as type *B* is concerned, this may make some sense as a test in which we want to pin the student down on one single point (probably for the sake of objective scoring). As teaching devices these types of exercises have only a limited value precisely because they do not force the student to produce complete patterns. After all, it is the entire pattern that has to be learned and that must become one of the student's speech habits. The student should not be made to chisel, so to speak, on only one building stone in order to make it fit into the construction.

(C) LESSON ORGANIZATION

What we have seen so far concerning types of drills and linguistic teaching methodology has, of course, an immediate bearing on the overall organization of the lesson and of the textbook. Any lesson organization which makes it impossible to have specific drills with a single emphasis on the new construction or vocabulary problem to be learned will be counter to linguistic principle.

The most obvious offender against linguistic principle is the lesson which consists of a set of grammatical rules (more or less extensively illustrated by examples), a series of vocabulary items, and exercises in which the student is expected to apply the grammatical rules and the vocabulary items, thus manufacturing Spanish—usually his own brand— according to a set of recipes.

The type of organization which deals with a single point of grammar, like the negative or the subjunctive, is not necessarily a saving device. As we have pointed out before, such classifications as the subjunctive or the negative may be, and are, often used to assemble a multitude of quite divergent structures of varying difficulty under a single heading. Moreover, the teacher who organizes his material according to such large grammatical categories will often fall victim to the temptation of covering the category in one lesson. This desire to be complete is understandable enough on the part of the teacher who knows the material and has organized it in his own way. But the organization which seems most logical and appropriate to the person who already knows the language is not necessarily the one that is pedagogically most suitable. We must learn to resist the temptation to give the rule, the exception to the rule, and the exception to the exception in one and the same lesson. The student who is trying to grasp the rather difficult "redundant" constructions need not be told in the same lesson and within the same breath that direct and indirect object pronouns of any person may be made emphatic by the use of *a* plus the corresponding disjunctive or prepositional pronoun, either before or after the cluster of verb with object pronoun, and that a similar phenomenon (with *de*) occurs with possessives, but of the third person only, although more commonly than not the possessive *su* is replaced by the definite article when *de usted de él*, et cetera, is added. Since learning a language means establishing patterns of behavior, it seems highly inappropriate to introduce exceptions to and complications of a pattern before the basic pattern itself and each of its normal variants has been firmly established by repetition and practice.

Another tempting but often inadvisable way of organizing the lesson is to take a semantic, rather than a grammatical, category as the basic unit of organization. One possibility is to organize around basic units of experience. This organization, usually tied in with the direct method, results in lessons built around experiences like *el almuerzo, en el cine, en la estación*. Just as the direct method itself, this approach is not necessarily in conflict with linguistic teaching; but it does take a great deal of careful planning to make the two compatible. Evaluating a lesson like *la comida* or *La Navidad en México*, the linguistically oriented pedagogue will not be primarily concerned with the questions "How lively and interesting is the story?" or "How many useful expressions does it contain?" His main concern will be "Does it contain new structures which are of particular difficulty for speakers of English?" "Are such structures singled out for specific and systematic drill?" and "Does it contain vocabulary problems that are not dealt with in specific exercises?"

The "concept approach" is another possible semantic category for organizing the lesson. The latter utilizes such categories as "the ways of expressing the future," "the immediate past," or "the idea of obligation." Much can be said for this type of organization, especially on the more advanced level of language teaching; it does present the material organized according to the viewpoint of the speaker wanting to use the particular language. It presents the grammatical and stylistic choices which the speaker must know in order to be able to communicate his thoughts. At the same time, it seems almost impossible to use this "concept approach" as the main guide for the organization of an elementary language class, for too many completely different and linguistically unrelated structures would have to be thrown together into the same lesson if the approach were to be followed through. A lesson dealing with the expression of the "immediate past" would have to contain a treatment of the present perfect tense; the *acabar* + infinitive construction; the *hace una hora* . . construction with the Spanish present indicative where English uses present perfect or present perfect progressive: *que estudio*—I've been studying; *que estoy aquí*—I've been here; *por poco me caigo*—I almost fell; and such forms as *recién, recientemente, hace poco, ahora mismo*. Similarly, a lesson dealing with the ways of expressing the immediate future would have to present the present tense (*Veo a Jorge esta trade*); *ir a* + infinitive, *pensar* + infinitive, *estar para* + infinitive, *estar a punto de* + infinitive, and adverbs such as *en seguida, en el acto, pronto, a poco, inmediatamente, dentro de poco*.

Perhaps the most important point to keep in mind in the organization of linguistically oriented teaching materials is that for any approach that relies primarily on habit-formation, the unit of instruction is not the lesson or chapter but the individual exercise: the drill dealing with a specific structure which adds a new building stone to the student's repertory. This does not mean that such an approach to language teaching is atomistic or that it does not see the overall problem. On the contrary, it looks at the student's acquisition of the language as a chain in which the individual exercises are the links that must be carefully connected with each other. If an exercise includes several difficulties, if it builds on problems not previously taught, this chain will be broken, and the student's knowledge will become fragmentary. But language study viewed as the formation of linguistic habit is a **continuum**, a progression from one link of the chain to the next, a progression which preferably should be allowed only after each link is solidly fashioned and anchored to its predecessor.

If we organize our teaching materials as **single-emphasis drills**, each one designed to establish a particular speech pattern, each drill, in a sense, becomes a lesson in itself; and the lesson as an overall unit of organization becomes a quite arbitrary unit. Linguistically oriented materials are thus apt to form a **continuum of drills and exercises.** Accompanying this continuum there should be, of course, exercises for review, examples of connected speech and stories (perhaps the unit of experience type), which provide a meaningful context for the learning of vocabulary and for the practice of the speech patterns acquired by the student. The typical lesson or unit might thus consist of, let us say, ten individual drills, followed by a story in which the ten patterns presented in those drills are used in context, and following this, there might be a series of questions about the story, which will give the student the opportunity to use the ten patterns in his answers. A variation of this organization may be to introduce the new patterns in the context of the story, then have the drills dealing with the new patterns, and the questions and answers calling for the contextual use of the patterns.

(D) VISUAL AIDS

There are various types of visual aids and many ways to use them in the language class. We shall comment on some of the most important categories from the linguistic viewpoint, beginning with those which are unrelated to structural linguistic teaching.

The most obvious way of using pictures is to employ them for the teaching of vocabulary items. The teacher may hold up a picture of a horse to the class, point to it, and utter the word *caballo*. He may then ask a question like *¿Qué es esto?* in the hope of eliciting the response *Es un caballo* from the class. Useful as this kind of pictorial aid may be, it has no immediate relation to the teaching of language structures.

Another possible use of the picture is to stimulate the description of a scene or action. A picture is presented to the student; the words for all the persons or objects in the picture and the actions taking place are described. Then the student is asked questions about what is going on. This kind of pictorial aid has several useful applications. If typically Hispanic scenes and typically Hispanic settings are chosen, a great deal of cultural information can be conveyed. The picture can also be used to good advantage for the contextual presentation of vocabulary items and of structures previously drilled or to be drilled. Since the description of even a very simple picture is apt to call for a variety of forms and patterns, it is an occasion for the use and testing rather than the learning of grammatical patterns.

Quite different use is made of the pictorial aid, if it is of the type in which every sentence to be learned by the student is accompanied by one picture. With this kind of pictorial aid two quite distinct possibilities must be differentiated. In the first method the picture is used to convey the exact semantic content of the sentence: the student hears the sentence *Un hombre entra en la sala* and sees the picture of a man entering a room. This kind of visual aid has been elaborated into a rather skillful teaching device, in which stick figures rather than personalized pictures are used.

These figures are systematically put through a series of actions which teach the student basic semantic concepts with the help of a basic vocabulary. This technique, an elaboration of the direct method, is again non-linguistic, insofar as it does not take its point of view of organization from the structure of Spanish, nor does it in any way consider the particular difficulties of the speaker of English.

The other approach, which combines an individual structure with a single picture, conveys not the exact meaning of the structure but rather the **visual reinforcement** of it. This visual reinforcement is supposed to be doubly effective if the picture is esthetically of high quality; we are at the opposite pole from the stick figures. The actual connection between the meaning of the sentence to be learned and the picture may be quite loose. Let us say, a picture of people skiing is accompanied by a sentence like *A los españoles también les gustan los deportes de invierno.* The value of this kind of use of pictures, aside from the obvious possibilities in the representation of a Hispanic cultural environment, lies in the supposed reinforcement of the structure to be learned. Whether such a reinforcement actually takes place (could it be that the visual impact rather diverts the student's attention from the language structure?) remains to be confirmed by experiments. Again, there is no obvious connection between the linguistic structural teaching approach and the pictorial aid.

A more linguistic use of the pictorial aid is made when it serves to teach a vocabulary item or construction which is difficult to learn because of the interference coming from the English speech habits. Such pictorial aids may, for instance, be used to reinforce the teaching of false cognates—these vocabulary items which resemble English words in form but which have quite different meanings: a picture of a man sitting in passive enjoyment of a concert may illustrate *asistir al concierto*; that of a man entering a bookstore may drive home the real meaning of *librería*. We may also use pictures to illustrate the meaning of *él tiene calor* versus *hace calor*, or *el café está caliente* versus *el sol es caliente*.

An extensive and very effective development of this idea, running to some 400 colorful and dramatic illustrations, has become available recently. It is in a form which makes it easily adaptable to use with practically any course or text material.

Other types of pictorial aids may also be brought into play in order to teach concepts and contrasts which are lacking in the native language. These include, for example, the familiar type of line graphs which illustrate the meaning of various tenses, such as the imperfect versus the preterite; or symbols such as squares or circles used to suggest ideas such as inclusion or exclusion (inside, outside, into, out of); or arrows or other symbols of relationship, associated with certain verb meanings or prepositions. The only limit to the use of this type of pictorial aid is the experience and imagination of the teacher.

A very direct application of the structural linguistic approach to the use of visual aids is the diagramming of sentence patterns. Various examples of the same pattern are presented to the student in such a way that the elements which fulfill identical functions in the pattern are lined up vertically and are put into the same "slot" in the structural frame. For example:

Nosotros	estudiamos	nuestra	lección.
Nosotros	bebemos	neustro	café.
Nosotros	llevamos	nuestros	libros.

The same method can also be used in the visual presentation of substitution exercises:

	yo	quiero	que	usted	salga	en el acto.
1.	—	ruego	—	—	—	—
2.	—	pido	—	—	—	—
3.	—	—	—	—	venga	—
4.	—	—	—	—	—	pronto.

This type of presentation is an important aid in the teaching of structure; in many ways it is more effective than lengthy grammatical explanation in making the student aware of basic similarities and differences between patterns and in making him conscious of grammatical word classes.

The pictorial chart may be more closely tied in with the structural approach when it is arranged to illustrate a grammatical category. For example, we may compose a chart which shows various situations, all illustrating uses of the verb *estar*, or we may construct a similar chart, illustrating the important verbs which take direct objects in Spanish while their normal English counterparts take a prepositional object. Such a chart might show the picture of a man waiting for a bus (*el hombre espera el autobus*), that of a student looking for a pencil (*el alumno busca el lápiz*), or a girl listening to the radio (*la muchacha escucha el radio*).

The composite chart of the type just mentioned is probably the most immediate application of pictorial aids to linguistic teaching, for it is this type of chart that can be used most effectively in the basic drill techniques of substitution, transformation, and expansion. A chart showing several objects or persons can provide the nouns to be substituted in a pattern. The teacher provides the pattern to be drilled, let us say, *Deseo que usted hable con el profesor*; and merely by pointing at different pictures, he elicits the responses, *Deseo que usted hable con la madre, Deseo que usted hable con el soldado, Deseo que usted hable con la criada*. The same chart may also be used to provide substitution items in a sentence like *Es un profesor viejo* to elicit responses like *Es una criada vieja, Es un soldado viejo,* and *Es una madre vieja.*

Even more useful for pattern drills is the chart which is composed of a series of action pictures. The student learns the basic sentence which describes each action taking place on the chart: *El profesor busca el libro, el alumno espera el autobús, la madre escucha el radio, el muchacho mira al policía*. Once each sentence has been learned and associated with the picture, the latter becomes an efficient instrument with which to trigger students' responses in manipulative pattern drills. For example, the basic sentence may be transformed into different tenses. By pointing at a particular picture and using a key word (for example, *ayer*), the teacher may drill his class to respond with a preterite: *el profesor buscó el libro, el alumno esperó el autobús*. The word *mañana* may be used to trigger a response in the future; *antes* for a response in the imperfect, and so forth. The teacher may ask the class, or individual students, to substitute different subjects in the actions of the chart— for example, he points to the chart and says *nosotros*, and the class responds with *buscamos el libro, escuchamos el radio*, et cetera. The basic sentences may be made negative or transformed into questions; the nouns may be replaced by pronouns; questions may be asked for the subjects or objects of the actions; and substitution words (for example, an adverb) may be suggested to be inserted into the basic sentences.

(E) THE LANGUAGE LABORATORY

There is no need to duplicate here the description of laboratory techniques found in several excellent texts which have appeared recently and which deal primarily with the subject of the language laboratory. While the laboratory is potentially a useful adjunct to any teaching approach, it is particularly useful—in some situations perhaps necessary—for the linguistic method. It is in the laboratory that two psychological principles utilized by the linguistic method can find immediate application: that language learning is primarily habit-formation; and that correct responses are learned better if they are immediately reinforced by reward.

In the classroom only one student can perform at any given time. It is true that by choral responses and answers the teacher may include more than two students in a situation. But the very fact that the student is performing in a group lessens his personal attention, his drives, and his motivation. The reward given for the correct response is directed toward the entire class and is thus less effective than that given to an individual. In any choral response there will be only a few leaders, and a large number of the students will be followers. For the latter the choral response exercise is in fact a repetition rather than a new reaction to a stimulus. But in the laboratory a large number of students can perform simultaneously. They can be rewarded simultaneously and immediately, for the answer they are supposed to give can be given on the tape. As soon as the student has finished his own response in any pattern drill, as soon as he has answered a question asked on the tape, the correct answer given on the tape can reward and reinforce the correct answer by the student. Even if the student's response has been wrong, the opportunity to be corrected immediately and in an impersonal manner is undoubtedly a distinct advantage over the type of correction which occurs hours after the student has made the mistake in his homework, or the type which occurs in front of his fellow students in the classroom. The latter point brings us to perhaps the most essential and obvious contribution of the laboratory: it is the only meaningful way in which the formation of language skills can be made part of the student's homework. A student sitting in silence in front of a book can hardly learn a language because he either does not perform or is likely to perform wrongly. He may perhaps develop some understanding of the pattern he is trying to analyze, though it is rather doubtful that he will develop this understanding by himself at home if he did not achieve it in the classroom under the guidance of the teacher. The main contribution homework can make is in the automatization of the responses, in fixing the correct answers in the student's mind. Where else but in the language laboratory (or in the presence of a private tutor) could this essential and (on the elementary level) only real function of homework be guaranteed? It thus seems that the laboratory functions best and can make its major contribution when it can be used in addition to or in conjunction with, rather than in lieu of, classroom instruction, and when it can assure flexibility in the amount of time needed by individual students to achieve mastery of learning tasks according to their individual needs and abilities.

The laboratory is no doubt the best place in which to locate the stimulus–response type of learning, the manipulation of patterns in transformation and substitution drill. The classroom is the place for explanation and above all for the use of the speech pattern in a situational context. In terms of a comparison we made earlier between language learning and football training, the laboratory is the practice field, the gymnasium, in which detailed operations involved in the game are drilled, and the classroom is the football field in which the actual game takes place. This does not mean that at times it may not be necessary to make their functions overlap. Obviously we may sometimes practice patterns in the classroom and, in turn, may sometimes prepare for the laboratory a little story followed by questions concerning it. There are many ways of enlivening laboratory work, but even then, the instructor planning the course should always keep in mind the principle that the laboratory and classroom are utilized best if there is a division, rather than a duplication, of work between the two.

The more we emphasize habit-formation in our teaching, the more the laboratory moves from the position of an adjunct to the language course to that of its very center in which all essential learning takes place. The concept of habit-formation by the immediate reward of correct responses has recently been combined with the idea of minimal-step learning in the Teaching Machine approach, in programmed Spanish courses. In any kind of programming, the material to be learned is broken down into a number of learning steps or frames. At the end of each step, an answer—hopefully the correct one—is elicited from the student and only the correct answer is confirmed or otherwise rewarded. In programmed learning, the laboratory becomes indeed the private tutor of the individual student. Responding to the stimuli provided by the machine, the student checks the accuracy of his answers against those provided by the machine. Ideally, the laboratory should then also furnish some sort of mechanical signal which confirms and further reinforces the correct response. It should also provide some sort of check which would allow the student to proceed to a new learning step only after the previous step had been thoroughly mastered. The possibility of incorporating these last two requirements to audio-lingual learning in the laboratory has been experimented with in various programmed courses. Although at the writing of this text none of the programmed Spanish courses have had any large scale application, it seems that programming—especially audio-lingual programming—will become an important part of foreign language teaching. Some of the details and assumptions concerning programmed learning (the underlying theory of learning, role of student motivation, size of the individual learning step), are still, and will undoubtedly remain, subject to dispute. But there is no doubt that programming can make a very significant contribution in at least one area that has been of concern to teachers: the individual student can be allowed to proceed at his own speed and the language laboratory turned teaching machine can be used to eliminate or at least alleviate the classroom situation which forces the slow and fast learner into the same learning pace.

PART TWO

CHAPTER V

General Phonetics
and Phonemics

(A) PHONETICS

The raw material of language consists of sounds. The science which is
concerned with the study of speech sounds is **phonetics**. Phonetics can
approach the study of speech sounds from two very different points of
view: it can study the properties of the sounds themselves, that is, the
exact nature of the sound waves as they progress through the air; or
it can study the way in which the sounds are produced by the human
speech organs. That branch of phonetics which studies the sounds themselves is called **acoustic phonetics**, and the study of the sound production
is called **articulatory phonetics**. Acoustic phonetics has made important
strides during the past years as the result of the discovery and perfection
of machines which allow us to analyze the speech sounds in great detail.
But from the viewpoint of the language teacher, articulatory phonetics
will continue to be the more important branch of phonetics.

There are several good textbooks in existence, all dealing in great
detail with the science of articulatory phonetics. In this chapter we shall,
therefore, summarize and review the most important concepts of phonetics which are useful to the teacher of Spanish, rather than try to give a
detailed account of the discipline. Phoneticians have for some time been
concerned with the creation of a phonetic alphabet. They have worked
out and are still attempting to perfect an **international phonetic alphabet**.
Ideally, such an alphabet would have one symbol and one symbol only
to identify without ambiguity any speech sound possible in any of the
languages existing today. In presenting the résumé of phonetics, we shall
emphasize only those sounds and symbols of both languages which are

55

of importance for the Spanish teacher. We shall follow the customary procedure of presenting phonetic transcriptions within square brackets: [ ]. We shall, however, make certain deviations from the International Phonetic Alphabet, in order to reduce its complexity for users of Spanish.

Speech sounds are traditionally classified as vowels and consonants. In the production of vowels the air stream passes through the larynx over the vocal cords, whose vibration creates sounds which are modified in the oral cavity by the other speech organs. At no time during the production of the sound is the air stream interrupted or impeded. In the production of consonants, however, the air stream meets a definite obstacle while passing through the speech organs which impedes or momentarily stops the sound.

Classification of Consonants

Voicing

Turning our attention first to the classification of consonants, we find that there are three possible criteria according to which they can be described. The first classification considers the already mentioned activity of the vocal cords. The actual mechanism which correlates the vibration of the vocal cords and the production of a consonant is quite complicated. But in somewhat simplified fashion we may say that we call a consonant **voiced** if the vocal cords vibrate throughout the production of the sound, while we consider a consonant **unvoiced** if throughout most or all of the production of the sound the vibration of the vocal cords is absent. On that basis we call the initial sound of English bin voiced, while that of pin is unvoiced; the initial sound of English father is unvoiced and that of veal is voiced.

The importance of voicing as a basis of distinguishing one consonant sound from another may be emphasized by comparing a number of pairs of words in which the only difference is that between a voiced consonant and an unvoiced one pronounced with the same position and movement of the tongue, lips, and so on:

Voiced consonant	Unvoiced consonant
din	tin
gap	cap
thy	thigh
edge	etch
tab	tap
van	fan

Manner of production

The second criterion for the classification of consonants considers the **manner of production**. We have already mentioned that in the production of consonants the air stream meets an obstacle. If during the production of the sound the air stream is completely interrupted, we call the sound a **stop**. A stop, then, is a sound which is produced by the act of closing and opening the path taken by the air during sound production. In this process of opening and closing, the air is often allowed to build up pressure against the obstacle and is then permitted to escape suddenly when the obstacle is removed. For this reason stop sounds are also frequently referred to as **plosives**. The initial sounds of the English big, tin, din, can, get, are all plosive or stop sounds. Stops may be either voiced or unvoiced:

Voiced:	[p]	[t]	[k]
	pin	**t**ip	**c**ut
	tip	**c**ut	**t**ack
Unvoiced:	[b]	[d]	[g]
	bin	**d**ab	**g**oal
	ta**b**	ta**d**	ta**g**

Another manner of production occurs in the initial sounds of chin and general. When producing a stop sound like the [t] in tin, the air stream is released suddenly after a brief stoppage. When, on the other hand, the obstacle is removed quite slowly, the air, instead of escaping with the explosion of the plosive, is allowed to pass over the obstacle more gradually. The result is that a fricative type of sound is produced. Instead of [t] as in tin, we get a sound that resembles [t] followed by an sh-like sound (transcribed [tʃ]), as in chin. In the word general, the initial sound is similar to [d] followed by [ʒ], which represents the sound heard in pleasure or azure:

Voiced:	[dʒ]	ba**dge**, **g**in
Unvoiced:	[tʃ]	ba**tch**, **ch**in

Although these sounds begin with a stop, they are called **affricates** because of the fricative element in them.

All sounds produced without any complete stoppage of the air stream are called **continuants** (vowels too are, therefore, continuants in the strict sense). Among the consonants we can distinguish different types of continuants. One important type is the **fricative**. In the production of the fricative the air stream passes over an obstacle; there is no complete closure, but rather a constriction of the speech organs, and throughout the production of the sounds the air is allowed to pass through the constriction. The initial sounds of the English father, veal, thin, this, sin, and ship are all fricative sounds, produced with air friction as it passes through a constriction of the vocal apparatus. Fricatives, like stops, may be either voiced or unvoiced:

Voiced:	veal	tee**the**	**azure**	**z**ip	
Unvoiced:	**f**eel	tee**th**	**Asher**	**s**ip	**hat**

The next comment concerns the sound [s]. How does it differ from the initial sound of thin (transcribed [θ]) with which so many speakers of foreign languages, such as Frenchmen or Germans, are apt to confuse it? For one thing, [s] is produced with the tip of the tongue in a different position than in the case of [θ]. This, however, is not the main difference. Both [s] and [θ] are also fricative sounds. This means that the air is creating friction as it passes through a narrow opening, but the shape of the opening is different for the two sounds. For [θ] (just as for [f] and [v]) the opening is wide from side to side and narrow from top to bottom. Such sounds are called **slit fricatives**. For [s] the opening is narrow from side to side and deep from top to bottom: [s] is called a **groove fricative**. The consonant sounds corresponding to the bold face letters in pleasure [ʒ] or shine [ʃ] or rose [z] are all **groove fricatives**. Since the grooved kind of opening results in these sounds having a hissing quality, they are also frequently called **sibilants**.

In another group of continuants there is a modification or narrowing of the speech tract, but without enough constriction to cause a fricative sound. These consonants, all of them voiced, are called **resonants**; the initial sounds of English man, news, lion, ran, and water, are examples of the resonants. In the initial sounds in man and neat or the final sound in song, the passage through the mouth is closed, but the passage through the nose is opened. For this reason these resonants are also called **nasals**. In the case of [l], as in lion, the aperture is partially closed by the contact that the tongue makes against the upper gum, but the air is allowed to escape freely at both sides of the tongue. The resonants produced in such a manner are called **laterals**. Finally, the resonants heard in water, yes, and ride have no actual point of closure, but only the rounding of the lips for [w], the gap between the front of the tongue and the gum-ridge (alveolae) in [y], the curling back of the tip of the tongue near the gum-ridge or the palate (in retroflex position) which produces the [ɹ] of ride.

These sounds are classed as **semivowels** or **semiconsonants—labial, alveo-palatal**, and **retroflex**, respectively.

Resonants:

Nasals:	**m**ap, ca**n**, sa**ng**
Lateral:	**l**ap, ca**ll**
Semiconsonants:	**w**ater, co**w**, **y**am, la**y**, **r**un
(or *semivowels*):	ca**r**

From the way we have characterized resonant consonants (without any complete stoppage or even real constriction and always voiced), it is also quite clear that there is little absolute difference in kind between resonant consonants and vowels. As a matter of fact, vowels may be classified as resonants, and the distinction between vowel and consonant—sharp and obvious if we compare vowels with stops or even fricatives—becomes blurred in the case of the resonant sounds and is difficult to make with any real precision. From the strictly phonetic point of view the distinction is therefore fairly arbitrary, and it is for that reason that the borderline sounds of [w], [y], and [ɹ] are, as we have just noted, called either semivowels or semiconsonants, according to their position in an utterance.

Two more manners of articulation must be considered: the **trill** or **vibrant** sound and the **flap** or **tap**. The latter is produced by a single rapid movement of an articulator. It may be compared to a very short stop sound; the [r] of Spanish *pero* is such a tap, produced with the tip of the tongue. A similar sound is heard in British speech, as in very ("veddy"). A vibrant consists of the very rapid alternation of sounds produced by the vibration of a flexible speech organ. The [rr] of the Spanish *perro* and *risa* is produced by the vibration or trill of the tip of the tongue. This sound is also heard in southern French; the [r] of standard French is produced by the vibration of the uvula.

Point of articulation

The third criterion in the classification of consonants is the **point of articulation**. This is based on the place of stoppage of the air stream or of maximum constriction of the speech organs. We note first that there are two lower articulators—the tongue and the lower lip. Consonants produced by the action of the lower lip are called **labials**. The lower lip may act with the upper lip, producing **bilabials** ([b], [p], [m], [w]), or against the upper teeth, producing **labiodentals** ([v], [f]). The tongue may make its contact or close approach with the tip (apex), the front, or the back (dorsum); when we are concerned with the shape of the tongue, we will describe a consonant as **apical**, **frontal**, or **dorsal**. On the other hand, the point touched or approached by the tongue must be identified in order to have an accurate classification of the consonant, and conse-sequently, the upper articulators alone provide the designations commonly used where the tongue is the lower articulator (except for English [ɹ] whose designation "retroflex" refers to tongue position). Table I summarizes the classification according to both articulators involved:

TABLE I

Lower Articulator	Upper Articulator	Name of Sound	Examples in English
lower lip	upper lip	1. bilabial	1. **pin**, **bin**
lower lip	upper teeth	2. labio-dental	2. **fin**, **vine**
tip of tongue	teeth	3. dental	e. **thin**
tip of tongue	gums of upper teeth (alveolae)	4. alveolar	4. **tin**, **sin**
tip of tongue (curled back)	palate	5. retroflex	5. **red**
front of tongue	gums of upper teeth (alveolae)	6. alveo-palatal	6. **chin**, **shun**
front of tongue	front of palate	7. prepalatal	7. **yet**
back of tongue	back of palate	8. palatal	8. **key**
back of tongue	velum	9. velar	9. **car**
back of tongue	uvula (back of velum)	10. uvular	10. (French: **rien**)

Note how the point of articulation shifts back as you say the English words given as examples in the table above.

It is, of course, possible to produce sounds which have their point of articulation even farther back than the uvula, namely, in the larynx. Thus, we can produce a stop just by the closure and opening of the vocal cords. This sound, a glottal stop (symbol [ʔ]), is produced in some languages (German and to a somewhat lesser degree English) before any word beginning with a vowel sound. Some speakers of English, especially along the Eastern Seaboard as in New York and New Jersey, say a glottal stop in a word like bottle [bɑʔl]. A **fricative glottal sound** is produced if the air stream is allowed to pass through the constriction created between the vocal cords without there being any further modification taking place in the rest of the speech tract: the [h] sound of have and her is such a glottal fricative.

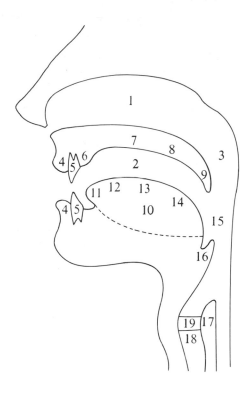

1. Nasal Cavity
2. Oral Cavity
3. Nasal Passage
4. Lips
5. Teeth
6. Alveolae, Gum Ridge
7. Hard Palate
8. Soft Palate, Velum
9. Uvula
10. Tongue
11. Tip of Tongue
12. Front of Tongue
13. Middle of Tongue
14. Back of Tongue
15. Pharynx
16. Epiglottis
17. Glottis
18. Larynx
19. Vocal Cords

Secondary features of consonants

Before summarizing our discussion of consonants, brief mention must be made of concomitant features, certain types of articulation which may accompany the articulation of a consonant. Thus the raising of the middle of the tongue against the palate may accompany the articulation of a consonant, which is then "palatalized." Or a rounding of the lips may take place while a dental or velar stop is pronounced, thus "labializing" that stop. For instance, the initial sound of English **quick [kwɪk]** can be interpreted as a **labialized stop**. The **aspiration** of a stop may also be an important accompanying feature. If, after the release of a stop and before the production of the following vowel, air pressure is allowed to build up immediately, a glottal fricative [h] will be heard between the stop and that vowel. This is normally the case in languages like English or German, in which most stops are aspirated. On the other hand, if after the stop the build-up of air pressure is delayed until the production of the following vowel, the stop will be unaspirated, as is normally the case in Spanish and the other Romance languages.

Consonants: summary

What we have reviewed here may seem to some a rather formidable array of terminology. Of course, there is no need for the student ever to hear most of it. The teacher, on the other hand, may find it quite useful to know the terminology of phonetics. Some control of this nomenclature is needed to follow important pedagogical discussions in professional journals; even more important, the control of the nomenclature implies a basic understanding of how sounds are produced. There is obviously no point in memorizing that "the English t is an alveolar unvoiced stop." The real point is that for the one who understands the nomenclature the rule gives in precise fashion the information about the pronunciation of the English t. Once that person knows how the English t is pronounced, he has no need to memorize the nomenclature, which is actually nothing but a condensed description of the pronunciation of the sound.

With this in mind let us review the terminology we have learned so far, with the help of Table II. In it, the points of articulation are given at the left in such a way that we move from the lips back as we proceed down the table. The manners of articulation are distinguished at the top of the table, as is the contrast of voiced versus unvoiced. Examples are taken from English, with written symbols representing the sounds whose spellings are underlined. A comparison of these English sounds with the consonants of Spanish will be made in the next chapter.

Classification of Vowels

Since vowels proper are all voiced and produced without any major obstacle to the air stream, they must be classified according to different points of view from those of consonants. The nature of any vowel depends on various factors, such as the position of the tongue, the position (front or back) of the highest point of the tongue, the position of the lips, the position of the lower jaw, and the aperture of the nasal passage. All of these modify the mouth resonator in different ways to produce vowels of varying qualities, whose possible number is almost unlimited. In order to classify vowels phoneticians have, therefore, had recourse to the system of the cardinal vowels. These cardinal vowels do not really exist as such in any language. They are sounds which can be produced by the tongue in certain well-defined positions. Other vowels actually existing in living languages may then be defined in relation to these "theoretical" cardinal vowels.

Certain vowel sounds of Spanish are so near some of the cardinal

TABLE II

The Consonants of English

Manner / Points of Articulation	STOPS		AFFRICATES		FRICATIVES				RESONANTS (all voiced)		
					slit		groove				
	voiced	unvoiced	voiced	unvoiced	voiced	unvoiced	voiced	unvoiced	lateral	nasal	semiconsonant
Bilabial	b (**bin**)	p (**pin**)								m (**man**)	w (**water**)
Labio-dental					v (**vat**)	f (**fat**)					
Dental					ð (**then**)	θ (**thin**)					
Alveolar	d (**din**)	t (**tin**)					z (**zinc**)	s (**sink**)	l (**late**)	n (**no**)	ɹ (**ran**)
Alveo-palatal			dʒ (**gin**)	tʃ (**chin**)			ʒ (**vision**)	ʃ (**nation**)			y (**yes**)
Velar	g (**goat**)	k (**coat**)								ŋ (**sing**)	
Glottal								h (**hat**)			

Note: There is some divergence among phoneticians in the selection of phonetic symbols. Some of the commonly used variants are:

for ʒ above, ž   for dʒ above, ǰ   for y above, j (since [y] is commonly used for the vowel of French **rue**)

for ʃ above, š   for tʃ above, č   for ɹ above, r

vowels that we can use them as illustrations, but we must turn to English and to French for approximate examples of others of these sounds.

If we raise the tongue as far as possible and push it as far forward as possible at the same time, we produce the sound [i], which occurs in Spanish *viví*. Keeping the tongue as far front as possible but dropping it as far as we can, we produce the sound [a] of French *patte.* If we again raise the tongue as far as possible, but now draw it back as far as we can, we say the [u] of Spanish *tú*. Dropping the tongue as far as possible while keeping it back produces the [ɑ] of French *pâte*.

We have now established four extreme positions: [i], maximum front and high; [u], maximum back and high; [a], maximum front and low; [ɑ], maximum back and low. The front series may be completed by two intermediate steps as the tongue is lowered from maximum high: [e] as in Spanish *peso*, [ɛ] about as in English bet; the back series, similarly, allows us to identify [o] as in Spanish *todo* and [ɔ] about as in English bought. We can now plot the position of these sounds in the form of a trapezoid, which is usually (and somewhat inaccurately) referred to as the **cardinal vowel triangle**:

High	1. [i] (Span. *viví*)		8. [u] (Span. *tú*)	
	2. [e] (Span. *peso*)		7. [o] (Span. *todo*)	
	3. [ɛ] (Engl. *bet*)		6. [ɔ] (Engl. *bought*)	
Low	4. [a] (Fr. *patte*)		5. [ɑ] (Fr. *pâte*)	
	Front		Back	

The above classification is based on the position of the tongue; we have simply assumed that the familiar rounding of the lips which is part of [o] and [u] and the spreading for [e] and [i] are taken for granted. It is possible, of course, to reverse this relationship, rounding the lips for the front series and spreading them for the back series, producing **secondary cardinal vowels** such as those heard in French *vu, peu,* and *peur*; but since neither English nor Spanish has sounds in this series, we shall dispense with a more detailed description of them.

In the next chapter we shall place the vowels of English and those of Spanish in relation to the scheme of cardinal vowels and, more importantly, in comparison or contrast with each other. In anticipation let us point out here that English uses a number of sounds at intermediate intervals: between [i] and [e], the [ɪ] of bit; between [ɛ] and [a], the [æ] of bat; between [u] and [o], the [ʊ] of good; in a position neither high nor low, neither front nor back, the [ə] of but (often transcribed [ʌ]). The

English [ɑ] of **fa**ther does not have a front counterpart like the French [a] of *patte*. Most important, the English vowels which seem nearest to [i], [e], [o] and [u] are, in fact, diphthongs. That is, they are combinations of vowels and semivowels as in s**ay** [sey], l**ow** [low]; or at the least, they clearly change their quality during the course of pronunciation.

A complete series can be illustrated by the following English words (the diphthongized vowels are shown, for simplicity, as simple vowels):

[i]	[ɪ]	[e]	[ɛ]	[aɛ]	[ə]
teak	tick	take	tech	tack	tuck

[ɑ]	[ɔ]	[o]	[ʊ]	[u]
tock	talk	toque	took	tune

(B) PHONEMICS

From the foregoing brief exposition of phonetics—the basis for analysis and description of the sounds of speech—it should be evident that any language may use a practically indefinite number of sounds. At the same time users of that language will actually differentiate only a specific number of units of sound. For example, in the English series of keen, kid, cad, conn, cup, and cough the initial [k] is articulated by the front of the tongue against the hard palate in keen, by the back of the tongue against the velum in cough, and in varying intermediate positions in the other words; yet speakers of English hear all these variants as "the same" sound. The initial [k] in these words is followed by a puff of air, or aspirated, while the [k] of skin is not; and the [k] of thick is ordinarily unreleased, that is, the air stream does not escape after it with an audible explosion, so that the sound is, so to speak, only half finished. Yet these variants too are felt to be "the same" as the [k] of skin or the [kʰ] of kin. The association of these variants into a unit perceived by speakers of English as one sound is denoted by the term **phoneme**. The variants are determined by position with relation to other sounds; these positions are mutually exclusive, or (to use technical terminology) these variants are found in **complementary distribution**. They are called **positional variants**, or **allophones**, of the same phoneme. When the symbol k is used to represent the **phoneme**, including its allophones or positional variants, it is conventionally written between slant lines, thus, /k/; the brackets we have used in the foregoing section indicate that our symbol—[k], for example—represents the sound as sound, not as a phoneme or unit of differentiation.

The concept of the phoneme will be clearer, perhaps, if we use again our analogy of the building stones of language. The phoneme, the smallest unit of sound which is distinctively differentiated by the speakers of a given language, may be regarded as the smallest building stone available to the users of that language. We may identify phonemes by comparing pairs of words whose sounds are all alike but one, such as pick, pit, or pit, pat, or pit, kit. Since users of the language recognize pick and pit as two different words, we take this fact as evidence that /k/ and /t/—the only sounds which differentiate the two words—are phonemes. We find that speakers of English consider kick and tick to be differentiated by the same pair of contrasting sounds, in spite of the phonetic difference between the aspirated [kʰ], [tʰ] of initial position and the unreleased quality of the final [k] and [t]. We now have information that [kʰ] and [k] are variants or allophones of one minimal building stone of English, the phoneme /k/; [tʰ] and [t] are allophones of /t/. It is by extended comparison of the differentiating sounds of large numbers of **minimal pairs**, such as the examples above, that linguists are able to group the large number of sounds which occur in a given language into the limited number of phonemes or differentiating sound units which characterize it.

The native speaker of any language is trained from infancy to perceive the specific phonemes of his language and the differences between them. Ultimately, it is only through these differences or **contrasts** that his language operates. What makes *le* and *ley* different words is the difference between /e/ (one phoneme) and /ey/ (two phonemes); the difference between *pero* and *perro* lies in /r/ versus /rr/, which are different phonemes. These differences, so obvious to any Spanish speaker, are at first difficult for speakers of English to hear and reproduce. English does not have /e/ and confuses both this sound and Spanish /ey/ with the English diphthong /ɛʸ/, as in bait. Since American English has neither Spanish /r/ nor Spanish /rr/, our students find these sounds not only hard to produce but harder to differentiate. Conversely, the Spanish speaker has great difficulty perceiving the differences between the English words seen /ɪʸ/ and sin /ɪ/, both of which he hears as Spanish /i/, or between bet /ɛ/, bat /æ/, and but /ə/, none of which occurs as a phoneme in Spanish. It is precisely because certain nearly similar sounds are heard as the same in one language, but as different in another, that the comprehension and pronunciation of foreign languages is so difficult. Our entire mechanism of perception and projection of speech sounds is geared to differentiating the phonemic contrasts of our own language

without conscious concern for the allophonic variations; and uncons-
ciously we try to project the same system of contrasts into the foreign
language, which organizes sounds differently into its own system of
phonemes.

The important contribution of phonemics to language teaching and
especially to the teaching of pronunciation lies in the fact that it has
simplified the task and systematized it. A speaker of any language produces an infinite variety of sounds as he speaks, but in doing so he is
only using a fairly limited number of phonemes. Phonemic analysis
teaches us to distinguish the unimportant from the important. We know
that our student must be able to hear and produce the phonemic distinctions of Spanish, or he will be able neither to understand nor to communicate. Phonemic analysis of Spanish and English shows us quite clearly
which of the Spanish phonemes will be difficult to learn for speakers of
English and must therefore be emphasized in our teaching. And finally,
phonemics provides us with a real understanding of the psychological
reasons for the foreign accent; the reason lies not so much in the English
speaker's inability to move his jaw muscles or tongue in the Spanish way,
but rather in the fact that his whole system of auditory discrimination
has been geared to the English phonemic differences. It is for this reason
that he is apt to find it difficult to distinguish between certain Spanish
sounds. Under the impact of phonemic theory our emphasis in the
teaching of pronunciation has been shifted to the teaching of auditory
discrimination as the initial step. **A student must be able to hear and
comprehend before he can be made to imitate and to speak.**

CHAPTER VI

Teaching Pronunciation

We shall now apply the concepts learned in the preceding chapter to the specific problem of teaching Spanish pronunciation. We will proceed by comparing Spanish and English consonants, vowels, and intonation patterns and by discussing Spanish orthography and pronunciation. Under each heading we shall try to summarize the major teaching problems and techniques which arise from our discussion. There are several excellent books dealing exhaustively with such subjects as English phonemics and Spanish pronunciation. Our purpose here is to focus our attention on the points with which every teacher should be familiar, rather than to give an exhaustive treatment.

In reading the discussion of teaching techniques, it should be kept in mind that we are thinking primarily of the senior high school and college level. Ultimately the acquisition of a good pronunciation by the student depends on a good pronunciation on the part of the teacher and his insistence on accurate (or at least increasingly accurate) repetition by the student. On the junior high school, and certainly the elementary school level, these are probably the main requisites of the teaching of pronunciation.

(A) CONSONANTS

Let us start by listing the consonant phonemes of Spanish; for each phoneme we shall give the phonetic symbol and a sample word in which the letter corresponding to the sound will be in boldface.

/p/	papá	/g/: [g]	golpe	/m/	mono, cama
/b/: [b]	bajo, vino	[g̊]	droga	/n/: [n]	nudo, lana
[b̥]	iba, favor	/f/	fino, café	[n]	ante, andar
/t/	todo, lata	/θ/	Zaragoza, hace	[ŋ]	cinco, ángel
/d/: [d]	daño	/s/: [s]	sino, cosa	/ñ/	caña
[d̥]	cada	[z]	desde	/H/	jugar, caja
[tʃ/	chulo, mucho	/l/	lata, escala	/rr/	rana, perro
/k/	que, capa, toca	/ĺ/	llama, calle	/r/	pero, corta, cantar

In addition Spanish has two semiconsonants which can be conveniently grouped with the consonants. They are

/w/ *huir, cuento*   /y/ *yo, leyeron*

These Spanish consonant phonemes can now be tabulated according to the criteria of classification discussed in Chapter V. Table III is arranged so as to permit a comparison of the consonants of Spanish with those of English.[1]

A comparison of the English and Spanish tables points out quite clearly some important facts:

The Spanish speaker learning English will have to learn the separate phonemic value of English /v/, which he will confuse with his allophone [b̥] of /b/; and of English /ð/, which he will confuse with his allophone [d̥] of /d/; he will have to learn /dʒ/, **judge** and learn that it is a separate phoneme from /tʃ/ **church**; he will have to learn /ʃ/ **shall** and /ʒ/ **treasure**. If he is Castilian or has had contact with Castilian speakers, he will easily learn /θ/ **thin**; but he may have difficulty discriminating /θ/ **thin** from /s/ **sin** if he is a Latin American.

The Spanish speaker will, of course, meet other problems besides those seen in the comparison of consonant phonemes. For example, he will have to learn to hear and pronounce final consonants such as

---

* Note that other transcriptions are used by some writers:

[tʃ]:	[č]	[rr]:	[R] [r̄]
[dʒ]:	[ǰ]	[ɹ] (English):	[r]
[ʃ]:	[š]	[b̥]:	[b] [β]
[ʒ]:	[ž]	[g̊]:	[g]
[y]:	[j]	[d̥]:	[d] [ð]
[H]:	[x] [h]	[ñ]:	[ɲ]

TABLE III
Comparison of Spanish and English Consonant Phonemes

Spanish

	Bi-Labial	Labio-Dental	Dental	Alveolar	Alveo-Palatal	Velar	Glottal
Stop	p [b]		t [d]			k [g]	
Fricative	[β]	f	θ [đ]	s z		H [ǥ]	
Affricate					tʃ		
Lateral				l	ĩ		
Nasal	m			n	ñ	[ŋ]	
Trill			rr				
Tap			r				
Semi-consonant	w				y		

In the above table the four pairs of consonants enclosed in brackets, and the similarly bracketed [ŋ], represent the most important allophones.

Observe that the symbol v is not used in either phonetic or phonemic transcription of Spanish.

English

	Bi-Labial	Labio-Dental	Dental	Alveolar	Alveo-Palatal	Velar	Glottal
Stop	p b			t d		k g	
Fricative		f v	θ ð	s z			h
Affricate					tʃ dʒ		
Lateral				l			
Nasal	m			n		ŋ	
Semi-consonant	w			ɹ	y		

/m/ some, /k/ tack, and /g/ dog, and (still harder for him) final consonant clusters such as /sk/ task, /rt/ art, and dozens of others which characterize English and are absent in Spanish.

The speaker of English has problems in his turn. While he has few obviously new sounds to learn (the /rr/ of *carro*, the /r/ of *caro*, the /H/ of *hijo*, and the allophones [ƀ] in *pavo* and [ǵ] in *agua*), he has serious problems of auditory discrimination arising from the fact that a number of sounds which are quite similar in the two languages are allophones in Spanish but separate phonemes in English. When he is speaking, his tendency to substitute English sounds for Spanish will not seriously impede the native listener's understanding, although it will sound very foreign. The English speaker's failure to produce the fricative allophones [ƀ] [ǵ] in *cebo* and *haga* will not confuse the Spanish-speaking listener because he makes no contrast in meaning between the normal [seƀo] [aǵa] and the foreigner's [sebo], [aga]. Some confusions could arise, however; for example, the English speaker's *cada*, pronounced with an English alveolar [d] (instead of the fricative Spanish [đ]), actually sounds more like *cara* than *cada* to the Spanish ear.

On the other hand, the English speaker has considerable difficulty understanding the Spanish speaker until he has learned to discriminate these differences. As sounds, English [d] is easily associated with Spanish [d], and Spanish [đ] with English [ð], as in lather. But in English meanings are distinguished by the difference between /d/ and /ð/:

/d/ ladder   /ð/ lather
    den   then

while in Spanish the difference is only that of positional variants, or allophones:

[d] *daño*   [đ] *cada*

The beginner who is not sufficiently drilled in recognizing the discriminations of sound in the distributions characteristic of the language he is learning will long suffer confusions with his own system—confusions which seriously impede his understanding of the spoken language. He will interpret [ƀ] as English /v/; [đ] as English /ð/; [ǵ] as English /k/, /r/, or /h/, or as no sound at all; he will try to react, subconsciously, to [s] in *casa* and [z] in *desde* as though they somehow signaled a difference of meaning, since in English face and phase are differentiated only by /s/ and /z/. And, of course, he will frequently hear Spanish /r/ as [d], and, on the other hand, he will fail to hear a difference between /rr/ and /r/ as in *morro, moro*.

Sounds which have some sort of counterpart in the native language of the learner are not necessarily easy to learn. Sometimes they are more difficult to learn than the completely new sounds because the interference of the native language is likely to be even greater than with the completely new ones. A case in point is the bilabial fricative [ƀ], which English speakers will tend either to convert into a stop [b] or into a labio-dental [v]. Learners who have mastered the completely new sound of /rr/ will often continue to mispronounce [ƀ], [g̵], and [H], all of which are nearer to English sounds than is /rr/.

Let us now examine the Spanish consonants systematically together with some methods for developing the auditory discrimination which must be learned before the beginner can reproduce the differences which are new to him. We shall take up these consonants according to the manner of articulation: stops (unvoiced, voiced); fricatives (unvoiced, voiced); laterals, nasals, tap, trill, and semivowels.

Spanish /p/, /t/, and /k/ are always unaspirated; they do not normally occur in final position. Since most English speakers are quite unaware that they aspirate English /p/, /t/, and /k/ as in pin, tin, and kin but do not aspirate in spin, step, and skin, some effort must be made to develop auditory discrimination between the two varieties in English; otherwise the learner will surely aspirate these stops in Spanish *papá*, *tino*, *quina*. A technique which has found increased acceptance of late is to contrast Spanish and English words which sound roughly similar, as

Spanish	English
papá	papa
pico	peak
tono	tone
tenso	tense
calma	calm
quina	keen

The difference between the aspirated stops of English and the unaspirated stops in Spanish can be illustrated by the teacher who has a reasonably good Spanish pronunciation; it can be done even more profitably in the language laboratory through the use of a tape recorded by a bilingual English–Spanish speaker. One might say that this method employs the pedagogical value of the minimal pair concept on an interlingual basis, modified, of course, by the fact that these words are differentiated by more than the one sound which is placed in contrast.

English /t/ and Spanish /t/ differ further in the "point of articulation," as the table shows. English /t/ is alveolar, while Spanish /t/ is dental—the tip of the tongue is against the back of the teeth. A similar difference applies to English and Spanish /d/ or, more accurately, to English /d/ and the Spanish allophone [d]. This basic difference in articulation should be observed not only because it makes some difference in the pronunciation of the consonants themselves, but also because it affects the pronunciation of the following vowels.

The voiced series /b/, /d/, and /g/ offers major difficulties. The plosive variants [b] and [g], as in *bota* and *gato*, are not importantly different from English /b/ and /g/; but the Spanish [d] is dental, in contrast with the English alveolar /d/, as noted in the preceding paragraph. More troublesome are the fricative allophones [ƀ], [đ], and [ǥ]:[1]

[ƀ], as in *haba* and *cava*, is a voiced bilabial fricative, a sound sometimes described as of "*v*-like character" but not made against the upper teeth. The possible confusions that this sound may cause have been mentioned above.

[ ], as in *haba* and *cava*, is a voiced bilabial fricative, a sound somewhat like the English [ð] of lather; it is not in contrast with [d] as is the English sound. This may lead to confusion of perception.

[ǥ], as in *haga*, is a voiced velar fricative, which does not have a commonly heard counterpart in English, although some speakers may pronounce words such as wagon, flagon, with less than full occlusion. As noted above, this sound may be misheard by learners in a variety of ways.

Two kinds of drill are useful to the learner mastering the variants [b] [ƀ], [d] [đ], and [g] [ǥ]:

1. The teacher may help in developing auditory discrimination of the contrast between English and Spanish by repeating a word such as *haba* three times, giving English [b] instead of Spanish [ƀ] in one of the repetitions; the students signal their perception of the difference by raising a hand when they hear the Anglicized variety of the sound. So, for example, a drill may be set up with the following as the teacher's "cue sheet":

---

[1] In the balance of this chapter, the transcriptions will show the fricative allophones, [ƀ], [đ], [ǥ], where they occur, even when the transcription is otherwise represented as being phonemic and is placed between slant lines. The same practice will be followed with the allophones [z] of /s/, and [ŋ] of /n/. This departure from standard practice in phonemic transcription seems justified by the rather marked character of the Spanish allophones mentioned.

haba:	[aβa]	[aβa]	* [aba]
iban:	[iβan]	* [iban]	[iβan]
cada:	[kaɖa]	[kaɖa]	* [kada]
lodo:	* [lodo]	[loɖo]	[loɖo]
haga:	* [aga]	[aǥa]	[aǥa]
digo:	[diǥo]	* [digo]	[diǥo]

2. The contrasts within Spanish should be exercised by series of drills of which the following are examples:

[b]	[β]
vez	*la vez*
voz	*la voz*
boca	*la boca*
un bus	*este bus*
un baile	*este baile*

[d]	[ɖ]
día	*ese día*
un disco	*este disco*

[g]	[ǥ]
gato	*este gato*
un gusto	*mi gusto*

The fricatives [β], [ɖ], and [ǥ] being accounted for as allophones of /b/, /d/, and /g/, the actual **fricative phonemes** are:

/f/, as in *café*, a voiceless labio-dental close enough to English [f] to cause no difficulty.

/θ/, as in *cabeza* and *dice* in Castilian speakers, is a voiceless dental fricative quite close to the similar sound in English **thing** and **bath**. The learner's problem does not lie in any difficulty in perceiving or imitating the sound, but in the controversial matter of "standard" versus "Latin American" pronunciation. There are cogent reasons for learning either variety and some arguments in favor of learning both.

Interference from English habits arises only when the learner is exposed to Spanish orthography; interference from alternate exposure to Castilian speakers and to non-Castilians can cause some confusion to beginners, who hear some words in alternate pronunciation, such as [diθe]: [dise], [kaβeθa]: [kaβesa], [boθ]: [bos], and so might erroneously say *[kaθa] for [kaθa]. In actual practice most learners experience very little difficulty in this potentially confusing matter, although there is no question that the teacher must be prepared to give clarifying exercises when they are needed.

/s/, with its allophones, [s] and [z]; here the problem is one of positional variation in Spanish, the sounds being different phonemes in English. There is very little learning problem involved except for a not uncommon tendency for learners to carry over English /z/ in positions calling for [s] in Spanish, as in *rosa* mispronounced * [roza]. While the Spanish [s] is more deeply grooved or closer to the teeth in some dialects, the English [s] is close enough.

/H/, as in *gente*, *caja*; there the tongue is higher in the mouth and tenser than in English /h/, so that friction is produced against the velum. The pronunciation of such words as *bájate* or *Méjico* with a relaxed or glottal /h/ as in English may be heard by a Spanish speaker as * [báate] or * [meiko], instead of [báHate/ or /méHiko/. It sometimes helps beginners to liken Spanish /H/ to the sound produced by a person blowing on his eye glasses before cleaning them.

Next in the table is the unvoiced alveo-palatal /tʃ/ which is sometimes classed as a stop + fricative. This sound is so similar in the two languages (compare **church** and *muchacho*) that there is very little learning problem. Some beginners, influenced by orthography, tend to carry over the /ʃ/ of *machine*, but this is very easily overcome.

The lateral /l/, a voiced alveolar lateral in *la* and *palo*, is pronounced with the tongue rounded upward toward the upper gums and palate, while in the English /l/ the tongue assumes a hollow or concave shape, low at the base. This tongue shape has a considerable influence on preceding or following vowels. In Spanish *mal* the /a/ is not noticeably modified as the tip of the tongue comes forward to make the /l/ against the upper gums; but in the English moll the low position of the base of the tongue as the /l/ is pronounced gives a marked diphthongization to the vowel, /maol/. (Before /t/ or /d/ the /l/ is articulated as a dental lateral, with the tip of the tongue against the upper teeth in position for the following dental stop: *alto* and *aldea*.)

The **nasals** offer a minimum of difficulty to English speakers. The /m/ is, perhaps, the most nearly identical sound in the two languages, both of which also articulate the variants of /n/ according to analogous circumstances: alveolar in most environments (English **no**, ca**n**e, illne**ss**;

Spanish *no*, *vano*, and *can*), dental before dental consonants (English anthem, Spanish *andar* and *antes*), and velar before velar consonants (English finger and syncopate, Spanish *finca* and *sangre*). The velar allophone is thought important enough to deserve a symbol, [ŋ]; the dental [n] (like the dental allophone of Spanish [l]) is worthy of mention more because it helps to emphasize the dental character of Spanish /d/ and /t/ than because the phenomenon of assimilation requires special attention.

The principal difficulty English speakers find in the Spanish nasals arises from the fact that in Spanish /n/ does not occur before the bilabial consonants /p/ and /b/. Words and prefixes which end in /n/ in all other positions end in /m/ if they stand before /p/ or /b/: compare the /en/ of *en Londres*, *en Ávila*, with /em/ in *en Burgos*; /kon/ in *con ella* with /kom/ in *con Pablo/*; /ben/ in *ven aldeas* with /bem/ in *ven pueblos*. This substitution is automatic in Spanish speech but is normally not reflected in orthography. The learner, consequently, may well use /n/ for /m/ in these positions, but the difficulty he may experience in auditory comprehension is more serious than his own mispronunciation. Special drills may be necessary to accustom the learner to the /m/ substitution in all such cases.

The alveo-palatal nasal /ñ/ must be regarded as a single phoneme, for it is not quite identical with Spanish /ny/: compare *viña* and *venia*. Some speakers may not, in fact, differentiate the consonant sounds as in *uña* and *unión*; but such uncommon minimal pairs as *huraño–uranio* permit the differentiation. When heard, the difference is that in /ñ/ the tip of the tongue touches the lower teeth, the front of the tongue presses against the hard palate, as the air escapes through the nasal cavity; practically at once the tongue moves away from the hard palate, producing a short fricative [y] sound. In /ny/, the tip of the tongue touches the upper gums, making an alvcolar [n], before releasing with the [y] sound. In Castilian Spanish there is an analogous difference between the /ĺ/ of *calle* and the /ly/ of *aliado*, as can be shown in the pair *se alió– se halló*. Spanish-American speakers in general substitute /y/ for Castilian /ĺ/.

We have now examined all of the Spanish phonemes shown in our table except /rr/ and /r/ and the semiconsonants /w/ and /y/. All English-speaking learners of Spanish, like all who teach Spanish to English-speaking people, are aware of the difficulty the /rr/ and the /r/ present. Both sounds are strange to American English, and the several sounds which characterize varieties of American English /r/ are lacking in

Spanish, although our learners stubbornly try to carry their own habits into the new language. Furthermore, the two phonemes /rr/ and /r/ are in contrast when between vowels, so that the difference must be both heard and reproduced, as in *carro, caro*; *pero, perro*; *poro, porro*; but in other positions the two sounds are not in contrast; in word-initial position, only /rr/ ordinarily occurs (although the orthography is *r*); in syllable-final position, the two sounds may actually be in free variation, as in *puerta* or *puerr-ta*. All of these facts make the mastery of /r/ and /rr/ a matter of great importance to the learner.

Certain devices have proved useful for teaching Spanish /r/ and /rr/ to English speakers:

1. It should be pointed out that English intervocalic /d/ is quite similar to Spanish /r/, especially in such words as caddy, madder, ladder. A common American pronunciation of butter, water, and Betty involves the same sound, in fact: /bəd'r/, /wɑd'r/, and /bɛdiy/.

If potter is pronounced with the Eastern or Southern dropping of final /r/, the resultant /pɑdə/ gives a good starting point for Spanish /pɑrɑ/.

The Englishman's "Veddy nice!" and the telephone operator's "th-dee" for "three" are also excellent break-through examples for the English speaker first learning the Spanish /r/.

2. A contrast drill can follow, in which the learner alternates English /d/ with Spanish /r/ in combinations like the following:

Written form	with English /d/	with Spanish /r/
para	/pɑdɑ/	/pɑrɑ/
caro	/kɑdo/	/kɑro/
cera	/sedɑ/	/serɑ/

3. He can now usefully contrast Spanish /r/ with Spanish [đ]:

> seda, cera, seda, cera
> cada, cara, cada, cara
> todo, toro, todo, toro

Such contrast drills can be useful, however, only if the student knows how to make the contrasting articulations here the voiced dental fricative [đ] in contrast with the voiced alveolar tap /r/.

4. Before attempting the contrast between Spanish /r/ and /rr/, some attention may well be given to the production of /r/ in other positions. In order of difficulty to the English-speaking learner, these are (a) post-consonantal, (b) final, and (c) pre-consonantal (or syllable–final).

(a)   Once the medial or intervocalic /r/ is learned, most students easily acquire /r/ after another consonant; some special exercise is, nevertheless, most helpful. In the following example the clusters are arranged according to the initial consonant—from labial to velar:

*pr*isa,	*pr*oa,	*pr*ensa,	*pr*udente
*br*isa,	*br*ota,	*br*uja,	*br*ea
*tr*es,	*tr*ino,	*tr*ono,	*tr*ama
*dr*apo,	*dr*oga,	*dr*ino	
*fr*eno,	*fr*ase,	*fr*ota,	*fr*uta
*cr*aso,	*cr*eo,	*cr*ía,	*cr*omo, *cr*udo
*gr*ano,	*gr*eco,	*gr*ito	*gr*oso, *gr*uta

Some special attention may have to be given to the groups /tr/ and /dr/. If the learner fails to place the tip of the tongue against the upper teeth, that is, if he starts off with an English alveolar /t/ or /d/, he will have difficulty making the tap /r/ at the same point of articulation, and a fricative sound somewhat like [ʃ] will be produced. This mispronunciation is annoying to Spanish-speaking people; it is easily avoided if the learner begins, as he should, with a dental /t/ or /d/.

(b)   Final /r/ is difficult for English speakers, for the tendency to revert to the English retroflex as in star (or to an Eastern or Southern suppression of the /r/) is strong, even after medial and postconsonantal Spanish /r/ is partly mastered.

A working solution—actually acceptable in some dialects of Spanish— is to release the final tap /r/, following it with an aspiration or a sort of voiceless [ə] which could be written [ə̥]:

cantar	[kɑntárə̥]
vivir	[biþírə̥]
comer	[komérə̥]

As this articulation is mastered, the supporting aspiration is allowed to become weaker until it practically disappears.

(c)   Preconsonantal /r/ is the most difficult articulation for English speakers, especially when the following consonant is dental /t/, or /d/. The rapid tongue movement from alveolar flap or "bounce" forward to the dental contact is entirely lacking in English. The tendency to revert to the English retroflex /ɹ/ is even stronger in this situation than in final /r/.

A working solution is similar to that for final /r/. At first, allow [ɹ] to follow the /r/, then accelerate pronunciation until the [ɹ] disappears:

árbol	[árɹƀol]	>	/árƀol/
arpa	[árɹpɑ]	>	/árpɑ/
arma	[árɹmɑ]	>	/ármɑ/
arco	[árɹko]	>	/árko/

This device will be particularly helpful when the following consonant is alveolar or especially, /t/ or /d/:

arnés	[arɹnés]	>	/arnés/
arsenal	[arɹsenál]	>	/arsenál/
arte	[árɹte]	>	/árte/
arder	[arɹḍér]	>	/arḍér/

5. The trill /rr/ must now be separately learned, before the contrast between /r/ and /rr/ is attempted.

Spanish /rr/ is not accomplished simply by "wiggling the tongue" against the alveolar ridge. The trill is actually a vibration of the slightly tensed tongue held against the alveolar ridge and caused to flutter by the pressure of the breath which forces the tongue away from the gum-ridge. In a sense the /rr/ begins at the diaphragm. A good deal of gymnastic practice is usually required before learners can consistently produce this sound.

6. After both /r/ and /rr/ can be produced at will, two important forms of exercise should be provided:

(a) Contrast drills to distinguish the two phonemes in minimal pairs:

pero	*perro*		
moro	*morro*		
caro	*carro*		
foro	*forro*		
vara	*barra*		
para	*parra*		
mira	*mirra*		
poro	*porro*		
maro	*marro*	(a plant)	(a game)

(b) Practice in /rr/ initial:

rata	/rratɑ/
ropa	/rroto/
ruso	/rruso/
ríe	/rríe/

even when preceded by article, pronoun, et cetera.

la rata	/la rrata/
la ropa	/la rropa/
se ríe	/se rríe/

We must now turn to the semiconsonants /w/ and /y/. The first of these is close enough to English /w/ so that little if any failure to understand is created. A good deal of interference is caused, however, by variants of Spanish /y/, which are actually very widespread.

1. Initial /y/, as in *yo*, *ya*, and *yanqui*, is pronounced by different speakers as [dʒ] (somewhat like English Joe), or [ʒ] (as in English leisure), or [y] (as in English yes). The fricative or affricate varieties are more typical of some dialect areas than of others; a given speaker may use one or more of these varieties. Since these sounds are, in Spanish, only variants of the one phoneme /y/, and since they never signal differences of meaning as they may in English (compare yes and Jess), the learner must learn to ignore the difference upon hearing Spanish; that is, he must learn to identify [dʒ] or [ʒ] with [y].

2. In some dialect areas ambiguity is caused by the absence of the Castilian phoneme /l̃/, which is absorbed into /y/ in Spanish America; this leads to confusions, as between the lexical items *halla* and *haya*, both pronounced /aya/, or *calló* and *cayó*, pronounced /kayó/. The learner who meets Spanish spellings early in his study has a special problem here, which may be aggravated again by the variant pronunciations, [aʒa], [kaʒó] or even [adʒa], [kadʒó]. Sporadic interferences of this type may be handled, if the need arises, by drills in pattern contrasts such as

| *Juan **halla** la casa.* | *No creo que **haya** tiempo.* |
| *El niño se **cayó**.* | *Su hermano se **calló**.* |

Except that the orthographical inconsistency adds an element of confusion to the learner, the problem is entirely analogous to that which may arise with ambiguous "words" at any moment, as in

| *Estoy en **la calle**.* | *Quiero que Vd. **calle**.* |

(B) VOWELS

In our discussion of general phonetic terminology we used vowels from French and Spanish, as well as English, as illustrations because the English vowel system is rather complex. Different linguists have advanced different interpretations of the English vowel system. There is no need for the Spanish teacher to understand in detail the technical problems involved in those interpretations. The principles are, however, important. Many English vowels are, in fact, diphthongs; if we say bee, we can note quite easily how the vowel corresponding to the ee glides upward during its production. What we are saying in fact is something like /ɪy/. If we say food, we can observe again how during the production of the vowel the sound changes; the tongue moves up and backward, and the lips become more rounded as we approach the end of the sound, which may be transcribed as /ʊw/. Starting with these considerations, some linguists have concluded that the vowel in words like bee, beat, and see or the vowel in do, shoe, is not just one building stone, but two: bee is not /b i/ but /bɪy/; food is not /fud/ but /fʊwd/. To be more specific, the vowel of bee is composed of a variant of the same vowel that is pronounced in bit plus a postvocalic variant of the same /y/ that occurs in the first sound of yes. The vowel of food is composed of a variant of the vowel of good plus a postvocalic variant of the same /w/ that begins the word water.

Other linguists have thought that they have found yet a third postvocalic vowel glide that is, in fact, a variant of a phoneme. Comparing the way words like cot and caught are pronounced (in some dialects at least), they felt that the difference between the two lies in the fact that the vowel of the second word is followed by a sort of neutral, voiceless glide which they interpret as the postvocalic variant of the sound /h/ of have, here.

It may be seen that the complexities and difficulties of English phonemes arise basically from one problem: how to interpret some of the English diphthongs; whether as one phoneme or as a combination of two. If we interpret the diphthongs as one phoneme, then the vowels of bet /bɛt/ and bait /bet/ are two different phonemes. If we interpret them as two, the vowels of bait consist of the same phoneme as in the vowel of bet, followed by the postvocalic variant of /y/, hence /bɛt/ versus /bɛyt/. This type of interpretation is found in several textbooks. The teacher using such books should understand the basic principle underlying this interpretation. From the pedagogical viewpoint the most important fact to retain is the diphthongal nature of the vowels and the existence of various glides which appear in English between vowel and following consonant. The exact phonemic interpretation of these glides varies from linguist to linguist and dialect to dialect.

For the purpose of illustrating the differences between English and Spanish vowels, it is probably easier to handle the following somewhat simplified scheme which considers the diphthongs as unit phonemes.

ENGLISH VOWELS

/i/ beat   /u/ boot
  /ɪ/ bit   /ʊ/ book
    /e/ bait   /o/ boat
      /ɛ/ bet   /ɔ/ bought
        /æ/ bat   /ə/ but
          /ɑ/ bottle

The preceding scheme is valid for large areas of the Middle West of the United States. For other areas some of the sample words do not fit. For instance, the pronunciation of hot by many New Englanders does not illustrate the /ɑ/ sound, and a word like father might be a better example for the sound in that area.

SPANISH VOWELS

/i/ *viví*   /u/ *luna*

/e/ { [e] *peso*   /o/ { [o] *cosa*
     { [ɛ] *tenga*   { [ɔ] *orden*

          /ɑ/ *casa*

The range of variants of Spanish /i/, /u/, and /ɑ/ is so relatively narrow that English /ɪ/ (bit), ʊ (book), and /æ/ (cat) have no counterpart in the Spanish sound system; any tendency of an English speaker to transfer such sounds into the Spanish system in stressed syllables is easily overcome. Spanish does have the positional variants [ɛ] and [ɔ], but since these sounds do not signal differences in meaning, as do the somewhat similar /ɛ/ (bet) and /ɔ/ (brought) in English, but simply occur in certain consonantal environments, they are easily and even automatically learned as mere variants or allophones of /e/ and /o/. Some phoneticians do not even recognize the [ɔ] sound as occurring in Spanish.

We may now compare the Spanish and English vowel system in such a way as to show approximate correspondences:

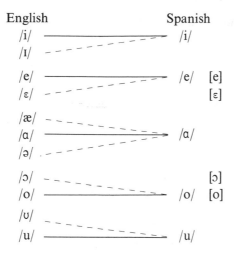

The above tabulation shows that the Spanish speaker learning English is faced with some real difficulties in learning to discriminate our complex set of vowel phonemes. The English speaker is not without his problems too. Interference of English habits comes from several sources beyond those shown by the table.

1.   The English vowel phonemes we have listed actually occur only in syllables bearing some stress; in general, the vowel of weak stressed syllables is either [ɪ] or [ə], regardless of orthography: incapacitate /ɪnkəpǽsɪtet/, evolution /ɛvəluʃən/, and monopolize /mənɑpəlaɪz/. English does not normally contrast unstressed vowels. A common illustration is the regular ambiguity between capital and capitol. Elicit and illicit are pronounced identically, and so are emit and omit in rapid speech—unless the speaker is aware of possible ambiguity or is given to hypercorrection.

Spanish, on the other hand, has the same five phonemes in unstressed syllables as in stressed syllables and so frequently distinguishes one word from another only by an unstressed vowel phoneme.

English speakers will tend to make mistakes in unstressed vowels, therefore, such as those in *Hasta la vista, amigo*, so that what is heard is * [ɑstə lə vɪstə, əmigə]. This tendency will lead to important mistakes in gender, mood, and person of the verb, or in vocabulary—mistakes which will often cause misunderstanding.

The solution to this tendency lies in ample drill with pairs of words in which the unstressed vowel is the only difference, as for example:

/ɑ/ and /o/ in contrast:	*cuenta*	*cuento*
	habla	*hablo*
	esposas	*esposos*
/ɑ/ and /e/:	*marcado*	*mercado*
	pintoras	*pintores*
	baldar	*beldar*
/ɪ/ and /u/	*pidiendo*	*pudiendo*

Extensive drills can be built to contrast every pair of the five vowel phonemes in this way. A strong tendency in English speakers will be to distort the drill by shifting the stress of the syllable in which the difference lies: * [habló] and * [hablá], for example. This only reverts to the English pattern, which makes phonemic distinctions only on stressed vowels. For many learners the tendency has been reinforced by exposure to old-school Latin teaching with its distorted "*amó, amás, amát, amámus, amátis, amánt; agricolá, agricoláe.*" The teacher must constantly oppose this tendency to distort on the basis of English habits.

2. A second area of interference lies in the fact that in English all the vowel phonemes are usually diphthongized to some degree, as we noted above. English speakers tend to carry this tendency into Spanish, with a strong foreign accent as the result, rather than a failure to be understood. When listening to a native speaker, however, the English learner may well be confused by failing to hear such differences as those between *le*/e/ and *ley*/ey/, and *ha*/ɑ/ and *hay*/ɑy/.

A **listening drill**, read by the teacher or by a taped voice, will help to develop the necessary discrimination in hearing. It contrasts English diphthongs with their similar Spanish relatives. The listeners indicate by a signal when they hear the non-Spanish pronunciation:

English /ɑy/ versus Spanish /ɑy/:	*hay*	**I**	*hay*
English /ey/ versus Spanish /e/:	**may**	*me*	*me*
	de	**day**	*de*
English /ey/ versus Spanish /ey/:	*ley*	*ley*	**lay**
English /iy/ versus Spanish /i/:	*ti*	**tea**	*ti*
	me	*mi*	*mi*
English /oy/ versus Spanish /oy/:	*voy*	*voy*	**boy**

3. An area of interference closely related to the foregoing arises from the fact that in English the consonants tend not to change their

point of articulation according to the adjacent vowels as much as is the case in Spanish. In English we tend to glide from the consonant position into the vowel position, then to glide off the stressed vowel before the next consonant. In Spanish, on the other hand, there is a tendency for the consonant to be somewhat assimilated to the vowel position rather than the opposite. For example, when the Spanish-speaking person is about to say "*todo*," he rounds his lips before he articulates the /t/, not after, and he maintains rounded lips until after the vocal cords have stopped vibrating; the tongue, meanwhile, has moved from the mid back /o/ position to the dental articulations of /t/ and /d/ with so direct a movement that it seems not to have changed during what the listener hears as the repeated vowel /o-o/. It is in this near absence of gliding tongue and lip movements before and after consonants that the difference between the English diphthongization and the Spanish "pure" vowel tendency lies.

A type of pronunciation drill which helps combat the tendency toward excessive lip movement calls for the learner to form the vowel called for by each example and to hold the lips in that vowel position while repeating the example. For instance:

> *Este es el esqueje que me venden.*
> *Las amas andan a atacar.*
> *Todos los topos no son toronjos.*

It is not easy to improvise examples using /u/ and /i/, which do not often occur in some positions. Semi-nonsense examples such as the following will serve, however.

> *Ví mi límite titiriti.*
> *Tú mudas muchas mulas nulas.*
> *Tú lulú su mumú.*

Throughout the teaching of the actual articulation of Spanish /i/, /e/, /o/, and /u/, it is necessary to remember that the tongue is higher than in the English counterparts, as well as tenser, and that the Spanish-speaking person rounds or stretches his lips for /u/, /o/ and /e/, /i/ more tensely and noticeably than does the American with his approximate equivalents.

4. Because the English diphthongs /ey/ (**bait**) and /oy/ **boy** are ordinarily made with an open variety of /e/ and /o/, so that phonetically

these syllable nuclei are more like [ɛy] and [ɔy], the English speaker tends to give a lower or more open sound to the Spanish /ey/ (seis) and /oy/ (voy). This tendency is largely overcome as a by-product of exercises which emphasize the relatively high position of /e/ and /o/ and which relate the Spanish diphthongs to the basic Spanish vowels.

(C) WORD BOUNDARIES AND LINKING

One major difficulty for learners of Spanish lies in the **linking** of sounds between words within phrase or breath groups. The foreigner would like to hear words separately; the speaker of English, in particular, is accustomed to a phenomenon known as **open transition or plus juncture** (/+/ juncture) through which he signals or hears a meaningful word boundary. Compare the normal reference to the home of the President of the United States, the White House, with the house in which Mr. White lives, the White house. In the former, there is little or no sound of /h/ after /t/, /Wʰaytaws/; in the latter, a definite shift from /t/ to /h/ can be felt, /wʰaythaws/. A still different transition will be heard in "a white house." The exact phonetic nature of this /+/ juncture is difficult to define, but the fact that English speakers use it to signal word boundaries makes them feel that Spanish speakers run their words all together.

Since Spanish speakers do in a sense run their words together, it is extremely important that learners be conditioned from the first to hear the normal linkings and to be aware of their character. We may indicate three major kinds of linking: (1) that which brings a final consonant or /y/ before a vowel; (2) that which brings a final vowel before an initial consonant; and (3) that which brings a final vowel before an initial vowel.

Let us examine the first type rapidly:

el agua	/elaǵwa/
los hombres	/losombres/
en abril	/enaƀril/
muy alto	/muyalto/

Such groups will be pronounced without pause, so that as the /l/, /s/, /n/, or /y/ is released, it is felt as part of the following syllable.

The second type brings with it a substitution of one allophone for another when initial /b/, /d/, or /g/ becomes medial, as it does when it is preceded by a word ending in a vowel:

bomba	/bomba/	*la bomba*	/laƀomba/[1]
gallo	/gayo/	*este gallo*	/esteǵayo/
daga	/daǵa/	*una daga*	/unaɖaǵa/

The third general type of linking involves adjacent vowels. In normal rapid speech this linking may change the "shape" of Spanish words through the actual disappearance of a vowel or the change of a vowel to /y/ or /w/. The following are the principal situations the learner must be trained to recognize:

1. When the final and initial vowels are the same, they tend to fuse into one:

su uña	/suña/
esto otro	/estotro/
una amiga	/unamiǵa/
mi hija	/miHa/

This phenomenon is normal in most speakers; it may at times alternate among "careful" speakers with a tendency to lengthen the fused vowel and even to make a slight change of pitch during the vowel, for example, /ese͡e\ko/, in order to differentiate *ese eco* from *es seco*. The learner's real problem is to hear the completely fused version.

2. Final /e/, /a/, and /o/ may disappear before certain vowels:

Pepe hizo . . .	/pepiso/
ésta es	/estés/
nada hizo	/naɖiso/
ella oyó	/eyoyó/
lo usamos	/lusamos/

While not uncommon, this phenomenon is not typical of "prestige level" speakers; the traveler will surely encounter it, but if he has learned the more basic discriminations and is familiar with normal forms and syntactical patterns, he will experience only moderate or occasional difficulty with it.

3. A final vowel forms a diphthong with the following initial vowel:

(a) Final /i/ becomes /y/:

si es	/syes/
mi amo	/myamo/
casi oscuro	/kasyoskuro/
mi uña	/myuña/

---

[1] Concerning transcription of [ƀ], [ɖ], [ǵ], see page 73, note.

(b)   Final /u/ becomes /w/:

su higo	/swiɡo/
tu edad	/tweḍaḍ/
tú andas	/twɑndɑs/
su hombre	/swombre/

(c)   Final /e/ may be replaced by /y/:

ese amo	/esyɑmo/
este hombre	/estyombre/
véndeme uno	/véndemyúno/

(d)   Final /o/ may be replaced by /w/:

barco inglés	/bɑrkwiŋglés/
no está	/nwestá/
no habla	/nwɑƀla/

This phenomenon will alternate with preservation of the separate vowel phoneme, /eseámo/, for example, according to the speaker's degree of education or the circumstances in which he is speaking.

There is no question that if learners of Spanish are sheltered from the common and normal phenomena we have been describing under the general head of linking, their comprehension of spoken Spanish will be delayed, if not permanently blocked. It is a temptation for teachers to create /+/ juncture where it does not naturally occur in Spanish and to maintain clear phonemic distinctions where phonemic substitutions actually occur. Such exaggerated clarity, while it gives the learner a sense of security and satisfaction, is actually a distortion of the facts of the language; and the security felt by the learner is a delusion, a blindfold which leads him inescapably into frustration and disappointment when he hears Spanish pronounced normally.

The solution is a considerable exposure to exercises spoken by the teacher (or by a recorded speaker), systematically arranged so as to accustom the learner to hearing the characteristic linkings of adjacent sounds. He must be drilled frequently, for example, in contrasts such as /bokɑ/, laƀokɑ/ and /deḍo/, /miḍeḍo/; others such as /mipɑdre/, /myaƀwelo/ and /su tío/, /swamigo/; phrases such as /byenenotros/. As was said above, developing knowledge of forms and structures helps to reduce the possibilities of confusion on the part of the learner, but there can be no substitute for well-planned practice in hearing and imitating.

Before leaving the subject of linking, we should point out briefly the fact that hesitation (as when a speaker gropes momentarily for a word) or certain styles of emphasis, or the like, may cause a Spanish speaker to make a /+/ juncture. This is not ordinarily a source of difficulty for the foreign learner, who might hear /el aǵwa/, /los ombres/, /la b̸omba/, except in the case of speakers of those dialects which use the allophone [ŋ] of /n/ in syllable or word-final position, and the allophone [ʰ] of /s/ in similar position. (This refers to the dialects whose speakers "*tragan las eses.*" Such a speaker might say /loʰ ombreʰ/ or /eŋ enero/, but a very little training enables a learner to recognize these variants.) In short, it is the normal transition, involving linking, which requires special attention on the part of the English-speaking learner.

(D) STRESS

Both English and Spanish utterances make use of **stress** or relative loudness as a device for signaling structural and lexical contrasts (grammatical or vocabulary differences). Each Spanish word has a syllable which is louder or more forcefully uttered than others, and each utterance has a principle stress or principle stresses.

English, for example, distinguishes the noun permit from the verb permit by a different placement of the stress. Similarly we differentiate address and address; contest and contest; a gentle man and a gentleman; and billow and below.

Since stress is a device for distinguishing meaning, it is a phoneme in English, just as the vowel and consonant sounds are phonemes. Stress is also a phoneme in Spanish, more important even than in English for distinguishing pairs of words which are otherwise alike:

/éstas/	these	/estás/	you are
/kánto/	song	/kantó/	he sang
/río/	river	/rió/	he laughed

Within the verb system, stress plays a very important rôle in certain contrasts:

/áb̸lo/	I speak	/ab̸ló/	he spoke
/preǵúnte/	ask!	/preǵunté/	I asked
/kantára/	(Imperf. Subj. of *cantar*)	/kantará/	(Future of *cantar*)

The greater difficulty for the English speaker, however, lies in the fact that English uses several degrees of stress, while Spanish has only two. English has a primary stress, / ´/, which is the main stress of a phrase or utterance; two degrees of intermediate stress, secondary / ˆ/ and tertiary / `/, and a weak stress / ˇ/. Characteristically, an English utterance alternates weak stresses with one of the stronger stresses, as in thĕ mân whŏ rêad thĕ mánŭscrìpt ănd táught thĕ lêssŏns, mâkĭng ùsefŭl cómmĕnts.

Sometimes two weak stresses come together, as in:

Yŏu nêedñ't bĕ trÿĭng tŏ cómfŏrt mê.

To the Spanish ear the English tertiary, secondary, and primary stresses all sound like strong stresses, alternating with weak stresses in what is sometimes called a "sing-song" pattern, like the rhythm of English verse: ˇ-ˇ-ˇ-ˇ- or -ˇˇ-ˇˇ, et cetera.

In Spanish there are only two significant degrees of stress, strong and weak. We shall use the symbols / ´/ for strong stress, and / `/ for weak stress in Spanish in order to avoid suggesting a contrast in length. In any group of words uttered rapidly together there will ordinarily be only one strong stress, as in

en Barcelona /èmbàrsèlóná/;

or, if there are two stresses or more, they will be of substantially the same force, as in

el señor de los bigotes /èl señór dè lòz ƀiǵótès/.

The weak-stressed syllables will be of approximately the same length and degree of loudness, and, in most important contrast to English, their vowel phonemes will be as distinct as in stressed syllables.

The errors the English-speaking person is likely to make, then, are (1) to carry over secondary or tertiary stresses and so introduce the English "sing-song" into the even series of Spanish weak stresses as, for example, * [ĕmbàrsĕlóná] instead of /èmbàrsèlóná/ or * [è] señór dĕ lôs bĭǵótĕs] instead of /èl señór dè lòz ƀiǵótès/; and (2) to pronounce the weak-stressed syllables with something like the /ɪ/ or /ə/ of English weak stresses instead of the actual Spanish phoneme: * [èl sĭñór də lòs bŏǵótĭz]. To the Spanish speaker these errors suggest an exaggeration of emphasis by the foreign learner, for the crescendo from a tertiary or secondary stress to the loudest or primary stress sounds to the Spanish ear like a signal of excitement or anger. For the English-speaking learner the effect of the Spanish speaker's absence of alternating stresses is that "you can't tell the syllables apart" or "he seems to talk like a machine gun." Obviously, then, this is an aspect of Spanish pronunciation which requires special attention by the learner.

Exercises in which large numbers of items are arranged so as to provide practice in the typical stress patterns will overcome much of the learner's difficulty, particularly if the drills are arranged to show contrasts. For example:

Two syllable utterances:

´ .	. ´
sea	control
tuyo	canté
libro	solí
súper	abad
cantan	cantar

Three syllable utterances:

. . ´	. ´ .	´ . .
aprender	mañana	único
contestó	minutos	rápido
cafetal	difícil	miércoles
capitán	contigo	médico

Four syllable utterances:

. . . ´	. . ´ .	. ´ . .	´ . . .
aprendera	aprendiendo	apréndalo	démoselas
escribiré	contribuyen	escríbame	cántemelo
simpatizó	simpatizo	simpático	dándotelo

Five syllable utterances:

. . . . ´	. . . ´ .	. . ´ . .
es muy alemán	esto es fácil	es muy rápido
los contribuyó	palabras vanas	los esdrújulos
él explicará	explicaremos	explicándolo
los compararé	los comparamos	comparémoslos

(E) INTONATION

We use this term here particularly to designate the patterns of pitch level, the relative highness or lowness of tone, and the changes which signal certain kinds of emphasis and phrase meanings. This includes the signals with which a phrase or an utterance ends. Linguists may also regard stress as an aspect of intonation; in any case, there is a close interrelationship between stress and pitch levels in Spanish.

Among the principal differences between English and Spanish intonation patterns we may first mention that English uses four significant pitch levels and Spanish, three. When English-speaking learners carry their English patterns into Spanish, they frequently give an effect of exaggerated forcefulness or brusqueness to their utterances by superimposing pitch levels characteristic of English on Spanish utterances. Perhaps the point might be made by contrasting roughly parallel utterances in English and Spanish, using a five-line staff to record the relative pitch levels:

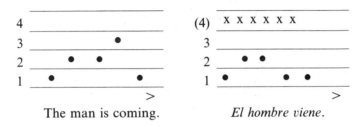

The man is coming.   El hombre viene.

In English, in such matter-of-fact statements, the pitch rises on the first stress, rises higher on the final stress, then falls back to the starting pitch. In Spanish, on the other hand, the pitch rises on the first stressed syllable and falls back to the starting pitch on the final stress.

If the statement is made emphatic in Spanish, it assumes the following shape:

¡El hombre viene!

If this contour is compared with the English one above, it will be seen that a **normal** statement pattern in English is similar to the **emphatic** pattern in Spanish. Now if we emphasize the statement in English, we use the level we have designated as 4:

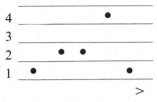

The man is **coming**!

Since Spanish does not make a four-level distinction, the effect of a higher pitch in its emphatic pattern would be merely to add more emphasis to what is already emphatic.

Unfortunately, direct contrasts between English and Spanish utterances like those attempted above are not easy to make in view of the differences of stress, syllabic cadence, and syntactical structure. Opinions differ as to the rôle of pitch or intonation patterns in linguistic analysis and, therefore, in comparative studies. Thus, our further comments will be confined to describing a few major intonation patterns and to one area of learning interference connected with English intonation and stress patterns.

Spanish and English both use a falling tone to mark the end of questions which ask information; these are questions which begin with interrogative words:

Where are we | going?   ¿A | dónde | vamos?

Both mark such questions with emphasis by using a higher rather than a lower pitch on the last stress:

Where are we go | ing?   ¿ A | dónde va | mos?

Both use a rising tone to mark the end of questions which call for a yes or no answer:

Are you coming?   ¿ Viene usted?

Both use a level or rising tone to indicate incompleteness of an utterance:

In this chapter, . . .   En | este capítulo, . . .

Quite detailed treatments of Spanish intonation patterns can be found in several of the recent textbooks and studies which are listed in the bibliography of this book. The teacher is referred to these for a more complete study of an area which has not yet been reduced to a wholly dependable set of classifications. Careful attention to native models, to the basic stress patterns, and to the general comments given here will help most learners to avoid the grosser errors of intonation. The teaching of intonation is an inevitable and necessary part of any good substitution or transformation exercise or any other type of pattern drill. The different intonations of questions and answers, statements and responses, and contrasts between one subject and another or one tense or another should be an integral part of the transformations guided by the teacher and performed by the student.

There is one aspect of the matter of stress and intonation which must be examined briefly, however, before we leave the subject. This is the fact that English can signal contrasts or points of emphasis in a given sentence by appropriate placing of stress and high pitch register. Take the simple, matter-of-fact statement, He is going to New York today. As we saw above, the typical intonation contour for unemphatic statements is:

He is going to New │ York │ today.

Observe how many different situations may be indicated by changing the point of highest pitch:

He │ is going to New York today.   (Not someone else!)
He │ is │ going to New York today.   (Although someone denied it!)
He is │ go │ing to New York today.   (He's not there yet, he's on his way.)
He is going │ to │ New York today.   (He is not coming from New York.)
He is going to New │ York │ today.   (Not somewhere else.)
He is going to New York to │ day.   (Not yesterday, not tomorrow.)

Spanish too may signal emphasis on some of these contrasts in a similar way, but some of them will be accomplished by actual changes in the structure of the sentence—use or non-use of pronouns or intensifying adverbs or a different word order. For example, the simple statement would ordinarily be in Spanish, *Va* │*hoy a Nueva* │*York* or *Va a Nueva* │ *York* │ *hoy*. The corresponding changes might be:

El | *va a Nueva York hoy*;   (or: *Es* | *él* | *quien va a Nueva York hoy*.)

Sí | *va a Nueva York hoy*;   (or: *Sí* | *que va a Nueva York hoy*.)

Va | *a Nueva York hoy*;

Va | *a Nueva York hoy*;

Es a Nueva | *York* | *adonde va hoy*

Va | *hoy* | *a Nueva York*   or   *Va a Nueva York* | *hoy.*

In a later chapter we shall return to the problems that may arise when English uses stress and intonation as a signal in situations which require a structural change in Spanish.

(F) SPANISH ORTHOGRAPHY

So far we have been discussing primarily those pronunciation problems which a speaker of English would encounter in Spanish even if he were not being taught to read and write it from the first. The introduction of Spanish spelling presents two new sets of pronunciation problems. The first set (not especially complex since Spanish has a fairly consistent system of spelling) is created by those instances in which Spanish speaking and writing do not correspond; the other set of problems arises because of the natural tendency of the student to give English responses to orthographic symbols when he is supposed to be reading Spanish.

1. Spanish orthographic symbols.

In Spanish the correspondence between writing and sound is much more predictable than in English. This does not mean that it is perfect, in spite of the oft-repeated claim that "Spanish is a phonetic language," an inexact phrasing of the belief that the Spanish system of spelling is entirely free of ambiguities. Let us examine the spelling of the Spanish consonant phonemes, proceeding from the stops to the semiconsonants, as shown in Table IV.

VOWELS

In standard Spanish the vowel sounds offer no serious spelling problems, with the important exception of those which may arise from the phonemic substitutions across word boundaries, which were discussed above in some detail. It is true that some students try at first to pronounce *sin* as [sɪn], *tema* as [tɪymɑ], *mula* as [myulɑ], et cetera.

TABLE IV

Phoneme	Written Symbol	Examples
/p/	p	padre, capa
/t/	t	tuyo, mata
/k/	c	capa, copa, cupo
	k	kilómetro
	qu	que, quina
/b/ [b]	b	bondad, ambos
	v	vino, enviar
[ƀ]	b	lobo, árbol
	v	cava
/d/ [d]	d	don, andar
[đ]	d	cada, arde
/g/ [g]	g	gano, goma, gula
	gu	guerra, guindo
[ǥ]	g	daga, sinagoga
	gu	azogue
/tʃ/	ch	muchacho
/f/	f	falso, café
/θ/	c	dice, ciprés
	z	caza, zorro, zumo

(this phoneme is replaced by /s/ in Southern Spain, and Spanish America; in non-Castilian Spanish the spelling c and z would occur under the phoneme /s/)

/s/ [s]	s	sin, cosa, las
[z]	s	desde, rasgo, las dos
/H/	j	jota, caja, jefe, Jiménez
	g	germen, gime
/l/	l	lata, calma
/ĺ/	ll	llama, malla

(this phoneme is replaced by /y/ in Spanish America; the spelling ll would occur under that phoneme)

/m/	m	mono, cama, calma
	n	un bravo, envío
/n/ [n]	n	cana, anda, nota
[ŋ]	n	finca, tengo, un gato
/ñ/	ñ	caña
/rr/	rr	carro, perro
	r	rana, río
/r/	r	carta, pero
/w/	u	cuatro, auto
	hu	hueste, hueco
/y/	i	fiambre, caigo
	y	yo, yerro, hay
	hi	hierro

The sort of exercise that quickly eliminates such interference is the same sort as that used to teach the vowel phonemes themselves, minimal pairs, except that this time written models and written responses are combined with the oral drill. For example:

mesa	*misa*	*mula*	*mola*
tela	*tila*	*tuno*	*tono*
senté	*sentí*	*bula*	*bola*

Large numbers of such pairs can quickly be assembled for use in drills of this sort.

The tendency to pronounce unstressed syllables with sounds like the English /ɪ/ and /ə/ will also be reinforced by the sight of written Spanish; practice like that suggested for developing familiarity with various stress patterns, but with written models, will help to eliminate this interference.

Spanish, then, offers two possible spellings of the sounds [b], [ǧ], [g], [θ] (or in non-Castilian areas three possible spellings of /s/), /H/, /m/, /rr/, /w/, and three possible spellings of /k/ and /y/. The specific spelling is dictated by rules of position, however, except for the spellings *b*, *v*, and initial *y*, *hi*; for non-Castilian speech, rules of position do not determine a choice as between *s* and one of the spellings *c* and *z*. Incompletely educated Spanish-Americans will, therefore, make mistakes in spelling such words as *vivo* ("*bivo, bibo*, and *vibo*"), will confuse the spellings of *casa* and *caza*, and will misspell *dice* ("*dise*") and *tres veces* ("*trez veses*"). Moreover, alternative spellings of some proper names are not uncommon, as *Cisneros, Sisneros*; *Salas, Sálaz*; *González, Gonsales*. Another common spelling error arises from the survival in writing of a symbol *h* which has no phonetic value at all, leading to such mistakes as "*hamor*," "*ambre*," "*ombre*," and "*handar*." In the main, the English-speaking learner has relatively little trouble mastering the spellings of Spanish, since in spite of these possibilities of confusion the system is quite simple and regular.

Looked at from the other point of view, we note that several of the written symbols may have more than one pronunciation value. This is the set of facts invariably presented by the standard beginning textbook. No special comment is called for here.

2. **English interference.**

The presence of written symbols serves to reinforce the tendency of the learner to transfer habits of his own speech into Spanish. Any teacher is familiar with the general run of mistakes of this kind:

1. Voicing of /s/ in words such as *rosa*.
2. Keeping of /n/ before a /b/ or /p/.
3. Injection of [ʃ] in words such as *estación*.
4. Pronouncing *quemar* as * [kwemɑr].
5. Spelling /kwota/ as * *quota*.

Other mistakes not directly suggested by orthography are also more likely to occur when the learner is reading, as, for example, the aspiration of /p/ /t/ /k/; low back /l/ as in *alma*; and "slighting" unstressed syllables. Any teacher could readily list many more specific instances of interference from English habits.

One of the most important areas of interference has only been mentioned incidentally. This is the strong tendency of English to mark word boundaries—whether by stress and intonation, by especially distinct pronunciation of consonants, or by glottal stop. Since Spanish is spoken in syllables rather than words, as we mentioned in our discussion of linking, the syllable boundaries in speech have no necessary relation to the word boundaries, that is, to the boundaries or spaces between the semantic units which appear on the printed or written page.

The native speaker of English is used to having many word boundaries clearly expressed in his speech. In addition he is apt to learn Spanish by remembering words. If he has read a Spanish sentence he retains a visual memory of how this sentence is divided into words. All this leads him to expect to find some sort of word boundaries when he hears a Spanish sentence. Since the Spanish utterance does not contain any clues as to where the word boundaries are, the student has a major comprehension problem. In writing, the semantic divisions of an utterance are marked by neat spaces between words; what the student sees is *Mi amigo Antonio ha entrado en una casa amarilla*. The transcription of what he hears is [Myɑmiǥwɑntónyoɑntráɖwenunɑkɑsɑmɑríyɑ]. The result of this lack of correspondence between orthographic representation and speech is, of course, that a student often will not recognize the spoken form of a sentence even though he may be perfectly familiar with its written form.

The lack of exact correspondence between Spanish sounds and symbols, the lack of word boundaries in speech, the possible interference coming from English orthography—all these add up to some rather formidable reasons why the learning of comprehension and speaking should in its initial stages be completely disassociated from the learning of reading and writing. To say that at that particular stage, and in a language like Spanish, speaking and comprehending on the one hand

and reading and writing on the other reinforce each other is simply not true; they interfere with each other and pull the learner's attention in opposite directions. The *dictado* for instance—one of the most frequently used teaching and learning devices in the Spanish class—is as such not a method to teach aural comprehension. It is primarily a test to find out (1) whether the student does comprehend Spanish and (2) whether he is mastering Spanish grammar and its orthography. If the student does not understand spoken Spanish to begin with, the *dictado* is not going to teach him to understand it. Of course, it is true that the *dictado*, if used frequently in the course, will contribute to the improvement of the aural comprehension of the student. But this will happen because the student is forced to listen to Spanish, and it would happen also and perhaps more effectively if the student were not forced to write down what he is hearing. The writing as such serves only one teaching purpose, a rather important one to be sure: to give the student who is already able to comprehend some practice in the use of Spanish orthography.

Since the Spanish system of orthography is so relatively regular, most teachers find very little to be gained by requiring their students to learn a system of phonetic transcription. Some advantage may be gained by use of the symbols [ƀ], [đ], and [ǥ] for the fricative variants of /b/, /d/, and /g/; some value may accrue to using /k/ for "hard" *c* or *qu* in contrast to "soft" *c* before *e* and *i*. In the main, however, it hardly seems worth the extra effort since other teaching devices can accomplish what the phonetic symbols suggest.

CHAPTER VII

Teaching Morphology

(A) GENERAL CONCEPTS

The smallest units of speech, the phonemes, have the power to differentiate meaning, but they themselves are meaningless. They are, however, combined into larger units, larger building stones which have recognizable meanings. The larger units are called **morphemes**. Morphemes are then the smallest units of speech which have identifiable meaning of their own.

Linguists identify morphemes in about the same way in which they identify phonemes, namely, by comparing utterances and observing the identical and different elements. Thus, if we compare *vamos* /bamos/ with *vais* /bais/, we can readily see that *va-* /ba-/ is common to both of them. It is therefore, a building stone that can be used again in other utterances like *vas* /bas/ and *va* /ba/. If we compare *vamos* /bamos/ with *vemos* /bemos/ or *somos* /somos/, we see that *-mos* /-mos/ is also a building stone that can be taken out of this utterance and used in another verb form. The comparison of *vais* /bais/ with *veis* /beis/ or *sois* /sois/ teaches us the same thing about the ending *-is*. Thus, *va-*, *ve-*, *so-*, as well as *-mos* and *-is*, are all morphemes of the Spanish language.

Morphemes are not necessarily identical with syllables or words: *vamos* is one word but two morphemes, whereas *va* is one word and one morpheme. (Of course, one may speak of a "zero morpheme" as the characteristic of the third person singular ending and so count *va* as two morphemes: /ba/ + /ɒ/. We shall not follow this technical practice here.) If we inspect a word like *iris*, we find that it has two syllables, but neither of the two, *i* or *ris*, appears anywhere else in the same recognizable meaning that it has in *iris*. Thus, the two syllables of *iris* are only one morpheme.

In the discussion of the phoneme we found that the same phoneme may appear in different forms according to the environment, thus having allophones. A similar statement can be made about morphemes. The very same building stone can appear in different forms according to its environment, and the same morpheme can have different **allomorphs**. For instance, the utterance "books" is composed of two morphemes, book and -s/s/, indicating plural. If we analyze the utterance "dishes," we find it is composed of dish and -es/ɪz/. Examining "hands," we see that it is composed of hand and the plural indicator -s, now pronounced /z/. Now /s/, /ɪz/, and /z/ all have the same meaning, that is, "plural," and the occurrence of these variants or allomorphs is predictable; /s/ occurs only after unvoiced consonants, /z/ appears only after vowels and voiced consonants, and /ɪz/ only after sibilants. All these three sounds are allomorphs of the same building stone, or morpheme.

It is clear from the foregoing that morphemes are essentially those elements of speech that we are accustomed to classifying as stems or roots, inflections or endings, and prefixes or suffixes. Morphology is the study of morphemes, of the types and arrangements of morphemes that characterize a given language.

We may identify **free morphemes**, such as Spanish *sal*, which we recognize as carrying **lexical meaning** ("salt") and which may be uttered alone or may enter into various syntactical patterns with other words without losing their dictionary meaning: *Me gusta la sal* and *No quiero sal*. We also identify **bound morphemes**, such as *-aba*, *-es*, which have no lexical meaning but do have a clear **structural meaning** and which cannot exist alone, but only as grammatical signals. Between these two extremes we have the "roots" of many nouns, most adjectives, and all verbs, and of adverbs in *-mente*, which convey lexical meaning but require the help of a bound morpheme in actual utterance; *hermos-* is a lexical morpheme which cannot be uttered without the addition of a morpheme for gender and number. And among bound morphemes we find a number we normally think of as being "words," such as *que* (not *¿qué?*), *de*, *lo*, *se*, *me*, and *para*, but which not only do not occur as free utterances, but are systematically limited to certain positions when they do occur, and which signal grammatical relationships rather than lexical meanings.

The teaching application of morphemic analysis lies principally in two directions.

One is the fact that the methods used in the identification of morphemes, namely, inspection for similar and different elements or the isolation of contrasts, are directly applicable to the presentation and drilling of the morphology of Spanish, just as they are to that of phonology. In other words, it is not that linguists have found out so much that is new about Spanish morphemes but that their methods clarify our problem in finding the best order and manner of presentation and in identifying the significant contrasts to be hammered home in appropriate pattern drills.

The second important contribution of morphemic analysis to Spanish teaching lies also in the application of a point of view rather than in a general discovery. This is the linguist's first concern with the spoken language, rather than the written form. For standard Spanish, however, the marked differences between oral grammar and written grammar are few. We are not referring here to differences between colloquial or conversational style and written or formal style. We mean that spoken Spanish differentiates the same inflectional morphemes as does written Spanish.

To make this point thoroughly clear, we may compare a few examples from French with corresponding ones from Spanish:

French			Spanish		
je parle	/ʒə/		*hablo*		o/
tu parles	/ty/	/parl/	*hablas*	/abl	as/
il parle	/il/		*habla*		a/
ils parlent	/il/		*hablan*		an/

In the French example above there is even complete ambiguity between singular and plural in the third person. The Spanish ending morphemes are so clearly contrastive that they free Spanish speakers from the necessity of using subject pronouns unless for emphasis or contrast.

French		Spanish
le livre	/lə livrə/	*el libro*
les livres	/le livrə/	*los libros*

In the French example the only spoken signal of the plural of the noun is in the form of the article. In the absence of such a signal a French noun is ambiguous as to number in speech, but in Spanish there is no question:

(*livre*)		*no hay libro*	/libro/
pas de (*livres*)	/padlivrə/	*libros*	/libros/

Since written and spoken grammar, or at least morphemics, are so nearly the same in standard Spanish, we shall dispense with phonemic transcriptions in this section unless a special problem makes it useful. This should not make us forget the constant danger to the student in learning written forms before oral patterns, a matter we have tried to emphasize consistently.

We shall now attempt to examine those morphemic patterns which signal the main grammatical relationships in Spanish, and we shall try to present those patterns as they appear, in oral Spanish, to the student who is trying to learn to speak and understand the language without the interference of orthographic representations.

A rigorous linguistic presentation would call for some revision of the terminology we are accustomed to, but we shall be able to preserve most of the standard terms. The reader must accompany us, however, in our attempt to clarify some of the familiar definitions. The most important revision is an attempt to **separate definitions** in terms of **structure or grammatical relationship** from a psychological or philosophical definition in terms of **meanings or ideas**. Both aspects are valid and important. Most of our habitual analyses of language have started from the second concept, that of meaning, or **semantic** criteria. In spite of occasional vagueness, errors such as forcing notions of "universal grammar" on specific languages whether they fit or not, and other weaknesses of which we are aware, traditional grammar has produced excellent and useful descriptions of numerous languages in their written and literary form.

From the pedagogical point of view the most serious drawback of grammatical classifications based on semantic criteria is the tacit assumption that we are dealing with a language just like the one we already know. A linguist who is interested in writing the grammar of a language with which he is not yet familiar (a rather typical situation for the anthropological linguist) cannot ask his native informant how verbs are expressed in his language. He must find this out himself. For this reason he is, initially at least, not much interested in the fact that some words express actions and others qualities or things. He must find out why certain words can be grouped into the same class. He must establish the purely formal characteristics that enable certain groups of words to express similar concepts and have similar functions. In the sentence, The father beats the child, we know, of course, that father and child are nouns and beats is the verb; but what interests the linguist primarily is how and why we know this. Thus we know that father and child are nouns because they are preceded by the, and we know that beat is a verb because it stands between the two nouns and because it takes an s in the third person singular. Linguists classify words, therefore, according to formal criteria, that is, criteria of form. Words belong to the same class because they can take the same ending or because they can be substituted for each other in the same syntactical patterns and may replace one another in the same "slot," or position. Now the point of view of the student studying a foreign language is basically similar to that of the linguist analyzing a new language. To find out that nouns are the names of persons, things, places, is no help in speaking or understanding the language. What the student must learn are the **formal features** that enable him to recognize and to use **word classes**. To define nouns as those words which may follow a noun marker (*mi, su, el, este*) may seem a rather strange and circular way of getting at a concept, but the pedagogical application of the procedure is quite clear; the student can be trained to recognize in written form, and especially in speech, the **noun markers** as clues for the following noun and this in turn will enable him to get a clearer understanding and auditory comprehension of the Spanish construction.

(B) THE NOUN AND THE NOUN MARKERS

In oral Spanish the plural is expressed by final [s] or [es]; these pronunciations are reflected in the corresponding spellings. Which allomorph applies is predictable from the final sound of the singular consonant + (-es), vowel + (-s), with only a few special cases such as proper nouns: *Los Moreno* + (zero); certain final stressed vowels: *sofás* but *rubís*; nouns ending in /s/ after unstressed final vowel: *análisis* + (zero). English speakers have little tendency to transfer the /z/ or /ɪz/ allomorphs to Spanish when the general absence of the phoneme /z/ has been established.

It may be said that gender in the noun is not a matter of inflection but of vocabulary. Nevertheless, the similarity between gender-number morphemes in the noun and those in the adjective helps in the learning of gender classes in the noun. For convenience, some of the principal gender classes are listed here with no attempt at completeness:

Characteristically **masculine**: nouns ending in *-o*, *-l* (*baúl, arenal*), *-d* (*césped*), *-or* (*profesor*), *-ema*, *-ama* (*sistema, drama*), also *día, mapa, poeta.*

Characteristically **feminine**: nouns ending in *-a, -ía, -dad, -tad, -ción, -ie* (*serie*), *-umbre*, also *mano*.

Characteristically having both **masculine and feminine** forms: Nouns standing for people, ending in *-o/-a*: (*hermano/hermana*); *-or/-ora* (*profesor/profesora*); *-ón/-ona* (*llorón/llorona*).

Of **either gender without form change**:

1. Nouns standing for people, ending in *-ista* (*el/la pianista*), *-ente*, *-ante* (*el/la agente, el/ la estudiante*). (Some speakers distinguish, however: *estudiante/estudianta*.)
2. Nouns with different meanings in different gender: *el policía/ la policía; el guía/la guía*.

The **noun markers** (also called determiners or determinatives) are a greater problem. English distinguishes number only in this–these and that–those, while Spanish distinguishes number in all cases and gender in most. They may be listed in such a way as to show those that express only the singular/plural contrast and those which also show the masculine/feminine contrast.

TABLE V

Singular		Plural	
Masculine	*Feminine*	*Masculine*	*Feminine*
un	una	unos	unas
el	la	los	las
este	esta	estos	estas
ese	esa	esos	esas
aquel	aquella	aquellos	aquellas
nuestro	nuestra	nuestros	nuestras
vuestro	vuestra	vuestros	vuestras
mi		mis	
tu		tus	
su		sus	

From the above arrangement we see that any of the Spanish determiners except *mi, tu,* and *su* and their plurals may serve as forms with which to introduce new nouns, since they all indicate the masculine/feminine contrast as well as that for singular/plural. Various types of transformation exercises can grow out of this fact. For instance, a student could be asked to substitute different nouns in a pattern like:

> *Este libro es grande. Es nuestro libro. El libro es bueno.*
> *Es un libro nuevo.* Substitute, for example, (1) *lápiz, automóvil, zapato*; (2) *casa, mesa, silla*; (3) plurals of the same nouns or others.

In due course the other demonstratives will substitute into appropriate slots.

Interference of English speech habits appears more noticeably in the student's pronunciation of Spanish and in his learning of syntactical patterns than in the realm of morphology or forms. One important instance of interference occurs in the area we are now discussing; this is the often-noticed tendency to equate his or her with Spanish *su* and their with Spanish *sus*. This confusion is magnified by the student's finding that Spanish *su* does not discriminate between his and her as he expects and wants it to do. Some help can be given here by working first with patterns involving *nuestro*, which students quickly learn, since the gender and number morphemes are like those already learned with other adjectives, such as *blanco*.

First, then, practice patterns such as:

> *Es nuestro libro.*   *Son nuestros libros.*
> *Es nuestra casa.*   *Son nuestras casas.*

Attention is drawn to the "adjective behavior" of this possessive. Then patterns are developed using *mi, mis, tu, tus*, but *not su, sus*:

> *Aquí está mi libro.*   *Aquí están mis libros.*
> *Aquí está mi casa.*   *Aquí están mis casas.*
> (similarly with *tu*)

Attention is drawn to agreement for number, like any two-form adjective. Students are told that *su, sus* behave in the same way, and that Spanish does not differentiate between his and her with these forms; they are then drilled:

(1)   *Juan tiene su lápiz.*
      María tiene su lápiz.   *Juan y María tienen sus lápices.*
          Repeat with *manzana* or other feminine noun.
(2)   *Juan y María están en su casa y tienen sus libros.*
      Juan y María están en su automóvil y tienen sus plumas.

(C) THE ADJECTIVE AND THE ADVERB

Spanish adjectives and nouns share certain characteristics: Many adjectives and many nouns have masculine and feminine forms /hermano/ hermana, hermoso/hermosa) while others have only the singular/plural distinction (capital/capitales and inteligente/inteligentes); the same number and/or gender morphemes or endings apply; they can be used in some of the same syntactical positions (Juan es inteligente/Juan es estudiante); and Spanish adjectives are often used as nouns (El viejo ha venido). The only major difference which allows us to assign words to one class rather than the other lies in the fact that genuine nouns are incapable of adverb formation or adverbial use, while adjectives can form adverbs (rápido/rápidamente) or can function adverbially, as in Juan habla alto, Vivieron felices. We may also note that adjectives may add suffixes, such as English -ness (goodness); Spanish -dad (maldad), -ez (brillantez), -ísimo (altísimo), while nouns may not add these same suffixes.

The only important problem in the learning of adjective morphology lies in the learning of two main classes: those which distinguish masculine /feminine and those which do not. The first group includes the very large number which follow the pattern blanco/blanca/blancos/blancas; adjectives of nationality which distinguish gender in the singular (alemán/ alemana) and form the plural, each gender on its own singular (alemán/ alemanes, alemana/alemanas); those ending in -ón, -án, and -or, which follow the same pattern as the adjectives of nationality; and, of course, the articles and the demonstratives.

The demonstratives, especially este, ese, are troublesome to many learners because the masculine plural involves a substitution instead of a mere pluralizing morpheme /s/: este/estos, ese/esos. Inevitably, the learner is confused when he encounters esto, eso; it is only natural that he attempt to substitute the masculine-looking /-o/ form for este, ese in accordance with the pattern /o, a, os, as/which applies almost everywhere else. The answer here is a contrast drill somewhat as follows:

Esto es un libro.	Juan me dió este libro.	Eso me gusta mucho.
Esto es un lápiz.	Juan me dió este lápiz.	Eso me gusta mucho.
Esto es un automóvil.	Juan me dió este automóvil.	Eso me gusta mucho.

Aside from the groups listed above, adjectives which do not end in /o/ have no distinguishing feminine forms: (un hombre inteligente/ una mujer inteligente).

The **formation of adverbs**—the distinguishing formal characteristic of adjectives—lends itself to drill in context, for instance, in substitution exercises in which the teacher suggests adjectives which the student changes to adverbs and fits into a pattern sentence:

Cue			Response
	Juan habla		
rápido	,,	,,	*rápidamente*
lento	,,	,,	*lentamente*
suelto	,,	,,	*sueltamente*

(D) THE VERB

Learning by Pattern Drills

The teaching of verb forms is naturally one of the chief problems for the Spanish teacher. The entire concept of conjugational endings is difficult enough for the speaker of English; the irregular patterns within the basic system add greatly to the complication. The fact that standard spoken Spanish reflects the written system permits, however, certain simplified presentations which utilize the principle of morphemic analysis without requiring the use of phonemic transcription.

It is customary to lay out verb paradigms as though each new conjugation, each new tense, and each new irregular verb represented a new learning problem in six-form blocks. As a result the usual textbook appendix lists several pages full of closely printed paradigms.

Now there is no question but that full verb tables are useful for reference and that they make it possible to observe the recurrent patterns that characterize the Spanish verb system. There is considerable question, however, as to the usefulness of teaching verbs exclusively on the conjugation basis. A presentation organized by minimal steps and using single-step transformation drills offers a much better basis for developing the automatic associations of person-number-tense-mood forms to the needs of communication.

For example, the learner may first meet a goodly number of first person singular forms through simple substitution drills, as:

Estudio con Eduardo. (Substitute: *hablo, camino, bajo, entro*)

He may then meet the third person singular in a similar way:

Eduardo estudia hoy. (Substitute: *habla, camina, baja, entra*)

He may then meet the first transformation:

> *Yo estudio, y Eduardo estudia también.*
> *Yo hablo, . . .*
> *Yo camino, . . .*

Through similar experiences of new forms, one step at a time followed by one contrast at a time, the learner may meet and master the numerous elements of the verb system with minimum dependence on the paradigmatic type of learning.

It is possible, however, that our learner may become as dependent on a specific series of transformations in order to produce a wanted form as the student who has been brought up on the old-fashioned conjugations and who has to recite "*comí, comiste, comió, comimos, comisteis*" in order to arrive at the desired "*comieron.*" For instance, he may have learned the third person plural *comieron* through a transformation drill such as:

> *Venden libros hoy; ayer vendieron libros.*
> *Comen carne hoy; ayer . . .* et cetera.

If he has also learned it through the transformation:

> *Juan vendió el libro. Juan y María vendieron el libro.*
> *Juan comió carne. Juan y María . . .* et cetera.

he has the reinforcement of two different contrasts. But the student must be freed from dependence on derivation and brought to the level of **instantaneous use of verb forms**. In order to accomplish this he must be required to work with drills which demand "choice" reactions from him. We may ask him to change the subject of a given sentence: *Comí carne ayer*; substitute *él, nosotros, tú, ellos.* This testing drill is at the same time an important contribution to learning. We may adapt transformation exercises into meaningful conversational patterns: *¿Comprende Vd? Sí, comprendo*; *¿Come Vd. carne? Sí, como carne.* Various natural patterns of question and response can be set up in this way. We may give a double signal for a test response: starting with a model such as *Vendo libros* we may give cues such as *Ayer él . . .* , *Mañana nosotros . . . Antes ellos . . .* and expect the student to complete the sentence with *Ayer él vendió libros, Mañana venderemos libros, Antes ellos vendían libros.*

Organization of the regular verb

Before many verbs have been learned, however, patterns begin to emerge; it seems evident that any clarifications which can make more meaningful to the learner the increasing mass of forms he must manipulate will be worthwhile. The following are some of the possibilities for helping the learner to find order and system in the Spanish verb:

1. There is no organic reason why the infinitive should be taken as the base form (since in itself it is a substantive rather than a verb), but in Spanish there is no strong reason why it should not. We take the infinitive, therefore, as the reference landmark which gives us the lexical base or root and the conjugation–class signal, or ending (-ar, -er, -ir). This lexical root will be used as the base for the formation of all tenses except the future and the conditional, where the whole infinitive will serve as the base form. In view of long-standing tradition among grammarians and teachers of Spanish, we shall use the term **stem** for the root or base.

2. While regular verbs are, traditionally, three conjugation classes (-ar, -er, -ir), the second and third conjugations are differentiated only in persons 1 and 2 plural of the present indicative (comemos/vivimos, coméis/vivís) and in the plural imperative (comed/vivid) as far as their endings are concerned, and so may be taken together as one conjugation class.

3. The vowel -a characterizes most endings of -ar verbs and -e, -i, and -ie characterize -er and -ir verbs.

4. All tenses except the preterite repeat a system of person differentiators or markers which is the same for both conjugation-classes, for indicatives and subjunctives, and even for the major share of irregular verbs.

This system of **person markers** is as follows:

yo: stem	vowel			nosotros: stem	vowel	-mos
tú: ,,	,,	-s		vosotros: ,,	,,	-is
él: ,,	,,			ellos: ,,	,,	-n

5. The tense–mood signals are (1) the vowel (or bisyllable, aba, et cetera which fills the vowel space, and (2) the stress position. These two signals work in conjunction; neither is more important than the other.

The tense–mood signals organize as follows:

	-ar			-er			-ir		
Present indicative: stem	o		stem	o		stem	o		Stress signal: on stem,
	a	s		e	s		e	s	1, 2, 3 s. and 3 pl.,
	a			e			e		on ending, 1, 2, plural
	a	mos		e	mos		i	mos	
	á	is		é	is		í	s[1]	
	a	n		e	n		e	n	

[1] The learner may be told that the tense-vowel -i- absorbs the personal ending -i-.

Present subjunctive:

		-ar			-er, -ir		Stress signal: on stem 1, 2, 3 S. and 3 pl.; on ending, 1, 2, pl.
	stem	e		stem	a		
		e	s		a	s	
		e			a		
		e	mos		a	mos	
		é	is		á	is	
		e	n		a	n	

Imperfect indicative:

		-ar			-er, -ir		Stress signal: on first syllable of ending throughout
	stem	aba		stem	ía		
			s			s	
			mos			mos	
			is			is	
			n			n	

Imperfect subjunctive (-ra):

		-ar			-er, -ir		Stress signal: on first syllable of ending throughout
	stem	ara		stem	iera		
			s			s	
			mos			mos	
			is			is	
			n			n	

Imperfect subjunctive (-se):

		-ar			-er, -ir
	stem	ase		stem	iese
			s			s
			mos			mos
			is			is
			n			n

Preterite:

Same stem as present, imperfect, et cetera.

This tense has special person indicators in 2nd singular and plural, 3rd plural.

	ar			er	ir		Stress signal: Stress always on ending (on first of two-syllable endings) in regular verbs.
stem	é		stem	í			
	a	ste		i	ste		
	ó			ió			
	a	mos		i	mos		
	a	steis		i	steis		
	a	ron		ie	ron		

Future indicative:

Stem is infinitive (or modified infinitive)

One set of endings fits all verbs, regardless of regularity or conjugation-class. These endings are, historically, the present indicative of *haber*:

				Stress signal: every ending is stressed. The infinitive as stem differentiates *hablé/hablaré*
he	stem	é		
has		á	s	
ha		á		
hemos		e	mos	
(hab)éis		é	is	
han		á	n	

Since both /e/ and /a/ appear as tense-mood signals in the future, while they usually signal different conjugation–classes, special cue–response drill may be required for firm learning of these endings.

Stress position differentiates
hablara/hablará
hablaras/hablarás
hablaran/hablarán

"Conditional" or "Past future"
  Stem: same as future

Stress signal: on first syllable of ending throughout

The above presentation of the regular verb system emphasizes the recurring pattern of -, -*s*, -, -*mos*, -*is*, -*n* as person-number indicators in all tenses except the preterite. It also emphasizes that within each conjugation-class the tense-mood signal is constant in present subjunctives, imperfect indicatives and subjunctives, and the conditional, although the stress changes position in the present tenses.

It may also be useful to note that even in the Spanish verb system a few ambiguous forms occur: the first and third persons singular are not differentiated in the present subjunctive, the imperfect indicative and subjunctive, and the conditional. Occasionally this ambiguity may call for solution by use of a subject pronoun. The only other ambiguity is that between the first person plural, present and preterite, in -*ar* and -*ir* verbs: *hablamos*, present/preterite and *escribimos*, present/preterite. In the rare cases of actual ambiguity as to tense meaning, an adverb easily resolves the confusion.

The formation of "compound" tenses is in part a morphological question, and in part a matter of syntax. The principles of patterning set forth above can be extended to the learning of these tenses, which we will not develop in detail here.

Irregular verbs

Spanish irregular verbs have been classified in a variety of ways by grammarians and linguists. For pedagogical purposes attempts to classify by different types of irregularity, except for the "radical changing" or "stem-vowel changing" verbs, seem to complicate rather than to simplify. The arrangements presented here frankly utilize the standard conjugational patterns as a starting point, although it should be pointed out beyond any possibility of misunderstanding that they are intended to interlock with pattern-drill types of exercise and not with "conjugating" as the device for exercising and learning.

In the arrangement followed here, the stem-vowel changing verbs are presented first as relatively large classes, then the unclassable irregulars are presented in a key form chart, and finally the spelling change verbs are presented, although they are not a problem of spoken Spanish but only of the written form.

Stem-vowel changing verbs

The "stem-vowel changing verbs" are more traditionally known as "radical-changing" verbs, because it is the radical or "root" vowel which changes. The term "stem vowel" is more usual among Spanish teachers.

In the following chart of the stem-vowel changing verbs, the first row of boxes gives a minimal statement of the nature and distribution of the changes. The second row identifies the visual signals, which we shall associate arbitrarily with the different changes, which are then arranged in the rest of the chart as a visual-aid device to assist in drills on these verbs.

The value of this device has been proved again and again in evoking oral responses in pattern drills. The scheme is introduced in steps as the several types of verb and the several tenses involved are met. The arrangement in a form like that of the paradigms assumes that the learner has passed the initial learning stages and has acquired some awareness of the paradigmatic arrangement. It does not require, however, that the orthographical system be known. In fact, the use of arbitrary symbols, rather than letters or actual model verbs spelled out, makes this device useful at any stage.

The students' attention is called to the two right-angled lines which emphasize the stress shift in the first two persons plural in the present tenses. The inner angle in the present subjunctive of Class III is made of broken lines to emphasize that the usual stress shift applies, although all six tense-forms have the same stem-vowel change in contrast with all the other present tenses. Thus a symmetrical arrangement, which emphasizes recurring patterns, also draws attention to what is different from one class or tense to another.

The successful use of this device requires presentation and rehearsal by the teacher in the classroom, after which it may be used by learners for home study and practice. With the appropriate section of the diagram on the chalkboard, the teacher works slowly through an oral

TABLE VI

"Radical-changing" or *"Stem-vowel-changing"* Verbs

These verbs are traditionally grouped into three types or classes, according to the pattern of changes in the stem vowel.

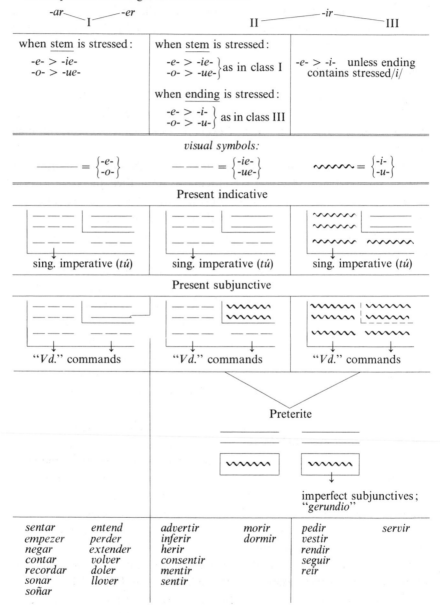

I (-ar, -er)	II (-ir)	III (-ir)
when stem is stressed: -e- > -ie- -o- > -ue-	when stem is stressed: -e- > -ie- } -o- > -ue- } as in class I when ending is stressed: -e- > -i- } -o- > -u- } as in class III	-e- > -i- unless ending contains stressed /i/

visual symbols:

——— = { -e- / -o- }   – – – – = { -ie- / -ue- }   ⌇⌇⌇⌇ = { -i- / -u- }

Present indicative

sing. imperative (*tú*) | sing. imperative (*tú*) | sing. imperative (*tú*)

Present subjunctive

"*Vd.*" commands | "*Vd.*" commands | "*Vd.*" commands

Preterite

imperfect subjunctives; "*gerundio*"

sentar	entend	advertir	morir	pedir	servir
empezer	perder	inferir	dormir	vestir	
negar	extender	herir		rendir	
contar	volver	consentir		seguir	
recordar	doler	mentir		reir	
sonar	llover	sentir			
soñar					

pattern drill, pointing to the spot on the diagram as each person–number form is cued and given by pupil response. Subjects may soon be dispensed with as cues, as merely pointing to the diagram elicits responses; students soon learn to "see" the diagrams mentally, even when they are not in sight and to respond directly with any desired personal form without needing to "conjugate mentally" in order to find it.

The "unclassable" irregular verbs

The remaining Spanish irregular verbs (with the exception of a few relatively rare ones) are shown in a "Key Form" chart which follows on pages 116 and 117. This tabular arrangement emphasizes the important fact that even the irregular verbs fall into recurring patterns, to which the listed forms are keys. The following are the most important points to be noted in explanation of this chart.

Present indicative: except for *ser*, *ir*, and *haber* all Spanish verbs have the same stem-ending arrangement in the second and third persons singular and the third person plural and have "regular" stem and ending in the first and second persons plural.

Present subjunctive: except for *poder* and *querer*, which are "stem-changing" verbs in the present indicative and subjunctive, the present subjunctive stem is the same in all persons in all the "unclassable" irregular verbs. Special key forms are given only for the first six verbs listed, since the rule-of-thumb which relates the present subjunctive stem to that of the first person singular of the present indicative applies to all the others.

Preterite: except for *ser* and *ir*, preterites of irregular verbs fall into only two specific patterns. Those with unstressed ending in the first person singular (the key form) all follow the same "strong" pattern—with only the deviation of *dijeron*, *trajeron*, and *-dujeron* and the purely orthographic adjustment of *hizo*. Those with *stressed* ending, such as *di*, *caí*, and *oí*, follow the regular pattern suggested by this ending. The other apparent complications are predictable spelling conventions applied to forms regular in speech.

Imperfect indicative: since this tense is "regular" except in *ser*, *ir*, and *ver*—and even these three pattern regularly on an irregular stem—a key form for this tense is listed only for these three verbs.

Imperfect subjunctive: in all these verbs the two sets of imperfect subjunctive endings, arbitrarily reduced to *-ra*, *-ras*, et cetera, or *-se*, *-ses*, et cetera, replace the final *-ron* of the third person plural ending of the preterite. This rule-of-thumb works, without exception, for *every* verb—

TABLE VII
Key Forms of the Common Irregular Verbs

Infinitive	Participles	Present Indicative	Preterite	Future	Singular Imperative
(1) ser	siendo sido *era* (imperfect)	soy somos eres sois es son sea (pres. subj.)	fui fuimos fuiste fuisteis fue fueron	seré	sé
(2) ir	(*yendo*) ido *iba* (imperfect)	voy vamos vas vais va van vaya (pres. subj.)	fui fuimos fuiste fuisteis fue fueron *vamos* replaces *vayamos* for first person commands.	iré	ve
(3) haber	habiendo habido	he hemos has habéis ha han haya (pres. subj.)	hube	habré	he
(4) saber	sabiendo sabido	sé sabes sepa (pres. subj.)	supe	sabré	(sabe)
(5) estar	estando estado	estoy estás esté (pres. subj.) accent all except 1st plural	estuve	estaré	(está)
(6) dar	dando dado	doy das dé (pres. subj.) accent 1st and 3rd singular	di	daré	(da)
(7) poder	pudiendo podido	puedo puedes (pres. subj. like stem-changing I.)	pude	podré	(none)
(8) querer	queriendo querido	quiero quieres (pres. subj. like stem-changing I.)	quise	querré	(quiere)
(9) andar	andando andado	ando andas	anduve	andaré	(anda)
(10) caber	cabiendo cabido	quepo cabes	cupe	cabré	(cabe)
(11) tener	teniendo tenido	tengo tienes	tuve	tendré	ten
(12) poner	poniendo puesto	pongo pones	puse	pondré	pon
(13) hacer	haciendo hecho	hago haces	hice (hizo)	haré	haz

	Infinitive	Participles	Present Indicative	Preterite	Future	Singular Imperative
(14)	venir	viniendo venido	vengo vienes	vine	vendré	ven
(15)	decir	diciendo dicho	digo dices	dije (dijeron)	diré	di
(16)	traer	(trayendo) traído	traigo traes	traje (trajeron)	traeré	(trae)
(17)	conducir	conduciendo conducido	conduzco conduces	conduje (condujeron)	conduciré	(conduce)
(18)	asir	asiendo asido	asgo ases	así	asiré	(ase)
(19)	caer	(cayendo) caído	caigo caes	caí (cayó, cayeron)	caeré	(cae)
(20)	oir	(oyendo) oído	oigo oyes	oí (oyó, oyeron)	oiré	(oye)
(21)	salir	saliendo salido	salgo sales	salí	saldré	sal
(22)	valer	valiendo valido	valgo vales	valí	valdré	val
(23)	ver	viendo visto veía (imperfect)	veo ves	vi	veré	(ve)
(24)	-uir type huir	(huyendo) huido	huyo huyes	huí (huyó, huyeron)	huiré	(huye)

Similarly for other verbs in which the sound -uir is heard, such as concluir, argüir (but not distinguir or delinquir, in which the u is not heard).

(25)	Vowel + -cer or -cir conocer	conociendo conocido	conozco conoces	conocí	conoceré	(conoce)

Similarly for most verbs in which -cer or -cir is preceded by a vowel. Major exceptions: cocer (stem-changing I.), mecer, hacer and decir; also -ducir group.

regular, stem-changing, irregular, and (in writing as well as in speech) the orthographical changing or spelling change verbs.

Future and conditional: the only irregularity to be learned here is in the stem, since there is only one set of endings for these two tenses, applicable without exception to all verbs. The stem, regular or not, makes no changes within the future and conditional of any verb.

Singular imperative: this is the only listed form which is not a key to others, since the plural imperative is always formed on the infinitive. In the chart parentheses enclose those singular imperatives which (regular or not) are identical with the third person singular of the present indicative.

In Table VII, irregular forms are underlined; forms showing orthographic "adjustment" in written Spanish and forms included as special reminders are enclosed in parentheses.

Verbs with spelling changes

In teaching which begins with hearing and repeating patterns of sound, the mastery of spelling change verbs should be much simplified. It is far easier for the student to learn to recognize conventional spellings of sounds which he has heard as regular (and in due course to spell them himself) than it is for him to proceed from what appears to him to be a visible irregularity. The latter is what occurs when he meets the written forms of these verbs first.

Verbs such as *tocar*, *pagar*, and *cruzar* should be learned orally in pattern drills in which, for example, the learner alternates *tomo/toco*, *tome/toque*, *toma/toca*, *tomé/toqué*, *tomó/tocó*, and so learns, orally, the complete regularity of *tocar*. Similar parallel drills will establish the regularity of *pagar* and *cruzar*. Only after the learner is in complete oral control of these verbs should he be exposed to the spellings—and then in such a way that he is made aware that the spellings are conventions; that they follow a pattern and are therefore predictable, and will occur in other verbs which have the same stem-final phoneme.

Verbs such as *vencer*, *recoger*, and *seguir*, should be acquired by a similar process. *Seguir*, of course, should be matched with the previously learned *pedir* (*vestir*, etcetera) in order that the stem-vowel change be acquired by analogy of sound and not be confused in the learner's mind with the problem of spelling -*go*, -*ga*, -*gue*, -*gui*.

A favorite stumbling-block in conventional learning is the orthography of forms such as *cayendo*, *cayó*, *cayeron*, and remembering the written accent on *creímos*, *creísteis*, and the like. Most of these difficulties seem to vanish when spelling is learned only after pronunciation, and as a system of predictable conventions.

One verb continues to defy many learners still. This is the useful *reir*, and, of course, its compound *sonreir*. A most successful device has been to incorporate *reir* into a pattern drill with *pedir* and *seguir*. The "feel" for *reir* is acquired through analogies like *pido/río, pide/ríe, pida/ría, pidió/rió*, contrasted with *pedimos/reímos, pedía/reía, pedí/reí*. Even the fusion of stem and ending in *rió, rieron, riendo* is usually acquired without question.

The reader is urged to reject the classification of verbs such as *conocer, parecer*, and the like as mere spelling-change verbs, which has sometimes been offered in textbooks. Since language is a system of sound symbols, any sound which is not predictably generated by the usual patterning of stems and endings is irregular. In *conozco, conozca* there is a /k/, not the normal product of the stem /konoθ–/ plus the regular endings /-o/, /-a/. Even though there are numerous verbs which have a similar "intrusive" sound in the corresponding forms, they should be regarded as forming a class of irregular verbs and not as spelling-change verbs.

Most spelling changes are made to reflect regularity of sound, and they will be most successfully taught that way, not as one more class of irregularity to be memorized by rote.

(E) WORD DERIVATION

In our discussion of morphemes we have so far distinguished between **roots**, those elements which carry the vocabulary meanings, and **grammatical morphemes**, which carry the structural or grammatical meaning.[1] There is still a third type of building stone which may be used in various circumstances with the same identifiable meaning, the various prefixes and suffixes which are used in word formation or derivation: the *-ero* which can be combined with a root such as *libr-* to form *librero* and which is used again with the same meaning of "person involved" in *carcelero, escudero, vaquero*; or the prefix *im-, in-* denoting negation, which appears in *imposible, injusto*, and *intolerable*.

Word derivation has little if any pedagogical application in the initial stages of the audio-lingual course. Whether any given prefix or suffix can be added to a specific root is not predictable; in other words, the existence of *clase* and *-ero* does not allow us to assume that there is a word * *clasero*. But in the vocabulary-building phase of the course and in the

[1] In discussing the Spanish verb, we have used the term "stem" rather than "root."

teaching of reading, it is quite essential that the student become familiar with the meaning of derivational suffixes and prefixes. This knowledge will enable him to infer correctly in a context the meaning of innumerable words which would otherwise send him to the dictionary.

The teaching of derivation suffixes or prefixes can be approached in two complementary ways: either through the teaching of "word families," words formed on the same root, or the teaching of series of words formed with the same derivational morpheme. Thus, the meaning of -*azo* can be made clear by teaching to the student a word series like *balazo*, *codazo*, and *sablazo*, and then inviting him to infer the meaning of *hachazo* and *zapatazo*. Or a series like *hablador*, *bebedor*, and *dador* can be presented in sentences in context, preparing the way for other sentences in which the student infers the meaning of *trabajador*, *amenazador*, and so on.

In the word-family approach the student is presented with sentences which use the family in a meaningful context: *El librero vendre libros en la librería, El relojero vende relojes en la relojería*. Basically, this method represents the extension of the pattern practice approach to vocabulary learning. Since many of the Spanish derivational suffixes and prefixes have recognizable English counterparts, we shall again touch upon the problem of derivation in the later discussion of cognates in vocabulary recognition.

CHAPTER VIII

Teaching Syntactical Patterns

(A) THE BASIC PATTERNS OF SPANISH:
NOUN AND VERB CLUSTERS

Derivational, lexical, and grammatical morphemes combine into larger units—words. The purpose of syntactical analysis is to determine just how words can be used and combined to make up larger units of speech such as phrases, clauses, and sentences. There are several methods of approaching the syntactical analysis of a language. The details of procedure and the comparative merits of these methods are relatively unimportant to the Spanish teacher. They deserve mention insofar as they have an obvious relation to teaching procedures.

One method of analysis consists of dividing an utterance into those elements which seem to be the basic constructions (usually two) of which the utterance is made up. These constructions are referred to as the **immediate constituents** of the utterance; they are then divided in their turn into their immediate constituents. (The term derives from the concept that such elements, or constituents, relate directly to one another without mediate or connecting elements; hence, non-mediate or "immediate.")

A sentence like "My sister's husband speaks Spanish quite fluently" divides into two immediate constituents: "my sister's husband" and "speaks Spanish quite fluently." The first immediate constituent, "my sister's husband," has, in turn, the immediate constituents, "my sister's" and "husband"; "my sister's" may finally be broken down into the immediate constituents of that phrase.

Another approach to syntactical analysis emphasizes the fact that syntactical units are related if they can alternate in the same slot in a frame; that is, in the same position and function in a sentence. Thus,

121

every syntactical unit is defined not only by its own makeup but also by the position which it can fill in a larger utterance.

These first two types of syntactical analysis have an obvious relationship to the expansion and substitution exercises. In the former the student is given a small sentence like *Mi amigo ha llegado* and is then asked to expand this utterance by successively adding elements like *esta noche, con su tío, a las ocho*, and *para visitarnos*. It has been pointed out before that the substitution exercise consists of successive replacement of one part of an utterance by items of similar value within the same structure; this type of exercise is, then, a principle of analysis converted into a teaching method.

Another type of syntactical analysis is based on the concept that the **entire syntax of a language can be described in formulas showing how utterances can be created from others by successive series of transformations.** In one of its applications, the process of transformation gives us a formal means of differentiating between apparently identical structures: dancing doll and bowling ball transform into doll that dances and ball for bowling; laughing gas accepts neither of these transformations, but is a gas that causes laughing.

Still another approach starts from the premise that one of the necessary constituent elements of utterances, of any syntactical unit, is an intonation pattern and that the surest way of identifying the component elements of utterances is through the study and isolation of such intonation patterns. Both approaches mentioned have pedagogical implications. The transformation approach opens up the possibility of teaching the entire system of syntax in a language through transformation exercises; the emphasis on the intonation pattern reminds us that such intonation patterns must be taught as integral parts of the utterance and that in Spanish the stress and breath groups we have mentioned earlier are not only phonetic but also syntactical units of Spanish.

There are at present no exhaustive analyses of Spanish using any one of the methods just described. Yet whatever method we may want to employ, the most essential facts concerning Spanish syntax are fairly obvious; we can perhaps best approach them by taking another look at **the concept of "word,"** which we have used in our definition of syntax. We would all call *les, la, no, tu, casa, nuestro, compro*, "words" and consider them as the units or building stones out of which syntactical constructions are made up. But our reason for calling all these units words is basically that they are listed as such in the dictionary and that they are separated from each other in spelling. If we consider the behavior of oral language alone, the concept of word becomes quite difficult to define. Linguists have tried different approaches. One way to define words is to ask a native speaker to pronounce connected utterances in such a way that he makes pauses within an utterance whenever such pauses would seem plausible to him. All the segments marked off by pauses could then be called words. Another way of getting at the definition of word is to call it a "minimum free form." This means a form that in actual speech could stand as an utterance by itself. The important implication of these definitions in the analysis of Spanish syntax lies not so much in the theoretical aspects concerning the definition of word, but in the perfectly obvious fact that according to the above definition *el*, *mi*, *lo*, and *se* could not qualify as words; no one would make a pause after *el* in *el automóvil* or after *se* in *¿Cómo se llama?* Neither is it possible to make an utterance like "*Mi*," or "*Lo*," except perhaps in answer to a question about Spanish grammar. Now whether we call such units "words," "affixes," or "bound forms" does not matter too much. What does matter is that we realize that elements such as *el*, *la*, *mis*, and *este* are indeed **bound to the noun** in actual usage and that others such as *le*, *nos*, and *se* are inescapably **bound to the verb**. The fact that a few of these "words" have two meanings (*la* and *los* may be bound to nouns as articles or to verbs as object pronouns, for example) does not upset this basic concept.

We may regard such forms as satellites of the noun or the verb; this helps us to realize that most utterances are made up of constructions or clusters: **noun clusters** or **verb clusters**. Each noun or verb cluster has a center or base, which is the noun or verb itself. Around this center are the noun or verb satellites and/or other free forms such as adjectives and adverbs modifying the nucleus.

Nuestro antiguo amigo	*no comprende*	*las nuevas ideas*
N	V	N
(noun cluster)	(verb cluster)	(noun cluster)

de este joven profesor.
N
(noun cluster)

The typical basic structure of the Spanish utterance is, of course, very much like the English. The noun construction may be used without a preposition, functioning as subject, direct object, predicate nominative, or appositive according to its position in the sentence, or it may be used after a preposition. In the latter case it becomes subordinate to either a noun or a verb construction:

$$\underbrace{Hablo}_{\text{V}} \ \underset{\leftarrow}{} \ \underbrace{de \ mi \ antiguo \ amigo.}_{\text{N}}$$

$$\underbrace{la \ casa}_{\text{N}} \ \underset{\leftarrow}{} \ \underbrace{de \ mi \ antiguo \ amigo}_{\text{N}}$$

The verb construction may also be used with or without a preceding preposition and may become dependent on other verb or noun constructions:

$$\underbrace{Se \ ha \ decidido}_{\text{V}} \ \underset{\leftarrow}{} \ \underbrace{a \ estudiar.}_{\text{V}}$$

$$\underbrace{Dieron}_{\text{V}} \ \underbrace{la \ orden}_{\text{N}} \ \underset{\leftarrow}{} \ \underbrace{de \ salir.}_{\text{V}}$$

Noun and verb clusters are also the basic elements of complex utterances involving dependent or subordinate clauses, adverbial or adjectival (relative). In the early stages, however, the main difficulties facing the English speaker learning Spanish lie within the formation of the basic clusters themselves, rather than in the arrangement of the clusters into sentences. Of course there are important exceptions, such as the different sentence orientation with which Spanish expresses "I like" or "I lack"; even these idiomatic structures are more quickly learned by students who have previously become at home with the behavior of articles, possessives, object pronouns, and the like.

The comparison of a few English and Spanish sentences will illustrate this point:

NOUN CLUSTERS	VERB CLUSTERS	NOUN CLUSTERS
Intelligent students	don't drink	a lot of wine.
Los estudiantes inteligentes	*no beben*	*mucho vino.*

The noun–verb–noun pattern is the same in both languages. The difficulties in Spanish concern the use of the article for generalizations; the position and agreement of the adjective in the first noun cluster; the formation of the negative and the inflection in the verb cluster; the correspondence of *mucho* to a phrase involving the article in English; and the agreement of the adjective and the contrast between its position before the noun and that of *inteligentes* after its noun.

Let us compare the constituent clusters of another pair of sentences:

VERB	VERB	NOUN
Without looking at him	he gave him	some money.
Sin mirarlo	*le dió*	*dinero.*

Again, there is overall similarity in the arrangement of the sentence pattern: preposition + verb cluster, verb cluster, noun cluster. The difficulties are within each group: infinitive instead of gerund after the preposition; absence of anything corresponding to English "at"; form and position of the object pronoun; absence of subject pronoun in the main verb cluster, inflection of the verb; form and position of the object (indirect) pronoun; and in the noun cluster absence of anything corresponding to English unstressed "some."

We should repeat that such parallelism in the arrangement of the basic clusters is by no means complete; we have mentioned one or two noteworthy exceptions. These examples do demonstrate the fact that the initial task, and perhaps the most difficult one, must be to teach the makeup of the noun and verb clusters themselves. In the case of the noun clusters, this means especially such matters as the use of the definite article for generalizations, with titles in direct address, when classifying by occupation, et cetera; the position of adjectives; and the formation and use of determinatives or markers (possessives, demonstratives, and so on). In the case of verb clusters it means the position of the pronouns, including such specifically Spanish problems as the "redundant" constructions, and the formation of interrogative and negative utterances. The special Spanish problem of use or omission of subject pronouns can be handled only in part in the framework of similar basic arrangements, for, as we shall see, this problem is most successfully solved through comparison of English and Spanish use of stress/intonation patterns as integral parts of the utterance.

The student will never be able to produce Spanish utterances with any degree of fluency or accuracy unless he can produce the composite elements—the noun and verb clusters—quickly and automatically. Noun clusters and verb clusters, once formed, may be mentally arranged into sentences, but this process of arrangement and assembly cannot be applied to the clusters themselves if anything remotely resembling control of the language is intended. Phonetically and syntactically, the clusters are units by themselves; they are the basic elements which make up the Spanish utterance. They are the units which must come to the speaker's mind already assembled and complete.

This does not mean that the learner should not have the analytic understanding of why *a* is used in *Veo a mi padre*, why no article appears in *Fulano es médico*, what circumstance controls the appearance of *se* in constructions like *Se lo doy a usted*. By itself, however, this analytic understanding of the structure of the cluster will at best make it possible for the student to construct it laboriously for the purpose of passing a written examination. In speech there is no time for going through such a building up process. In speech the clusters must become available, readily and automatically, as units.

The best way to secure this automaticity is to cause each type of cluster and each variant to be used over and over again in sentences in which the complex cluster being learned remains constant while other elements are changed. For example, we may ask the student to substitute different subjects in a sentence like *Juan tiene mi nuevo lápiz azul*; while incidentally drilling the different forms of the verb, the student is using the noun cluster *mi nuevo lápiz azul* over and over again and committing this four-word cluster to memory. We can achieve the same purpose by asking the student to substitute other verbs such as *ve*, *deja*, and *quiere*, or we can have him replace the noun itself with others such as *libro*, *corbata*, *papel*. In such **substitution drill** we change one item within the frame, or even within the noun cluster, but we keep the **structure intact** and so accomplish automatic learning of the point at issue. If our concern is with the forms and position of possessives, we may now signal substitutions such as *tu*, *su*, *nuestro*; with each of these we may alternate a masculine and a feminine noun (as *sombrero/corbata*), or the singular and plural of a single noun. So, progressively, the student masters minimal steps involving forms, word order, and agreements and learns to handle a complex cluster as a unit.

Similar procedures will apply in teaching verb clusters. For example, the cluster *no se la he* + past participle can be set up in an exercise in which the student is asked to answer questions replacing nouns by pronouns:

> *¿Ha leído usted la carta a su amigo?*
> *No, señor, no se la he leído.*
> *¿Ha escrito usted la carta a su amigo?*
> *No, señor, no se la he escrito.*
> *¿Ha explicado usted la carta a su amigo?*
> *No, señor, no se la he explicado.*

The drill may be continued substituting *dado*, *mandado*, *presentado*, and so on. The difficult verbal cluster *no se la he* remains constant and is repeated over and over by the student and becomes automatic because the student is more consciously aware of the series of different past participles he is substituting. Similar drills are used for variants of the cluster; in one series, a masculine noun will replace *carta* and the cluster becomes *no se lo he*; in another, the subject of the question may become *Juan* and the cluster becomes *no se la ha*; or again, the indirect object in the question may become *me*, *¿Me ha leído usted la carta?* and the cluster learned in the reply becomes again *no se la he* as the student learns by repetition that *se* means one thing in response to one utterance and something else in response to another.

When within one drill, rather than a series of separate drills as outlined in the foregoing paragraph, we ask the student to change elements within the cluster itself, we are teaching the assembly of the cluster. If we use nouns of different gender or number in successive questions, the student must choose among *lo*, *la*, *los*, and *las* in constructing the reply. If we change the indirect object to *nos* or *me* or the subject to *ustedes* or *ellos*, in successive questions the student must choose among different person-forms of the verb and react to "you–I" or "me–you" relationships in assembling his cluster in response. Exercise of this type is, of course, also useful and necessary, but if used alone, it may leave the student exactly where we do not want him to remain: at the stage, that is, where he must assemble each cluster out of its component elements. Such problem or testing drills must be alternated with the kind of exercise which drills each complete cluster as a unit.

If our exercise procedures leave the learner at the "assembly" stage, he will never develop the automatic control of such fixed contrasting patterns as *démelo*, *no se lo doy*, *cómprela*, *no la compre*, or *quiero decírselo*, *se lo digo*—all of which lend themselves admirably to substitution-type pattern drills.

(B) THE TYPES OF SYNTACTICAL SIGNAL

In the preceding section we have shown that a major problem in the initial stages of learning Spanish is mastering the noun clusters and verb clusters out of which sentences are built. While we have touched on the differences between English and Spanish in composing the elements into clusters, we have particularly emphasized the importance of types of exercise arranged to develop automaticity rather than an assembly process.

We must now prepare to examine some of the differences in the patterns of construction through which English syntactical habits interfere in the learning of Spanish. Let us first examine briefly the devices which both languages use to signal the relationships of words, their interdependence rather than their lexical or dictionary meanings. In both English and Spanish these devices are (1) word order, (2) inflection, (3) agreement, (4) function words, (5) replacement words, and (6) stress and intonation.

(1) **Word order** is a fundamental device in both languages. In spite of the bad grammar of such a substandard utterance as Him and her went with you and I, there is no doubt as to the meaning because the word order signals the subject-verb relationship. In Spanish, however, subject-verb relationship is less clearly signalled by word order alone, since we may say *Juan viene mañana* or *Viene Juan mañana* or *Mañana viene Juan* or even *Mañana Juan viene*. In other structures, however, word order may be as fundamental a signal in Spanish as it is in English.

(2) **Inflection** of a form, that is, a change in ending or in some other element of a word, may by itself signal important relationships, such as person, number, tense, and mood in a verb or plural in a noun. In English, for example, the difference between him and he is an inflectional difference which signals case of the personal pronoun; in walks, the /-s/ is an inflection which signals person and number of the verb.

(3) **Agreement** signals relationships between words by an accord, usually shown by endings. Spanish has, of course, a much more extensive system of inflections and agreements than does English. English nouns have no grammatical gender; English adjectives have no inflection for gender or number, with the exception of this/these and that/those; and "regular" verbs have only four forms (walk, walks, walked, and walking) and many irregulars have fewer (put, puts, and putting; can and could; ought). English object pronouns do not distinguish dative (indirect object) from accusative (direct object) by form, et cetera. Even in Spanish the system of agreements is often a matter of custom rather than of necessity. A foreigner's *El casas son hermoso* would sound barbaric to the native ear but would probably be understood. This observation must not be taken to suggest any careless attitude toward the matters of form and agreement; it is intended only to emphasize the fact that other devices, such as word order and intonation, are essential factors of the grammatical system and must not be neglected.

(4) **Function words** are those whose principal service is to relate one part of an utterance to another, as do prepositions and conjunctions, or

to express **grammatical concepts** such as "future" in he will go, "past before present" in we have seen, or "mode" (attitude) in he won't sing. Functions words may, of course, have a more or less clear lexical content as well; there is a difference in lexical meaning between up the tree and down the tree, although our confidence in lexical meanings may be somewhat shaken by remembering that after we cut the tree down we can cut the tree up. The importance of function words to sentence structure lies in their grammatical meanings, the way in which they relate noun or verb clusters to other noun and verb clusters, the way in which they increase the range of time-mood concepts, and so forth.

English makes somewhat greater use of function words than does Spanish to signal variations in verb meaning, since Spanish has so extensive an inflexional system: shall-will ('ll) as future signals or as signals of intention; do-does-did (don't-doesn't-didn't) as signals of the interrogative or negative; should-would ('d) as signals of conditional, with the complication of should-ought to, would-used to; may-might as mood signals (so that you may understand) but also conveying aspects of Spanish *poder*; will you, won't you, aren't they, can't he, et cetera, as "question tags," all corresponding to *verdad* or *no es verdad*.

Spanish too makes extensive use of function words. All teachers are aware of the many problems prepositions cause, since they so often refuse to behave as their counterparts do in English. Subordinating conjunctions are interwoven with subjunctive constructions; Spanish does have more or less similar verbal auxiliaries, such as **have** gone, *han ido* and **can** come, *puede venir*; but others do not correspond, He says he **will go** *Dice que irá* and **Will** you go? *¿Quiere Vd. ir?*

(5) **Replacement words** are principally those known as pronouns, words which replace lexical items. Like function words, replacement words often signal grammatical meaning through form or position (he, him; *nosotros, nos*), and may serve as markers as well as replacers: *este libro; éste*.

(6) **Stress and intonation**, as we know, signal such important matters as questions (together with word order or specific signals such as interrogative words); conclusion of a statement; pause after incomplete statement; and various types of emotional overtone. Intonation is the only signal which differentiates such Spanish utterances as the statement, *Va Juan* / ⌐⌐ /, from the question, *¿Va Juan?* /⌐⌐ /; subject-verb relationship is not necessarily signalled by word order in Spanish, and Spanish lacks a function word like English do-does. English, on the other hand, uses only stress or intonation to establish contrasts, as in

I know you; I don't know him, which Spanish signals with specific structures, *Le conozco a Vd.*; *no le conozco a él.*

The fact that an English function word may or may not have a "corresponding" function word in "corresponding" use in Spanish or that one language may use a different function word in certain constructions or that a function word may signal a relationship which the other language signals by inflection, word order, or intonation—this lack of systematic correspondence between the two languages in the selection and arrangement of the signalling devices is a major source of difficulty; the structural system of the mother tongue, which is a matter of automatic habit, interferes with the acquisition of the system of the foreign language.

The construction of successful exercises depends in large part on the teacher's awareness of the mechanisms of interference between the English system and that of the foreign tongue, an awareness which the successful student also comes to share as he alternates appropriate pattern drill with analysis and construction or problem type exercises in which he must make choices. Examples of some of the most noteworthy conflict points follow; a treatment of the present scope cannot attempt a complete comparative analysis of Spanish and English syntax.

(C) MECHANISMS OF INTERFERENCE: DIFFERENCES OF MEDIA

We can compare utterances of English and Spanish which have the same structural meaning in both languages: statement, question, possession, and so on. If different media or types of signal are used in the same type of utterance or if different media are used to convert one type of utterance to another, we may expect that the speaker of English will have trouble with the Spanish utterance.

Let us give a few examples of uses of different media in Spanish and English:

(1) **Inflection and/or agreement in Spanish, not in English**

Usted lee el periódico.	You read the paper.
Ustedes leen el periódico.	
Nuestro libro, nuestra casa	our { book, house
nuestros amigos	{ friends

(2) **Inflection in Spanish, not in English**

La veo; le doy el libro.	I see her; I give her the book.
Los veo; les doy el libro	I see them; I give them the book.

(3)   **Inflection in English, function word in Spanish**
My sister**'s** house.   *La casa **de** mi hermana.*

(4)   **Function words in English, inflection in Spanish**
I'll sing.
I'm going to sing. } *Cantar**é**.*

(5)   **Word order in English, function words and inflection in Spanish**
I want to tell him the truth.
Quiero decirle la verdad.
I want him to tell the truth.
Quiero que (él) diga la verdad.

(6)   **Function words in English, intonation in Spanish**

He speaks Spanish.	*Habla español.*
Does he speak Spanish?	*¿Habla español?*
We **are** going.	*Vamos.*
Shall we go?	*¿Vamos?*
Let's go.	*¡Vamos!*

Teachers are well aware of the foregoing types of difference and, in the main, experience shows that some of them cause little interference because the Spanish does not seem especially strange to the learner, and others are well controlled by any of a variety of standard teaching procedures. This is less true when the learner is less aware of the nature of the syntactical signal, especially if **stress** or **intonation** signals different meanings in the two languages.

(7)   **English and Spanish use different intonations**

Charles speaks Spanish   { *Carlos habla español.* (Statement)
   (Statement)   { *Carlos habla español.* (Emphasis)

Charles speaks Spanish?!   *¿Carlos habla español?*   (Question)
   (Surprise or doubt)

(8)   **Stress in English, word order and/or function words in Spanish**
(a)   A Spanish teacher   *un profesor de español*
     A Spanish teacher   *un profesor español*

It must be granted that stress alone is not always a sure signal in such English utterances; an ambiguous English utterance may be rendered by different structures in Spanish according to the meaning established by supplementary signals or a wider context.

(b) I'm giving this money to <u>John</u>. *Le doy este dinero a <u>Juan</u>.*
I'm giving this <u>money</u> to John. *Le doy a Juan este <u>dinero</u>.*
I'm giving <u>this</u> money to John. *Le doy a Juan <u>este</u> dinero.*
I'm <u>giving</u> this money to John. *Le <u>doy</u> este dinero a Juan.*
<u>I</u>'m giving this money to John. *<u>Yo</u> le doy a Juan este dinero.*
I <u>am</u> giving this money to John. *<u>Sí</u> que le doy este dinero a Juan.*

In the above examples we observe that English may move an emphatic stress from one element of an utterance to another with no other change in the structure. Spanish also has an emphatic stress, which may coincide in position with that of the English utterance as in the first and fourth examples (emphasis on last element in the sentence or on the verb), may accompany a change in word order as in the second and third examples, may accompany a subject pronoun not present in the other examples, or may accompany an adverb of emphasis as in the last example.

The position of emphatic stress may coincide in the two languages when it falls on the subject (Spanish subject pronouns are likely to be used only when they carry emphatic stress), on the verb, or on a cluster which comes last in the sentence; but when English emphasizes any predicate element other than the last, Spanish typically places the corresponding cluster last, even though the stress falls on a determinative, as in *este dinero* (third example above).

(c) I see <u>him</u>; I don't see <u>her</u>. *Le veo <u>a él</u>; no la veo <u>a ella</u>.*
<u>She</u> is coming; <u>he</u> is staying home. *<u>Ella</u> viene; <u>él</u> se queda en casa,*
<u>I</u> see <u>you</u> and <u>you</u> see <u>me</u>. *Yo te veo <u>a ti</u> y tú me ves <u>a mí</u>.*
<u>My</u> house and <u>your</u> house. *Mi casa y la casa de <u>Vd</u>.*
<u>His</u> book, not <u>her</u> book. *El libro <u>de él</u>, no el libro <u>de ella</u>.*

Most textbooks and many teachers are at a loss to help learners to master these problems of subject pronouns and redundant constructions that "may be used or not." More than anything else, traditional attempts to analyze the problem are based on the concept of clarity. The real issue is one of contrast, and the mechanism of contrast in these examples is for English stress, whereas in Spanish it is **a change in structure plus stress**. Spanish object pronouns and the possessive *su-sus* do not accept emphatic stress, while their English counterparts do.

In this area we have not only the need to master a number of different noun and verb clusters; we must also resolutely set up patterns of contrast between English and Spanish. Only by so doing will we head off a tendency to say * *Le veo* on the basis of English I see **him** or * *Me gusta* on the basis of **I** like it, or will the student learn to use subject pronouns for contrast by emphasis and not otherwise.

(D) MECHANISMS OF INTERFERENCE: PATTERN CONFUSIONS

The difference in media and the sheer necessity of learning new forms and vocabulary are only partially responsible for the student's difficulties. The difference in media is not even one of the major obstacles. The most difficult problem is, as pointed out in Chapter II, the one created by the student's attempts to equate parts of Spanish and English constructions. If the student can predict with absolute certainty that Spanish will always use an inflection, let us say, whenever the English uses a function word, his problem will then be merely to learn the specific Spanish form, and there will be no further difficulty. A language in which all media, although different, existed in a one-to-one correspondence with the media of another language would be merely a coded form of that other language. The most persistent problems faced by the student are not those created by radical differences, but those due to a partial similarity or overlap between the two languages which the student extends by analogy into an area in which the overlap does not exist. An examination and analysis of mistakes made by hundreds of students on French examinations at the University of Michigan showed that actually only a small percentage (15% to 20%) of all mistakes are due to what one might call complete lack of learning, meaning that the student simply did not know a French word or form. The majority of mistakes (60%) were traceable to students having "learned" some French–English correspondence which was then extended into an area where it does not exist. As we have noted in Chapter III, language study has a unique position among other subjects insofar as the most frequent source of error, namely, interference, is not due to absence of learning but is built into the learning mechanism itself.

In the following discussion we shall try to trace the most frequent sources of errors caused by this parallelism and correspondences between Spanish and English. The categories we can establish there are not absolutely rigid. In some cases English may interfere with a particular Spanish construction for more than one reason, and assignment to one or the other category has to take place on a somewhat arbitrary basis. Still, we hope that our discussion and examples will cover the most important cases of structural interference due to parallelism and correspondence.

We may define as **parallel constructions** all those in which each Spanish element corresponds to an element in the English construction; in both the Spanish and English constructions the corresponding elements make the identical contribution to the total structural and lexical meaning of the utterance, for example:

1	2	3	4	5	6
Yo	*puedo*	*ver*	*la*	*segunda*	*casa*
I	can	see	the	second	house
(1′)	(2′)	(3′)	(4′)	(5′)	(6′)

Such constructions are not very often missed by the student. But as we have pointed out before, this idea of a $1 = 1'$, $2 = 2'$, $3 = 3'$, and $4 = 4'$ correspondence becomes the basis of errors elsewhere.

Constructions which systematically correspond between the two languages, although different in some greater or lesser respect, we shall call **pattern correspondences** rather than parallel constructions. Spanish is systematically different from English in its regular nonexpression of an uncontrasted or unemphatic pronominal subject. Where this difference from English is not the phenomenon being observed in a given group of examples, we shall regard the structure as parallel for our purposes in the following comparisons and contrasts.

In the following pages numerous examples will be given, showing various types of interference arising from pattern confusions.

1. **Parallel or near parallel constructions exist, but do not always correspond to the same lexical items:**

(a) **Different types of object structures**

I speak of John.	*Hablo de Juan.*
I think of John.	*Pienso en Juan.*
I dream of John.	*Sueño con Juan.*
I count on John.	*Cuento con Juan.*
I ask for Robert.	*Pregunto por Roberto.*
I ask for water.	*Pido agua.*
I pay for the book.	*Pago el libro.*
I pay the bill.	*Pago la cuenta.*

The problem illustrated above concerns, both fortunately and unfortunately, some of the most frequently used verbs of the two languages. Others are *esperar* (to wait for), *mirar* (to look at), *buscar* (to look for). We say unfortunately because their frequent occurrence gives the English-speaking student many opportunities to make mistakes, but fortunately since the very frequency of these constructions makes it comparatively easy to build them into the patterns and practice materials of the early part of a Spanish course.

It seems advisable (1) to drill the construction of these verbs in exercises especially designed for that purpose, such as a substitution exercise using different objects, as in *busco el libro* (*la casa, los papeles,* et cetera); *miro el mapa* (*la mesa, el automóvil,* et cetera) and (2) to use these verbs freely as substitution items when drilling with other more complex syntactical patterns. It would be just as easy to use *pagar la comida* or *espero la clase* as substitutions in a pattern drilling the use of the subjunctive, as to practice these patterns with *comprar un lápiz* or *ver la silla,* and it would be more profitable.

(b)   **The connection between verbs and dependent infinitives**

I can work.	*Puedo trabajar.*
I must work.	*Debo trabajar.*
I know how to work.	*Sé trabajar.*
I want to work.	*Quiero trabajar.*
I have to work.	*Tengo que trabajar.*
I begin to work.	*Empiezo a trabajar.*
I work to eat (in order to eat).	*Trabajo para comer.*
I forget to eat.	*Me olvido de comer.*
I try to eat.	*Trato de comer.*
Don't fail to come.	*No dejes de venir.*

An example like "we are to leave," *hemos de salir,* involves the additional factor of noncorrespondence of lexical items; that is, "we are" is not equated with "*hemos*" except in this pair of idioms.

As shown above, both Spanish and English have dependent infinitive constructions with and without connecting function words. The situation is complicated by the fact that Spanish has several possible function words (*que, a, para,* and *de*; note also *sueño con llegar* and *pienso en viajar*, which are not parallel to English infinitive constructions). English has basically only one function word with dependent infinitives, which is "to"; but note "know **how to**" and "go **in order to**".

Again we are involved in an extremely frequent series of constructions with conflicts between English and Spanish that can lead to ingrained errors in the learner's speech habits. Special drill is necessary; a mere list of verbs requiring *a*, *de*, and the like, or nothing before the dependent infinitive cannot by itself solve the problem.

They permit me to work.	*Me permiten trabajar.*
They oblige me to work.	*Me obligan a trabajar.*
They invite me to work.	*Me invitan a trabajar.*

The above examples are, of course, similar to those in the preceding group.

(c)   **Subject–object reversal**

A friend bothers me.	*Me molesta un amigo.*
I need a friend.	*Me falta un amigo.*
I like my friend.	*Me gusta mi amigo.*
I like the teacher.	*Estimo a la profesora.*

These correspondences, since they are not quite parallel in either the first or the last examples, illustrate an area of semantic involvement in syntactical matters that obliges us to relate our drills to meanings. Substitution–transformation drills cannot always set up a mechanical criterion to signal only one of a series of semantically related structures.

2.   **Parallel constructions exist in Spanish and English, but the parallel is broken by Spanish constructions which have no counterpart in English.**

(a)   *Ser* and *estar* and certain idioms

He is tall.	*Es alto.*
He is young.	*Es joven.*
He is sick.	*Está enfermo.*
He is tired.	*Está cansado.*
He is wrong.	*Está equivocado.*
He is right.	*Tiene razón.*
He is hungry.	*Tiene hambre.*

The grammatical distinctions involved in contrasting *ser* and *estar* with adjectives must, of course, be pointed out to the student, as must the category of expressions which use *tener* and a noun, but control of phenomena of this type can be achieved only by a great deal of well-arranged pattern drill, especially of contrastive type.

Generally similar to the above are the following cases:

The coffee is cold.	*El café está frío.*
The sea is cold.	*El mar es frío.*
The man is cold.	*El hombre tiene frío.*
It is cold.	*Hace frío.*

(b) **Nouns modified by the indefinite article**

He is a good student. He is a famous architect.	*Es un buen estudiante.* *Es un arquitecto famoso.*
He is an architect.	*Es arquitecto.*

As long as the singular noun is modified by an adjective, the noun construction after *ser* parallels (or, as in the second example, corresponds to) English. But without a modifying adjective, Spanish does not distinguish between noun and adjective after *ser*, as in *es arquitecto* and *es inteligente*.

(c) **The position of adjectives**

a good student	*un buen estudiante*
a young student	*un estudiante joven*

The whole question of adjective position in Spanish is complicated by a number of factors which require analysis at considerably more length than is available here.

(d) **The position of the object pronoun**

Give me the book. He is giving me the book. He wants to give me the book.	*Déme el libro.* *Está dándome el libro.* *Quiere darme el libro.*
He gives me the book. Don't give me the book.	*Me da el libro.* *No me dé el libro.*

Spanish uses the object pronoun after the verb, as in English, only in a limited number of constructions, but these would be enough to establish the idea of parallel in the learner's mind if they were learned first and would tend to lead to such errors as * *Juan da me el libro*. For this reason the nonparallel construction should be learned first, and contrastive drills used when the postverbal position is learned.

These correspondences can be complicated by the fact that English has the alternative, he is giving the book to me, and Spanish the alternative, *Me está dando el libro* and *me quiere dar el libro*.

(e) **Direct object nouns**

I see the house. He crossed the river.	*Veo la casa.* *Cruzó el río.*
I see the man. He hears my brother.	*Veo al hombre.* *Oye a mi hermano.*

The quick mastery of such a phenomenon as the "personal *a*" is accomplished by **pattern drill**. We may first ask the student to substitute different subjects in such examples as *Juan ve a mi hermano*; then we may have him substitute other verbs, such as *oye*, *deja*, and *llama*; then he can replace the object noun itself with others, such as *padre*, *amigo*, *hermana*, and *profesor*. In this way phrases like *a mi hermano*, *a mi padre*, become automatic. A **parallel drill** involving noun objects which are not personal is set up next and finally a **contrastive drill** which emphasizes the choice which must become automatic. The model might be *Veo la casa pero no veo a mi padre*. We then substitute different pairs of objects, such as *el automóvil—mi hermano*, *el árbol—la profesora*.

3. **A pattern correspondence is broken by Spanish**

(a)

It is hot. It is cold. It is good weather.	*Hace calor.* *Hace frío.* *Hace buen tiempo.*
It is pleasant (weather).	*Hace un tiempo agradable.*
It is sunny.	*Hay sol.*
It is rainy.	*El tiempo está lluvioso.*
It is raining.	*Llueve.*

In the last two examples there is a break in the English parallel between it is rainy and it is raining, but many speakers of English are not aware of this and try to say * *hace lluvia* by analogy with *hace calor*.

(b) **The use of the definite article for generalization**

I am buying meat.	*Compro carne.*
I don't eat much meat.	*No como mucha carne.*
I like meat.	*Me gusta la carne.*

This type of break in parallel requires an explanation of the concept and a series of drills arranged to contrast the partitive (which is fortunately similar in English and Spanish) with the generalization.

(c) **Infinitive versus gerund after prepositions**

After closing the book, . . .	*Después de cerrar el libro, . . .*
Before closing the door, . . .	*Antes de cerrar la puerta, . . .*
Without seeing the house, . . .	*Sin ver la casa, . . .*
On buying the house, . . .	*Al comprar la casa, . . .*
By studying the lesson, . . .	*Estudiando la lección, . . .*
While studying the lesson, . . .	*Mientras estudia (Vd.) la lección, . . .*

Our traditional grammars teach quite thoroughly the use of infinitives after prepositions in Spanish, but important exceptions make breaks in the correspondence, each of which calls for a pattern drill of its own.

(d) **Dependent infinitive construction versus subordinate clause**

I permit him to study.	*Le permito estudiar.*
I forbid him to study.	*Le prohibo estudiar.*
I ask him to study.	*Le pido que estudie.*
I want him to study.	*Quiero que estudie.*

The break of correspondence in the above case requires special sets of contrast drills, especially because there seems no theoretical basis to differentiate those verbs which require the subordinate clause (when there is "change of subject") and those which permit, or more frequently take, the infinitive construction.

If the learner first meets the construction, *le permito estudiar*, which is a near correspondence to English, he will tend to create, by analogy, * *le pido estudiar* or * *le quiero estudiar*. For this reason the subordinate clause equivalents should be learned before the student meets the alternative infinitive construction with *permitir, mandar, dejar, hacer, invitar, aconsejar*, and a few other verbs.

(e) Indicative versus subjunctive in a subordinate clause

I shall talk to him if he comes.	*Le hablaré si viene.*
I shall talk to him when he comes. after before	*Le hablaré cuando venga.* *después que* *antes que*

Here the common error is to say * *si venga*. This error is caused not only by analogy with *cuando venga*, but also by false analogy with the imperfect subjunctive in *le hablaría si viniera*. Drill in terms of the structure, such as contrasting *si viene* with *antes que venga*, is much more effective than attempts at conceptual analysis in overcoming this error.

I know he will come tomorrow.	*Sé que vendrá mañana.*
I think he will come tomorrow.	*Creo que vendrá mañana.*
I hope he will come tomorrow.	*Espero que vendrá mañana.* *Espero que venga mañana.*
I doubt that he will come tomorrow.	*Dudo que venga mañana.*
I don't think he will come tomorrow.	*No creo que venga mañana.*

The "break" in correspondence can in large part be accounted for by the clues given by the pattern itself. The subjunctive appears almost automatically after certain expressions used in the main clause: *querer, pedir, mandar, hacer, obligar; dudar, negar, creer* in the negative; expressions of emotion such as *alegrarse de, temer, tener miedo de*. There is no need for an exhaustive review here of these expressions and categories, which are presented in any Spanish grammar.

The point is that these expressions must be taught as **signals for the use of the subjunctive in the subordinate clause.** The student's ability to use the subjunctive actively depends primarily on exercises through which automatic habits are developed. Such exercises might consist of substitution drills, as for example:

> *No creo que Vd. lo sepa.*
> *Dudo_____*
>
> *No es posible_____*

or

> *Quiero que vaya Juan.*
> *que venga María.*
> *que salga Ernesto.*

Drills which require a choice of indicative or subjunctive are a next step:

> *Creo que Juan está aquí.*
> *No creo_____*
>
> *Me parece_____*
>
> *Es dudoso _____*

This does not mean that the student should not be made to understand the meaning of **the subjunctive as the reflection of an attitude** signalled by the main verb (or by other sentence elements in adjective and adverb clauses). A grasp of the meaning of the subjunctive is especially necessary in learning those cases in which the surrounding structures are potentially or entirely ambiguous and in which the use of the subjunctive rather than the indicative carries a differentiation of meaning not signaled elsewhere in the construction:

> *Arregla la cosas de manera que siempre caen.*
> versus
> *Arregla las cosas de manera que siempre caigan.*

or

> *Busco una casa que tiene dos puertas.*
> versus
> *Busco una casa que tenga dos puertas.*

or

> *Espero que vendrán a vernos.*
> versus
> *Espero que vengan a vernos.*

or

Nos habla cuando viene.

versus

Nos hablará cuando venga.

If well-designed and ample drill on the clearly signaled structures is first provided, at least some of the ambiguous cases can be associated with the others by further exercise, in such a way as to convert "subjunctive thinking" into habit.

(f) Time expressions

I am here for two weeks.	*Estoy aquí por dos semanas.*
I have come for two weeks.	*He venido por dos semanas.*
I worked for two weeks.	*Trabajé (por) dos semanas.*
I have been working for two weeks.	*Hace dos semanas que trabajo.*

(g) Lexico-syntactical problems

Many more examples could be given of English constructions which have divergent or multiple correspondences in Spanish. Some fall partly in the category of vocabulary problems but at the same time involve structural elements, as, for example, correspondences with English "take":

Take a book.	*Tome Vd. un libro.*
Take a swallow.	*Tome Vd. un trago.*
Take it home.	*Llévelo a casa.*
Take a walk.	*Dar un paseo.*
Take a trip.	*Hacer un viaje.*
Take a bath.	*Bañarse* or *tomar un baño.*
Take a nap.	*Echar una siesta* or *dormir la siesta.*

(h) Imperfect versus preterite in the verb

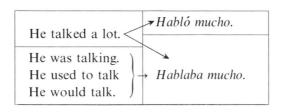

The correct use of the one tense or the other depends largely on a grasp of their meaning; pattern drill and structural clues do not solve all the problems, although they can, if well arranged, reduce the difficulty of learning considerably. Drills can well be arranged in a sequence which takes advantage of such structural correspondences as there are:

(1)   Whenever English uses one of the structures was talking or used to talk and when would talk is interchangeable with used to talk, Spanish imperfect is the regular correspondence.

(2)   Whenever talked may be replaced by was talking, used to talk, or would talk without change of meaning, Spanish imperfect is the regular correspondence:

$$He \begin{cases} \text{talked a lot} \\ \text{used to talk} \end{cases} \text{when he was a boy.} \qquad hablaba$$

$$When\ I \begin{cases} \text{lived} \\ \text{was living} \end{cases} \text{in the country.} \qquad vivía$$

$$I \begin{cases} \text{drank} \\ \text{would drink} \end{cases} \text{horchata while in Madrid.} \qquad bebía$$

(3)   Whenever a specific signal of beginning, ending, or specific duration is present, Spanish *preterite* is the regular correspondence of English talked, sang, was, saw, et cetera.

(4)   A number of common English verbs do not usually appear in the "progressive" forms and so do not safely permit the test substitution of Section 2 above. For example:

$$\overset{1}{} \qquad \overset{2}{}$$
He was sitting on the porch. He **was** tired; he **had** a headache; it
$$\overset{3}{} \qquad \overset{4}{} \qquad \overset{5}{}$$
seemed hot to him; he **knew** it was late; he **thought** his wife was
$$\overset{6}{} \qquad \overset{7}{}$$
coming; he **believed** she would be there soon; he **saw** the trees; he
$$\overset{8}{} \qquad \overset{9}{} \qquad \overset{10}{}$$
heard the brook; he **felt** the breeze; he **could** smell the flowers. He
$$\overset{11}{} \qquad \overset{12}{} \qquad \overset{13}{} \qquad \overset{14}{}$$
liked this time of day; he **loved** and **needed** rest. He **hoped** it would
$$\overset{15}{} \qquad \overset{16}{}$$
last; he **wanted** to stay there; he **wished** it would never end. He
$$\overset{17}{} \qquad \overset{18}{}$$
remembered other pleasant evenings; he **forgot** his troubles. Yet he
$$\overset{19}{}$$
feared it could not last.

A large share of the tense errors made by English-speaking learners of Spanish arise from the absence of different signal structures in English with verbs of the sort given in the foregoing passage. These verbs have in common the fact that they do not denote **visible action**, but mere existence, mental processes, sensory process, and emotions.

Recognition of the source in the native language of this difficulty makes it possible to construct drills which simplify the learning. For example:

> He was sitting on the porch; he was tired.
> She was reading a book, although she had a headache.
> They were dancing, but they knew it was late.

(5)   Description in the past does not lend itself to the *was —ing* or *used to* — substitutions in English; much description is accomplished with was, were, and had:

> The house was white and had a large chimney.

Other simple pasts may be used in description: her eyes twinkled; he limped. Exercises which contrast description with "stopped action" can be devised:

> He crossed the room; since he limped, it took five minutes.

The student's ability to use the subjunctive in conversation or to make the right choices of imperfect or preterite or to react automatically to any of the other thorny choices arising from the existence of more than one construction in Spanish corresponding to a given construction in English will depend primarily on his having been provided with well-designed exercises so arranged as to make habits dependable and automatic.

4.   Pattern correspondence between English and Spanish is broken by English

In some instances the student's difficulty is evidently created by the fact that English is not consistent in its own pattern. The student is unlikely to see this lack of consistency in his native language and may be confused by the resulting break in Spanish–English correspondence.

(a) **English verbs not using the progressive tense**

English	Spanish
I have been studying Spanish for two years.	*Hace dos años que estudio el español.*
I have been reading for two hours.	*Hace dos horas que leo.*
I have been here for two days.	*Hace dos días que estoy acquí.*
I have known him for years.	*Hace años que le conozco.*

In this case Spanish will consistently use the present tense for an action begun in the past and continuing into the present. English uses the perfect progressive tense to convey the same meaning. But this correspondence is broken with those English verbs (be, know, like, see, need, understand, want, et cetera) which are not usually used in a progressive form, and this peculiarity should be pointed out to the learner.

The above-mentioned problem exists also, of course, in the case of past action, as in I had been studying (= *estudiaba*) but I had known this for two years (= *sabía* . . .).

(b) **Different indirect object structures**

English	Spanish
I want to tell him the truth.	*Quiero decirle la verdad.*
I want to ask him the truth.	*Quiero preguntarle la verdad.*
I want to explain the truth to him.	*Quiero explicarle la verdad.*
I want to hide the truth from him.	*Quiero ocultarle la verdad.*

English	Spanish
They sent him the hat.	*Le mandaron el sombrero.*
They gave him the hat.	*Le dieron el sombrero.*
They put the hat on him.	*Le pusieron el sombrero.*
They took the hat from him.	*Le quitaron el sombrero.*

This consistent Spanish pattern, with the troublesome break in the English correspondence, is always the subject of a paragraph in Spanish grammars. It is obviously material for a series of habit-forming pattern drills. It should be observed, however, (and we have pointed this out in another connection) that there is less difficulty for the learner when one structure of the foreign language corresponds to two or more in the native language than when the contrary is the case.

(c) **Spanish "dative of interest"**

English	Spanish
I forgot the address. I dropped the book.	*Se me olvidó la dirección.* *Se me cayó el libro.*
My cup got broken.	*Se me rompió la taza.*
An idea occurred to me.	*Se me ocurrió una idea.*
I was offered a job.	*Se me ofreció un puesto.*

This multiple break in correspondence can be complicated still further by other acceptable English equivalents, such as "The address slipped my mind"; "The book fell down on me"; and "A job was offered to me." No doubt the answer to interference from English lies in ample substitution and transformation drill within Spanish.

(d) **Adverb clauses**

before he comes unless he sings	*antes que él venga* *a menos que él cante*
so he may understand	*para que él comprenda*
without his knowing it	*sin que él lo sepa*

Once more we can observe that a break in parallel in English may prove to be only a minor source of interference when the pattern in Spanish is consistent, as this one is.

5. **Spanish seems to break the consistency of its own pattern**

This category is similar to that given in 3 above; the difference is that the break in consistency does not necessarily involve a break in parallelism or correspondence with English; the learner's error will be caused by his wrong extension of a Spanish pattern rather than by the interference of English.

(a) **Subjunctive versus indicative in adverb clauses**

> *Le hablaré en cuanto venga.*
> *... cuando venga.*
> *... con tal que venga.*
>
> *... si viene.*

A similar example was given in Section 3(d), as a break in pattern correspondence with English. It was also pointed out in that place that analogies within Spanish lead the learner to the erroneous . . . * *si venga.*

(b) **Use of the definite article**

> *Voy al campo.*
> *Voy a la carnicería.*
> *Voy a la escuela.*
> *Voy a la iglesia.*
>
> *Voy a misa.*
> *Voy a clase.*
> *Voy a casa.*

Breaks of this sort practically have to be learned as lexical items. They should be used liberally in pattern drills which are basically concerned with some more important syntactical contrast.

(c) **Personal object** *a*

Veo	*a*	*dos amigos.*
Fusilaron	*a*	*un soldado.*
Necesito		*dos obreros.*
Tengo		*tres hermanos.*

Since so much emphasis is given to the use of *a* as the signal of a "personal object noun," the learner is likely to extend this construction erroneously to instances in which the object noun is not specific in its reference. This distinction has value as a signal for the choice between indicative and subjunctive in relative clauses. The further extension of this analogy to objects of *tener* is not a very common error in actual experience.

6. **An English construction type has no counterpart in Spanish**

There are many English constructions which cause interference in corresponding Spanish patterns simply because the student transposes the English construction literally into Spanish; the mechanism of a "break" in parallelism or even correspondence does not appear to be involved.

(a)   **The indirect object marked by word order alone in English**

> I gave Robert the papers.
> { *Le dí a Roberto los papeles.*
> { *Le dí los papeles a Roberto.*

In Spanish the indirect object noun must be marked by *a* regardless of word order.

> { I give him the book.
> { I give her the book.
> *Le doy el libro.*

Beginners may try to mark gender in Spanish by using *lo* or *la* as the pronoun, by analogy with I see him, *Lo veo,* and I see her, *La veo.* The structure through which Spanish does mark gender in indirect object pronouns has no counterpart in English, of course:

> *Le doy el libro a él.*
> *Le doy el libro a ella.*

(b)   **Passive construction with following direct object or infinitive complement**

> He was given a new watch.
> *Le dieron un reloj nuevo.*
> John was given a car.
> *Le dieron a Juan un automóvil.*
> He was not allowed to go.
> *No le dejaron ir.*
> I was ordered to do it.
> *Me mandaron hacerlo.*

This English structure is a fruitful source of fractured Spanish for the unwary. It calls for some especially arranged exercises. Interestingly enough, expressions like the distorted * *Fuí dicho* for I was told, crop up frequently in the work of advanced students who have acquired a degree of fluency in Spanish and who, launching into "self-expression," carry over English interference which earlier exercises had been organized to avoid.

(c) Relative clause without relative pronouns

The house I bought . . .	*La casa que compré . . .*
The house I lived in . . .	*La casa en que vivía . . .*
The man you saw . . .	*El hombre* $\begin{cases} que\ vió\ Vd.\ .\ .\ . \\ a\ quien\ vió\ Vd.\ .\ .\ . \end{cases}$

The formation of a relative clause without a relative pronoun does not exist in Spanish. Translation exercises built around the formal or puristic "The house which I bought" or "The man whom you saw" will not block interference from this more normal English pattern; pattern drill within Spanish will do so.

(d) Questions beginning with "whose"

Whose is that house? $\Big\}$ *¿De quién es aquella casa?*
Whose house is that?

Whose house were you living in? *¿De quién es la casa donde Vd. vivía?*

The lack of parallel between English and Spanish with the interrogative *whose* is complicated further by the existence of the relative adjective *cuyo* in Spanish.

The man whose daughter sings . . .
El hombre cuya hija canta . . .

Thus this problem could have been presented in Section 3 above as a break in pattern correspondence.

Many examples may be added to this sixth category. A few more common English constructions which are a direct menace to accuracy in Spanish, are listed here:

a friend of mine
I am studying Spanish this year.
the three of them
all of us
we Americans
Swimming is good exercise. (verbal noun in **-ing** in general)
a hanging rope (verbal adjective in **-ing**)

I wash my hands.
He had me come in.
I had eggs and toast.
He who . . .
The one who . . .
Did he? No, he didn't! (or any negative or interrogative pattern using
   do)
how fast, how much, how long, et cetera.

There is no need for us to give here the correct Spanish equivalents, nor the faulty word-to-word translations into Spanish which are (alas!) only too familiar to the Spanish teacher. The question is what to do about them. Evidently the corresponding Spanish constructions must be made the subject of special drills. Since the problem does not involve any pattern conflict within Spanish, the best type of exercise to be used is the substitution drill. Overt comparison of the Spanish construction with the English counterpart may often be helpful. The authors of this book have quite successfully used the device of writing constructions like "a friend of mine" on the blackboard and crossing them out, thus warning the student against literal translation. Yet while such a device tells the student what not to do, the positive remedy must always be with the active practice of the Spanish pattern.

7. **Spanish uses different function words or replacement words (pronouns) corresponding to a single English replacement or function word**

In this kind of interference the problem is created by multiple word correspondence rather than by syntactical patterns alone. Since the words involved are either pronouns which have no independent lexical meaning or function words which express structural meaning rather than lexical meaning, we include this category in our discussion of syntax. Actually, the differentiation between function word and lexical word is not a precise one, and the category of interference to be discussed here partly overlaps the following chapter on vocabulary problems. The problem involved is also in some respects similar to that in examples (a) and (b) of Section 1 above.

In this category there seem to be two distinct possibilities: either the function word to be used depends on a lexical item in the structure, or it depends entirely on the structure itself. Example (a) will illustrate both possibilities:

(a) *Para, de,* or *a* following an adjective introducing a dependent infinitive

English	Spanish
I am ready **to** leave.	*Estoy listo **para** partir.*
I am willing **to** go.	*Estoy dispuesto **a** ir.*
I am happy **to** leave.	*Estoy contento **de** partir.*

In the above example the use of *para, de,* or *a* depends on the preceding adjective. It is in no way dependent on the construction itself, and correct usage should be established by substitution exercises which force the student to use different adjectives (*pronto para, alegre de, inclinado a*) in the above construction.

In other instances, the choice of a function word—or of none—is signaled by a structural clue which can be pointed out to the student. A case in point is the contrast between the two examples:

It is hard to study!
¡Es difícil estudiar!
This lesson? It is hard to study.
¿Esta lección? Es difícil de estudiar.

The infinitive may be regarded as subject of the impersonal *es* + adjective and so will have no function word, but in the construction noun (pronoun) + *es* + adjective, *de* must be used when the noun subject is the logical object of the action of the infinitive.

The two types of construction may be contrasted in pattern drills:

—*¿Es agradable oír al artista?—Sí, el artista es agradable de oír.*
—*¿Es fácil comprender el discurso?—Sí, el discurso es fácil de comprender.*

(b) Spanish function words corresponding to English "what"

What do you want?	*¿**Qué** desea Vd.?*
What are you thinking about?	*¿En **qué** piensa Vd.?*
What is geometry?	{ *¿**Qué** es la geometría?* { *¿**Qué** cosa es la geometría?*
I know **what** you are doing.	*Yo sé **lo que** Vd. hace.*
Do you know **what** he is doing?	*¿Sabe Vd. **qué** hace?*
Do you understand **what** he is doing?	*¿Entiende Vd. **lo que** hace?*
What I want is money!	***Lo que** yo quiero es dinero.*

What is the capital?	*¿Cuál es la capital?*
What are the largest cities?	*¿Cuáles son las ciudades más grandes?*
What a wind!	*¡Qué viento!*

The learner may easily be lulled into a false sense of security by the number of situations in which *qué* is the equivalent of English what—and then be trapped by constructions calling for *lo que, cuál,* or *cuáles.* The above examples underline an essential point made earlier in this book: the student must learn **complete structures**, not just words. The only solution to the learning of function words in appropriate structures is practice in suitable pattern exercises. For example:

—*¿Sabe Vd. qué tiene Juan?*   —*Sí, yo sé lo que tiene.*
—*¿Sabe Vd. qué dice Juan?*   —*Sí, yo sé lo que dice.*

Some explanation may be necessary, such as the difference between *qué* asking for a definition and *cuál* asking for an identification; context exercises can again drive this home:

—*¿Qué es la geometría?*   —*Es una ciencia matemática.*
—*¿Qué es un hombre?*   —*Es un animal inteligente.*
—*¿Qué es un libro?*   —*Es un texto impreso.*

—*¿Cuál es el jefe?*   —*Es el más alto.*
—*¿Cuál es la capital?*   —*Es Bogotá.*

(c)   Conjunctions, prepositions, and adverbs

He came before my departure.	*Llegó antes de mi partida.*
He came before I left.	*Llegó antes que yo partiera.*

English uses a number of function words as prepositions (before a noun construction) or as conjunctions (before a dependent clause), while Spanish differentiates, as in *después de—después que, desde—desde que, hasta—hasta que,* and so on. Some learners are confused by these contrasts, which are further complicated by the variants *antes de que* and *después de que*; besides pointing out the structural difference, the instructor should provide substitution–transformation exercises in which the student is asked to replace *antes de* by *antes que, hasta* by *hasta que, después de* by *después que*—or vice versa—and to make necessary additional changes:

Me dijeron la verdad después que se fué el jefe.
después de . . .
Juan habiá salido antes de la llegada del jefe.
antes que . . .
Guardamos silencio hasta que se puso el sol.
hasta . . .

The pair *sin—sin que* involves a pattern break in English, not in Spanish, and deserves special drill:

| They went without my permission. | *Fueron sin mi permiso.* |
| They went without my knowing it. | *Fueron sin que yo lo supiera.* |

English differentiates preposition "because of" and conjunction "because," a pattern break which has led countless students to the barbarism * *porque de eso*. This pair corresponds to the pattern *por— porque*, just like *hasta—hasta que* except that the symmetry is obscured by the English inconsistency and by the Spanish orthography which makes "one word" out of *porque*. The correspondence is further complicated, of course, by the common equivalent *a causa de*. In any case, because and because of call for special exercise.

A somewhat similar phenomenon occurs with certain common adverbs and prepositions:

I've seen you **before**.	*Te he visto **antes**.*
Come **before** seven.	*Ven **antes de** las siete.*
He comes **near**.	*Viene **cerca**.*
He is **near** me.	*Está **cerca** de mí.*

Among other items in this group may be mentioned *fuera—fuera de*, *dentro—dentro de*, and *delante–delante de*. Only occasionally, however, does it seem necessary to make a special effort to keep a student from attempting to say * *Está fuera de*.

Altogether, there are numerous instances of conflict arising from two or more function words or pronouns corresponding to a given English word. We shall conclude our discussion of problems of interference in syntax by enumerating a few additional cases without giving detailed examples or analyses.

(1)   The problem created because Spanish has one set of object pronouns used only as satellites of the verb, the direct and indirect object

pronouns, and another set used as objects of prepositions. The related problem created by the identity of these prepositional pronouns with the subject pronouns in all forms except *yo*—*de mí* and *tú*—*de ti*.

(2)   The difference between Spanish equivalents for English relative whom and interrogative whom: *el hombre que vió Vd.* and *¿A quién vió Vd.?*

(3)   The use of *nadie, alguien, alguno*, and *quienquiera* for anybody in different situations; and the corresponding possibilities for *nada, algo*, and *cualquiera cosa* to identify with anything. An abundance of examples in pattern drills will, as usual, provide the cure, although the learner should be made aware of the negative value of *nadie* (not . . . anybody) and *nada* (not . . . anything).

(4)   The forms *ese, esa, aquel*, and *aquella*; the corresponding stressed (pronoun) forms, *ése*, et cetera; the neuters *eso* and *aquello*; and the ubiquitous *que*—all possibilities for the one English function word "that" in different structures.

(5)   The special problem of two degrees of remoteness for the demonstrative "that"—*ese* or *aquel*.

Rather than multiply examples, let us refer the teacher to almost any set of semester examination papers. A restudy of the typical errors will show how many of them arise from multiple correspondences of the sort we have been discussing and will reinforce with impressive testimony the necessity for learning function words as part of structures and not as vocabulary.

One point should be stressed again most emphatically. Our discussion was based primarily on comparisons of English and Spanish because English interference is the enemy against which the teacher is constantly fighting. We must know the exact nature of the enemy—the psychological and linguistic mechanism which may cause the student's errors. But all of this docs not mean that overt comparison between English and Spanish is necessarily the best way of fighting the enemy. Just how much direct comparison between the two languages should take place depends on various circumstances. The authors' view is that in the beginning course such overt comparison should be brief and should be restricted to the interference discussed under types 4 and 6 in the preceding pages. It can be used more freely in review courses for remedial purposes. It is of prime importance in active phases of advanced composition and translation. In the beginning courses it is probably more advisable to use pattern contrasts within Spanish as a teaching tool, even though the underlying problem may be at least partly due to

English interference. The danger of using the method of comparing English and Spanish is obvious; the student, instead of using Spanish patterns freely and without reference to English, may become confused by the discussion of English–Spanish differences and comparisons. The understanding of the nature of interference is necessary equipment for the teacher, but not necessarily for the student. For the latter it can in no way substitute for the drill and actual use of the Spanish speech patterns themselves.

CHAPTER IX

Teaching Vocabulary

Everyone seems to have a working concept of what constitutes a word, in spite of the fact that we do not have a clear-cut linguistic definition. Learning meanings of these semantic units and learning their behavior as parts of speech or members of **form classes** is so obviously a major part of the process of learning a language that to most learners, and to many traditionally minded teachers, it often looms up as the major learning problem. Unfortunately, this concern for vocabulary learning can obscure the basic importance of learning structure; the preceding chapters have, we hope, amply demonstrated the dangers of inadequate or improper attention to structure at the level of sound, forms, and syntax. We now turn to the problems which surround the teaching of words as the bearers of the content of utterances.

We have already mentioned that function words which signify relationships and grammatical meanings belong properly to the realm of structure or syntax. There are other word groups we can exclude from the consideration of vocabulary teaching. First are the pronouns (or replacement words), which in a sense have no independent meaning of their own. Then there are words whose use depends very largely on grammatical considerations; the exact use of words like some, any, neither, more, et cetera, and their counterparts in Spanish, such as *algo, nada, más, ni,* is more of a grammatical than a lexical problem. They were discussed in our consideration of syntax rather than vocabulary, for the correct usage of these words depends primarily on learning them within a structure. For example, the use of *nada* in *No tengo nada* or in *No trabajo nada* must be learned as part of the total construction, and it does not seem advisable to teach such words separately as lexical terms.

The "content" words, on the other hand, are the words on which the **lexical** part of the total meaning depends. They are the nouns, verbs, adjectives, and derived adverbs which are the lexical meat of the utterance. When we speak of vocabulary, or content words, or lexical items, we shall be referring to words of this type and not to function and replacement words like prepositions, conjunctions, or pronouns.

We note from the start a high degree of parallelism and overlap between English and Spanish vocabularies, just as we did in comparing the syntactical structures. We find similar advantages to the learner and similar disadvantages in interference arising from breaks in parallelism and inconsistencies in the overlapping of meanings or uses of words. Let us look first at the hazards or disadvantages of the many similarities or correspondences.

(A) INTERFERENCE MECHANISMS IN VOCABULARY LEARNING

Just as we cannot always be sure whether an item is best treated as a function or structural word rather than a lexical or content word, so we cannot always clearly determine when structural factors are responsible for interference in the learning of vocabulary items. The typical cause of interference of the sort we refer to here is of the same character as that we noted in the case of structures: an overlap or correspondence in an area of meaning is extended by the learner into another area where the overlap no longer exists. The basic problem in all the categories of interference we shall describe is the learner's identification of an English word or concept with a Spanish word or concept on a simple one-to-one basis.

A common example of error arising from this false extension of analogy is the translation of the word time by *tiempo*. Having learned *No tengo mucho tiempo* and *Llegó a tiempo*, the learner goes on to formulate the incorrect * *Lo he visto tres tiempos* or *¿Qué tiempo es?* Mastery of the correct *Lo he visto tres veces* and *¿Qué hora es?* may to a large degree be accomplished by pattern drill, since the different equivalents for English time do occur in recognizable structural situations. At the same time, conceptual understanding of different areas of reference or meaning will also help to remove confusions and make the appropriate distinctions automatic.

In our discussion of the types of interference, we shall start with those in which structural problems seem to contribute most importantly and then go on to those in which differences in the underlying concepts seem to be the principal cause of difficulty.

1. Similar lexical meanings occur in different structural types.

The Spanish lexical meanings of the words in bold type do not conflict with English meanings in a series of expressions like the following:

Acabo de estudiar mi lección.	I have just **studied** my lesson.
No me acordé de subir.	I did not **remember** to go up.
Me he olvidado.	I have **forgotten**.
Mandó llamar al médico.	He had the doctor **called**.

The problem arises from differences in the constructions involved in the two languages, and the solution lies in identifying those structural conflicts associated with specific lexical items and in providing ample pattern drill. It should be noted that many of these items are of the kind often classified as "idioms" in conventional texts. We shall discuss the matter of "idioms" in detail later in this chapter.

2. Different Spanish lexical items reflect a single English item in different structures or contexts.

In this category the difficulty is caused not so much by overlapping in lexical meaning as by similar or identical lexical meanings being expressed by different words in different structures. Say, tell, speak, and talk all have meanings basically similar to Spanish *decir, contar,* and *hablar.* The fact that it is not possible to establish a one-to-one correspondence between any of these will cause considerable difficulty to the student. These English and Spanish words cut up, so to speak, the same semantic area, but they do it somewhat differently. The use of *decir* versus *hablar* versus *contar* must be learned through the use in context and especially through the observation of whatever structural clues are available.

For example, *decir* is used before a subordinate clause:

Le dije que no quería salir.	(English: say, tell)
Le dije que no saliera.	(English: tell, order)

or before a noun or noun cluster:

Me dijeron la verdad.

or with a replacement word as object:

Me lo dijeron.

Hablar is used before a prepositional phrase:

> *Hablamos de muchas cosas.*   (English: talk or speak)
> *en voz alta.*

or before names of languages:

> *No hablo japonés.*   (English: speak)

or without complement:

> *No quiero hablar.*   (English: speak or talk)

Contar is used before nouns (or with replacement words):

> *Nos contó sus aventuras.*   (English: tell)
> *Nos las contó.*

Since each of these verbs may take a noun or pronoun object, conceptual differences must, of course, be explained and exploited at the same time that pattern drills can make most reactions a matter of habit.

The great difficulty of establishing mutually exclusive categories is shown by the first two examples with *decir* above: there is a conceptual difference between *decir* followed by a clause in the indicative and *decir* followed by a clause in the subjunctive; the difference is **signaled by structure**. In this instance English has a similar conceptual "split" within the verb tell, shown by a dependent infinitive in English in contrast to a dependent clause: Tell him **not to go**, tell him **that I'll go**. Insofar as the structural inconsistency is the problem, this is the sort of difficulty treated in Section 1 above. But insofar as tell the truth = *decir la verdad* must be distinguished from tell the story = *contar el cuento*, the problem is conceptual. This is the subject of the next section.

3. Different lexical items correspond to a given English item.

So long as the different concepts involved are clear to the English speaker, this category does not usually present a very great problem. Signals in the immediate context ordinarily are sufficient to make the learner accept and quickly learn the difference between I left the room—*Salí del cuarto*—and I left my book in the room—*Dejé mi libro en el cuarto*. Breaks in vocabulary correspondence of this kind are legion, and the phenomenon is well known to teachers and textbook writers, so well known that often, unfortunately, some of the split correspondences are overlooked when exercise material is being prepared. The teacher oriented in analyses of the sort this book has been attempting and practiced in the concepts of pattern drills will spot confusions in student reaction or weaknesses in textbook exercise in terms of the kind of interference which is at work, and will be able to improvise pattern drills almost instantaneously to lead students safely across the barriers of interference.

Such problems in vocabulary correspondence as take a drink, a book, the train (*tomar*); take a walk, a step (*dar*); take a trip, exercise (*hacer*); take a bath (*bañarse*) prove to be more a case of not knowing the Spanish equivalents than of confusing them. English "two-part verbs," combinations such as run across, run over, call up, call on, get up, get on, get off, and "independent" meanings of some of the same verbs such as "get rich" and "get money" would seem to suggest trouble for learners of Spanish, since these English items involve so many different meanings; but here again the usual difficulty seems to be simply not knowing the Spanish equivalents rather than confusing them. Evidently the conceptual differences between expressions such as get ("become" or "obtain") and get up, get on, and so on, are far too obvious to an English speaker for him to be led to use a word that he associates with get (*ponerse* and *conseguir*) in the meaning of get up or get on.

Somewhat more subtle splits in meaning may be resolved by simple diagrams or pictures together with frequent use in exercises which exploit the concepts of transformation or expansion drills at the same time that they provide the clues of lexical or semantic context. For example, different types of leaving may be expressed in Spanish by *salir* (*de*), *partir*, and *abandonar*; in addition to the structural variation there is the subtle difference between going out (*salir*), departing (*salir* or *partir*), and going away from (*abandonar*). A diagram will help:

So also will pattern drills based on differentiating models, such as:

> *Salimos de la casa.*
> *El tren sale a las diez.*
> *Voy a partir mañana.*
> *Abandoné mi pueblo cuando era joven.*

Much more difficult are two or more lexical items corresponding to a single item in English, where the conceptual difference is not obvious to the English speaker. Whether a given learner finds a given split correspondence obvious or not seems to depend to some degree on his linguistic sophistication, but it is still possible to predict that more difficulty will occur with items such as *saber* versus *conocer, andar* versus *correr* ("the watch runs," "the boy runs"), and *tomar* versus *llevar* than with *salir* versus *dejar*. Any teacher or advanced student of the language can easily extend this list.

Since the problem of clarifying these splits of meaning is subtle, a combination of teaching devices must be used instead of attempting to alternate purely structural drills with others purely semantic. We must, of course, highlight whatever structural clues there are. For example, we can emphasize that *saber* may appear before a subordinate clause, while *conocer* ordinarily does not. So in a pattern drill we may set up a series of clause substitutions:

Sabemos que Juan trabaja. (Substitute: *donde está ahora, cuando viene, que no estudia*, et cetera)

and another series in which noun objects are substituted:

Conocemos al profesor. (Substitute: *señor López, médico, amigo,* et cetera)

Then by alternating substitutions from the two drills, the appropriate choice of *sabemos* or *conocemos* is made a matter of habit. This will help to narrow the possible area in which mistakes will be made purely because of confusion of concept. The surrounding structure alone does not determine the choice of *saber* and *conocer* in all cases, however. There are no purely structural clues to the difference between I know the poem, *Conozco el poema*, and I know the poem, *Se el poema*, or *Conozco el problema* and *Sé la solución*. Obviously, then, the conceptual difference must be explained—by amplifying the context, by the use of pictorial aids where that is possible, by the use of synonyms or antonyms, and by discussion in English. A great deal of pedagogical work remains to be done in this particular area, to which structural linguistics, because of its preoccupation with the purely formal clues and ways of expressions, cannot contribute greatly.

The category we are discussing here is a rather broad one, and various other types of vocabulary interference belong to it. For instance, the variation of meaning which Spanish may produce by using the same adjective either before or after the noun belongs here:

un hombre pobre	*un pobre hombre*
una casa nueva	*una nueva casa*
una noticia cierta	*cierta noticia*
el padre mismo	*el mismo padre*

Pattern practice, asking the student to place such adjectives before or after the noun, would be an entirely meaningless gesture in the absence of differentiating signals in the context which would make clear the conceptual differences; English "poor" and "new" do not normally express the differences involved, although "sure" and "correct" versus "a certain," and "himself" after the noun versus "same" before the noun do signal corresponding differences. These instances reveal again how extremely complex are the relationships involved here; at the same time they indicate how inextricably problems of structure and problems of vocabulary may be interrelated.

To this difficult category belong also many items having basically similar lexical meanings, such as catch, pick: *coger*, but in which the Spanish word may have a connotation in certain contexts, regions, or social strata not matched by the English counterpart. Only appropriate explanation, warning, and use in context, together with exercise in the use of synonyms or other devices which save the situation, can solve vocabulary problems of this disturbing type.

At this level of the language the increasing cultural sophistication of the learner and his expanding acquaintance with the *mores* and characteristics of the people whose language he is learning become factors of major importance and provide the basis for many distinctions that purely structural linguistics cannot isolate.

4. Misleading cognates

So far we have discussed interference due to a partial overlap in meaning; there is, of course, also interference due to partial overlap in form, the so-called "false friends" or misleading cognates. By these we mean in the pedagogical, not linguistic, sense any English and Spanish words which have a great resemblance in terms of orthography or sound but which have basically different meanings. Many textbooks contain lists of these *amigos falsos*, so that we need not give numerous examples here:

Spanish	English
lectura	lecture
asistir	assist
conferencia	conference
facultad	faculty
alumno	alumnus

These cognates have, of course, a close historical relationship and some degree of semantic relationship. They cause more difficulty than do the apparent cognates—words in which the relationship of orthography or sound is purely fortuitous, as in *red*/red, *pan*/pan, and *can*/can. A goodly number of cognates conform completely as to orthography, as doctor, error, and chocolate; they will never sound alike. Quite often they will overlap only partially in meaning, as do the "false friends" listed above.

This partial overlap in meaning is a major source of difficulty to the learner. The fact that English edit, editor relate to the same general area of activity as do Spanish *editar, editor* leads the learner to confusion as he tries to learn that Spanish *editar* means to publish, Spanish *editor* is a publisher, while Spanish *revisar, revisor* correspond to English edit and editor—except that a publishing executive, also called editor in English, is in Spanish a *director*. As a matter of fact, the more closely we watch the exact connotation and nuance, the more the concept of the "real friend" becomes vague, and the dividing line between "*amigos*" and "*amigos falsos*" is one of degree, since there is never absolute overlap in the usage of different words of different languages. There is, rather, a progression from "friends" (almost complete overlap) to "false friends" (no overlap at all).

A speaker of English trying to communicate in Spanish will almost automatically put heavy reliance on the English–Spanish vocabulary correspondences. The most obvious and common of the false friends must therefore be pointed out and contrasted with the real Spanish counterparts of the English words. The problem is not solved by a list of misleading cognates in the appendix of the textbook, but by specific exercises. Perhaps the best way to bring the false friends into focus is to use them in contrasting contexts, as in *No voy a la **biblioteca**, porque he comprado el libro en la **librería**. En su **conferencia** el profesor habló de sus **lecturas** de historia. Voy a **ayudar** a mi hermano; no puedo **asistir** al concierto.*

5. Confusions within Spanish

There are instances in which the source of confusion lies within the Spanish system itself, rather than in lack of consistency of correspondences between English and Spanish. We saw some cases of this in comparing syntactical structures, this may occur in lexical items as well, as in the confusion of meanings of *más* and *mas* or in the closely similar word forms *partida*/*partido* and *fondo*/*fonda* or in the forms of *sentar*/ *sentir*. An example of confusingly similar expressions is the pair *Me faltan dos pesos* and *Me hacen falta dos pesos*. On the whole, learners of Spanish have only sporadic difficulty with this sort of interference; when it occurs, the similar Spanish words or expressions can be explained in terms of synonymous structures or fuller contexts. For example, the learner may be taught to associate *No hallo dos pesos* with *Me faltan dos pesos* and *Necesito dos pesos* with *Me hacen falta dos pesos.* Then he can be asked to respond with one expression or the other to such statements as *Acabo de contar mi dinero*: ____ ; *Quiero comprar cigarillos; para comprarlos,* ____ .

6. Idioms

The last examples bring us to the general problem of the idiomatic expressions. From the linguistic viewpoint the very idea of idiomatic expression is in need of clarification; we can, of course, call any expression or structure or vocabulary usage in which Spanish and English are not parallel "idiomatic." From the linguistic point of view this definition, in which features of one language are defined in terms of the peculiarities of another, would be meaningless. From the purely pedagogical point of view it would not be too useful either. We have already noted that absolute parallelism between English and Spanish rarely appears with consistency in the realm of structure and that it certainly is not a typical situation. From the viewpoint of English more of Spanish is "idiomatic" than not. A meaningful linguistic approach to the concept of idiom must be based on Spanish criteria alone. Simplifying the problem somewhat, we may suggest that we should call an "idiom" any form the meaning of which cannot be deduced from the meaning of its components. *El tocadiscos* (although it does not correspond to its English counterpart, phonograph) is not an idiom because its meaning is deducible from that of its components. But the construction *hay que* + infinitive is an idiom, since its meaning is not clearly deducible from that of each of its components. Therefore, its meaning must be learned like a vocabulary unit. In the realm of teaching vocabulary and lexical meaning, we must thus be on the lookout for all expressions which have a total meaning which is in no way predictable from the meaning of the component parts. *Buscar algo* (to look for something) and *tener hambre* (to be hungry) are structural problems from the viewpoint of English but to call them idioms does not seem to be useful. Real idioms, we suggest here, are such expressions as *darse cuenta de algo, todo el mundo, de vez en cuando, en seguida, hacer caso, ya lo creo, guardar cama, en vez de, cada vez más*, and *¿Qué tal está?*

Such expressions must be learned as units; where they seem complex to the learner, the meaning of the full expression must be contrasted with the meanings of their individual components in other situations: for example, one must contrast *vez* in *una vez, tres veces*, et cetera, with the expressions *de vez en cuando, en vez de*, and *cada vez más*; and where an element appears in several idioms, as does *vez*, the several expressions must also be used in contrast.

(B) TEACHING OF "COGNATES"

So far we have considered English and Spanish similarities and over-laps only as a problem, as sources of interference. There is, of course, little doubt that the existence of cognates (words similar in form and meaning in both languages) is also a great help which must be exploited to the fullest. In the teaching of cognates two situations should be distinguished: teaching them as "active vocabulary" and teaching them for recognition purposes as passive reading vocabulary. In the first situation they are likely to constitute a special pronunciation problem. The similarity in form intensifies English interference—the possibility of English reaction to Spanish orthographic symbols, as, for instance, the reflex /ʃən/ instead of /syon/ in such words as *comunicación* and *extensión*. In either situation it is helpful to point out to the student the general pattern of cognate correspondence, but it is only in the passive reading situation that the student should be encouraged to rely on that pattern alone. Cognates taught for active use should be taught in connected speech patterns and in active production, and the student should be warned against the active use of any cognate that has not been expressly presented in the vocabulary materials. The pattern of correspondence between Spanish and English words to be presented here allows the student who is reading Spanish to deduce the meaning of Spanish words within a context. They are not predictors which enable the student to make up his own "cognates" for active use.

In many cases the Spanish words and English words are orthographically identical or differ only in minor spelling patterns which do not create any problems in identifying the Spanish "cognates," such as English mortal, Spanish *mortal* or English responsible, Spanish *responsable*.

Some of the more important cognate patterns in the realm of noun or adjective endings are (omitting all those which are orthographically identical):

English	Spanish	Examples
-ace	*-acio*	palace–*palacio*
-ade	*-ada*	brigade–*brigada*
-ance, -ancy	*-ancia*	abundance–*abundancia*
-ant	*-ante*	constant–*constante*
-arian, ary	*-ario*	centenarian–*centenario*
-ence, -ency	*-encia*	tendency–*tendencia*
-ent	*-ente*	accident–*accidente*
-ice	*-icio*	precipice–*precipicio*
-ion	*-ión*	infusion–*infusión*
-ism	*-ismo*	socialism–*socialismo*
-ist	*-ista*	artist–*artista*
-mony	{ *-monia*	ceremony–*ceremonia*
	{ *-monio*	patrimony–*patrimonio*
-tion	*-ción*	station–*estación*
-ty	*-dad*	charity–*caridad*
-y	{ *-ia*	academy–*academia*
	{ *-ía*	energy–*energía*

The above list is only partial—perhaps twice as many more ending correspondences for nouns can be given. A list for adjectives would be nearly as long. We confine ourselves to a few very common patterns:

-ant	*-ante*	abundant–*abundante*
-arious, -ary	*-ario*	precarious–*precario*
		ordinary–*ordinario*
-ct	*-cto*	perfect–*perfecto*
-ent	*-ente*	confident–*confidente*
-ite	*-ito*	infinite–*infinito*
-ive	*-ivo*	intensive–*intensivo*
-ose	*-oso*	verbose–*verboso*
-ous	{ *-oso*	luminous–*luminoso*
	{ *-o*	continuous–*continuo*

There are also some patterns of correspondence among verbs. A great many English verbs which end in an orthographic ("silent") -e, that is, which end in a consonant sound, correspond to Spanish verbs of the -ar conjugation: *examinar, inspirar, causar, curar, combinar, imaginar, conservar.* Many other English verbs lack any distinctive ending and may correspond to Spanish verbs of any of the conjugations: desert–*desertar*, admit–*admitir*, and comprehend–*comprender*. Some verb-ending morphemes shape into patterns of correspondence:

-fy	*-ficar*	signify–*significar*
		certify–*certificar*
-ute	*-uir*	substitute–*substituir*
		constitute–*constituir*
-ate	*-ar*	impersonate–*impersonar*
		implicate–*implicar*
-ize	*-izar*	specialize–*especializar*
		theorize–*teorizar*
-duce	*-ducir*	produce–*producir*
		deduce–*deducir*
-duct	*-ducir*	conduct–*conducir*
		induct–*inducir*
-eive	*-ibir*	conceive–*concibir*
		perceive–*percibir*

Among the many suffixes which transform Spanish word roots into other words of more or less derivative meaning, few have a noticeable similarity to English. For example, Spanish *-ino* corresponds to English *-ine* in *alabastrino* and *elefantino*, but many derivative words such as *azulino* and *blanquecino* do not have English counterparts; the noun suffixes *-dad* and *-ción* have been included above.

Among prefixes more cognate correspondences occur. Most of them will be recognized at sight, at least when they are prefixed to cognate roots, as in **exam**ine–*examinar*, **in**correct–*incorrecto*, **con**clude–*concluir*. With relatively few exceptions these prefixes will be recognized when heard as well as when they are seen. It hardly seems necessary in this place to spell out many examples.

The English initial clusters of s + consonant, while not prefixes in the same sense as those we have been discussing, do need to be compared systematically with the cognate words which in Spanish begin with a "supporting" or prothetic /e/: spirit–*espíritu*, station–*estación*, et cetera.

Mention should be made in passing of the very frequent use of *a-*, *en-*, *em-*, and *des-* as verbal prefixes, as in *tornillo–atornillar*; *botón–abotonar*; *botella–embotellar*; *freno–enfrenar*; *hoja–deshojar*; and *pluma–desplumar*. This is but one of many forms of word-making in which parallels or partial parallels with English may open the way for learning other items which hardly correspond at all.

The recognition and learning of the pattern of cognates of English and Spanish is really a special application of the process we referred to at the end of the chapter on morphology: the learning of the derivational cognates. In some cases the main roots of the words as well as the derivational morphemes are cognates, as in stupidity–*estupidez*, and in others the derivational morpheme may not be a cognate of English while the root of the word is. At any rate, the recognition of the derivational suffix or prefix and its subtraction from the stem will usually reveal the cognate. For example, once we know that *-eza* is a noun ending, we can recognize the cognate and with it the total meaning of *delicadeza*, *alteza*, *grandeza*. Once we recognize the prefix *des-* as a derivational prefix, indicating "negation" or "contrary to," we can make an informed guess at the meaning of *descompuesto*, *descargar*.

(C) GENERAL PROBLEMS IN TEACHING VOCABULARY

The main contribution which linguistics can make to the teaching of vocabulary lies in those aspects which have been discussed under Sections A and B above: the comparison between English and Spanish vocabulary and the process of derivation. There are many other aspects of the teaching of vocabulary—less directly connected with linguistics— which are nevertheless important. We shall mention them briefly. First of all, there is the perennial problem of what words to teach, the problem of determining which words are the most "frequent" and thus most necessary. This problem has often been obscured by the failure to differentiate between function words, grammatically determined words, and replacement words, on the one hand, and content words on the other. The former are comparatively few in number and are a necessary and inevitable part of the utterance. From the point of view of active production, they must be taught as part of the structure; from the point of view of passive recognition, they practically need not be taught at all. Their frequency of occurrence is so great that they teach themselves. As far as the content words are concerned, their frequency depends entirely on circumstances and so does the necessity of knowing them. If someone wants to say something about the gearshift of a car, he needs to know the word for that object; whether the word is frequent or not is quite irrelevant in that particular moment. Many of the frequency lists which have been established are based on works of literature, often heavily weighted with 19th century novels. To use them as guides for the construction of teaching materials makes sense only insofar as it is our aim to prepare the student to read literature. If it is not, then this type of frequency list is of comparatively little use.

Recent studies have shown that even this value is less significant than was formerly believed, for carefully controlled rechecks have shown that after the first 750 to 1000 most common words—including all the structural words—there is actually no validity at all in rankings by second thousand, third thousand, et cetera. It seems, in fact, impossible to determine the frequency and usefulness of content words from any absolute point of view.

Another possible approach taken to vocabulary frequency is the one used in the construction of Basic English and the Spanish methods based on the same general principle (*Spanish Self-Taught Through Pictures*, et cetera). There the words included in the course are not those which are determined by a frequency count but those judged absolutely necessary to express essential concepts and those which, in turn, can be used to express other concepts. The goal is the greatest possible economy. Hence all possible synonyms are avoided, as are the vocabulary items which can be adequately expressed in terms of others.

A third approach to frequency is one based on attempts to observe the words and concepts which are most common, universal, and essential in everyday speech. One such attempt was subsidized by the government of France in order to determine the minimum amount of French which would have to be taught to inhabitants of the French colonies. Another was conducted in Puerto Rico in recent years. The resultant lists are quite different from those based exclusively on written sources.

Analyses of this kind represent the "real" spoken language, not one that has been subjected to artificial simplification for pedagogical purposes, as in the "Basic" concept approach, nor one heavily weighted with literary vocabulary. Therefore they include, quite necessarily, the essential function words of the language, and they provide the wherewithal for the development of easy and natural communication in the shortest possible time. As far as the "content" words are concerned, however, even those selected in this manner are subject to the basic objection mentioned above: "essential" vocabulary is that required by what the speaker needs to communicate at any given moment, not that culled by any statistical process.

One more aspect of the fallacious statistical approach to vocabulary learning should be mentioned. Studies of running pages of current novels, stories, and plays have shown that a foreign learner will find practically as many new words per page on the thousandth page that he reads, as, for example, on the five-hundredth. While 40% or more of all the words on any page are among the most common, most of them are function words, pronouns, and the like. If, say, another 30% of the words are found in such a list as the Keniston *Standard List of Spanish Words and Phrases*, the reader is still faced with the remainder—the words of very low frequency according to existing word counts and words which do not appear at all in the statistics. No one knows for sure how many thousand pages a learner must read before the percentage of new words per page comes down to a level which permits reading without significant vocabulary problems, but it is clear that it is many more than we were led to think by the earlier enthusiasms over the frequency studies.

We shall return briefly to this phase of the vocabulary-learning problem in connection with the development of the skill of reading in the final chapter. Since the linguist concerns himself primarily with the spoken language and with structure, he can contribute little that is tangible to the problem of vocabulary learning in the larger environment of life, literature, and society. Our concluding remarks here are concerned primarily with vocabulary learning as part of the acquisition of basic skills.

The "overall" method of teaching vocabulary has been a subject of controversy and discussion for years. The preceding pages should make our views quite clear. Linguists join direct methodologists and others in strongly opposing the teaching of English–Spanish equivalents out of context and especially in the learning of lists of words. Such teaching will lead the student to structural fragmentation and to the most serious and often ridiculous errors in the use of vocabulary. In general, a vocabulary item should never be learned without putting it into the context of an utterance. Of course the student will be forced to use a dictionary at times, but if he consults the dictionary when reading Spanish, the context will be provided by the passage. On the other hand, if he consults it for the purpose of forming a Spanish sentence himself—a situation which should typically arise only in the more advanced stages of instruction—he must be trained to pay special attention to the sample sentences and contexts provided in the dictionary. Dictionaries which do not provide concise examples of the usage of words are obviously less than useless for composition or translation work.

Other methods of presenting vocabulary include explanation in English; explanation or definition in Spanish (*un perezoso es un hombre que no quiere trabajar*); the use of synonyms or a series of synonyms (*de prisa*: *rápidamente*, or *feliz*: *contento*); or of antonyms (*perezoso es el contrario de industrioso*). The last three methods used have the obvious advantage of "staying within Spanish." They do have certain disadvantages: for instance, the Spanish explanation may often not be clear and synonyms and antonyms never define with 100% clarity and precision. Yet they seem preferable to explaining or giving the equivalent in English. In a Spanish–to–Spanish association, both members of the association (for example, *levantarse = ponerse de pie; joven ← → viejo*) are useful. In an English–Spanish association one of the members is quite useless from the Spanish teacher's viewpoint. Thus, as we have pointed out in Chapter IV, the use of English seems indicated only if the Spanish explanation becomes confusing or uneconomical.

Not only in the matter of frequency but also in the problem of overall method, much confusion is evidently due to the failure to distinguish function words and grammatically determined words from content words. The former operate as part of, or are closely tied to, structure. To learn them correctly is primarily a matter of habit formation and automatic response, reinforced by the understanding of the grammatical structure. The content words, on the other hand, function because they refer to specific concepts and objects in specific situations. They must be learned in association with such specific situations. It is, therefore, in the realm of vocabulary building that organization according to situations of "units of experience" seems particularly appropriate.

In a linguistic approach we inevitably teach the function words and the grammatically determined words and their operation, and we should supply enough content vocabulary to "make the structures work" and to relate the structures to objective reality. Expansion of vocabulary is a later phase of learning, one to which the linguist's direct contribution becomes progressively less as the learner enters higher levels of cultural and literary sophistication.

CHAPTER X

Conclusion: The Cultural and Literary Context

The necessity of learning at least lexical meaning in a definite situational context brings up an important problem: What kind of context? When and at what stage should the context include literature, or "cultural" material? Again, these questions have been dealt with and discussed at length in many other publications. They are tremendously important questions, but they are beyond the realm of linguistics and thus beyond the scope of this text. We shall attempt only very brief answers. Culture, in the sense in which it is used by most linguists or cultural anthropologists, is the entire complex pattern of behavior and material achievements which are produced, learned, and shared by the members of a community. Language is part of culture, perhaps its most central part, because it is largely language that makes the learning and sharing of behavior possible. Being the central part of culture, it is probably also the best key to that culture. Once more, since it operates within a culture, it should be learned within contexts and situations which are part of that culture. Cultural anthropologists—some of them linguists—have tried to analyze the cultural patterns of society in a way that corresponds closely to the structural analysis of the linguistic patterns. These cultural patterns (for example, the structure of family life, child rearing, attitude toward parents and children, and basic similarities in points of view which reappear in different forms in all of those areas) should ultimately become apparent to the student of the foreign language. Those patterns of Spanish culture which clash with American patterns should receive special attention. Not only is the understanding of

172

Spanish a key to the understanding of Hispanic culture, but the reverse is also true. So far we have distinguished the lexical and the structural levels of meaning, but within a specific context there is often also the cultural level. Unless we understand the cultural situation in which an utterance is made, we may miss its full implication or meaning. The tie of language study with culture is not an "option" to be discussed in terms of the preferences of the individual teacher but actually a practical necessity. A student who reads about a Colombian going to a *farmacia* and pictures him going to an American drugstore is not getting the full meaning of what he is reading. A student who encounters a Spaniard's use of *Dios mío* and equates the effect of this exclamation with that which the literal equivalent might produce in an American environment does not grasp the cultural meaning level of the situation.

Linguists have usually tried to associate elementary language study with culture in the anthropological sense, rather than with "culture" as we so commonly use the word to mean the great artistic and literary achievements of a civilization. In some cases this may simply be due to the linguist's association with departments of anthropology rather than with departments of literature. There seems, nevertheless, to be some valid reason for the tie of language instruction with anthropological culture rather than Culture (and Literature), at least at the beginning level. The very understanding of literary works often depends on the grasp of the cultural environment in which their plots, characters, and themes operate. Of course, it is quite possible to approach culture through the literary work. Nor do we want to question the judicious use of literary works or the value of the learning or memorization of poetry in elementary courses. But we must keep in mind that the facets of culture presented in a literary work may be atypical; particular care must be taken to choose literary works which will produce a real understanding of culture, rather than the one-sided impression that could be gained from *Zaragüeta*, for example, or from the more naturalistic scenes of *Cañas y barro* or the evocative sketches of an Azorín. And what is said about the teaching of culture applies even more so to the realm of language: the language of the literary work is apt to be atypical. As a matter of fact, many literature scholars and linguists believe that the very essence of literature may be defined by its use of special structure and vocabulary. This is obviously the case in poetry. The very possibility of appreciating a literary work depends often on recognizing the departures it makes from the structure and vocabulary of normal, everyday speech patterns. Only after we have "learned Spanish" can we really appreciate the individual particularity, the style, of a Valle Inclán, an Azorín, or a García Lorca. There are great dangers in using the fruits of virtuosity as represented by the style of such authors as the vehicle for the learning of the language by beginners.

Yet there can be little disagreement with the argument that it is important to learn to read in the foreign language, so long as language study is a part of education in general, rather than training in a specialized skill for a specific practical end. Most educators would subscribe to the view that the reason for the inclusion of language study in our schools and colleges is educational rather than vocational and that some acquaintance with literate culture should form a part of the objective and content. Since we are writing here for teachers of foreign languages in our schools and colleges, we would be remiss if we did not say at least a word about the development of reading skill.

A learner who has been well trained by audio–lingual methods in the manipulation of patterns, and who controls all the important structures of the language is well prepared for learning to read rapidly and well. As we have shown in Chapter VI, Spanish orthography is relatively quite consistent. The first use of printed material should be vigorously overlapped with continuing practice in structures and intonational patterns, and immediate attention should be given to the visual recognition of the same inflections and agreements and the same phrasings—noun clusters, verb clusters, and organization of sentence patterns—as those practiced orally. As the learner reads, he must be kept moving, so that the cadences, stresses, and intonation patterns are triggered in him by the series of visual signals. At first he should meet no new vocabulary until he is completely skilled at recognizing these structures. Only then, and by an extension of the processes of substitution and transformation, can he begin to meet the problem of absorbing new content words without disruption of his awareness of structure.

Let us imagine that the black spaces in the following lines represent words that the reader does not recognize. In spite of these gaps the reader can tell quite a bit about the situation, and he should have practically no question about the organization of the sentences:

Recuerdo muy bien la primera vez que le ví. Estaba sentado en medio del patio, el ____ desnudo y las ____ ____adas en el suelo y reía silenciosamente. Al principio, creí que ____aba o sufría un tic pero, al llevarme la mano a la ____ y ____ar la vista, ____i que tenía los ojos ____os y reía con ____. Era un muchacho ____, con cara de ____, de piel ____a y ____a y pelo ____o y negro. Sus compañeros le ____aban, ____os a la sombra del ____ y uno con la ____ afeitada le ___ó desde la ____. La ____ al hombro, me acerqué a ver.

Assuming that our learner has been taught to read through this much before he tries to solve the meaning of new words, or look them up if he cannot solve them, he now goes back over the passage and looks for cognate words whose meaning is further clarified by the context. In the first two blanks he comes upon *torso* and *palmas*, and he begins to fill in the picture. The blank ending in *-aba* is a verb, and the verb is often the key to the content of a statement, so he looks up *bostezar* and finds that "At first I thought he was yawning or suffered a tic but . . ." Skipping over the phrase between commas, he wants to know what "I did" (___*í*). He at once recognizes the cognate *descubrir* and realizes that, contrary to what "I" thought at first, "I discovered that his eyes were ____ed and he was laughing with ____." He may want to get to the description in the next sentence, or it may seem more essential to get at what the friends (*compañeros*) were doing (*le ____ aban*). Possibly he recognizes the cognate *espiar*, or perhaps he has to look it up to realize that this boy's friends "were watching him, ____ed in the shade of the ____."

Now if we know ahead of time that the narrator was on guard duty in the guardhouse of a squalid army post, we might feel that we have a clear enough picture of the situation for the moment and decide to move on through the story, after which we would certainly find on another reading that many more of the words which at first were unknown have now taken on meaning. But note how much of this general sense of understanding is an outgrowth of the familiarity with structure that our earlier work with pronunciation, forms, syntax, and word-learning has provided; we know which words are nouns, which verbs, and which adverbs by the signals of ending morphemes, determiners, order of pronouns, and other structural signals we have come to know. Drawing upon the help of overlapping word forms and meanings, on the recognition of derivational suffixes and prefixes, and on the increasing complexity of our feeling for context and our growing linguistic and cultural sensitivity, we develop skills of inference, we learn to make the intelligent guess, we absorb word stocks by a process that becomes more and more like that of osmosis or like that which operates in our native tongue.

This process may be further illustrated by paragraphs in which made-up or "nonce" words represent a number of the nouns, adjectives and verbs. At first glance the result seems ludicrous to the sophisticated reader; but the situation is very close to that faced by the less experienced reader of a foreign language—or even one reading in his own language when the content involves vocabulary beyond the reader's experience.

As one reads through these paragraphs, it should become obvious that the assimilation of new vocabulary can be made more real and useful when the reader has learned how to make the "intelligent guess," even when he is left without the help of cognate vocabulary or of recognizable compounds within the language in question.

Example 1

The dogs were morping, the storts were singing, an acpul breeze was blowing through the moppins. A young man lay under a shady moppin, dreaming of his lum friend. Suddenly a murch rang out across the spibbing brook. The young man choomed his head with a start. At first he was spleetled, but then he molanized that it was only a loker poonting at a stort. As he copt up, he was at first unminely on his feet. He recovered his sloopance minchly, however, and strode off to find his lum.

Example 2

Una mañana de zuroto llegan los zuroteantes al campo; aparecen con el tolar y el sol. Llegan por tren, mirnados de maletas, quípidos por falta del aire libre y del sol. Les gusta el campo, pero tienen frilio a las vacas, los perros y los otros porinetos. Van a la cocina a pedir mate. Esa nolduba aromática que olvidan en la ciudad aquí les parece necesaria, como el aire o el pan. . . . Antes de irse a la cama, piden que les mardoquen caballos para el día siguiente. Se embuetan temprano, porque piensan levantarse temprano. Pero la mañana siguiente son los últimos en aparecer, a pesar de sus incolsos.

At this stage we may say that there is truth in the old adage that we learn to read by reading, just as we learn to live by living. But it is also true that the dividends returned from the investment of well-founded mastery of the structural patterns of the language will accrue as long as the learner continues to use the tongue he has learned and to familiarize himself with the culture of which that language is a manifestation.

Questions for Review
and Discussion

CHAPTER I: THE MEANING OF APPLIED LINGUISTICS

1. What extreme points of view obscure general understanding of the relationship between linguistics and language teaching?

2. What ideas about the application of linguistic science to language teaching seem to emanate from special or limited areas of interest?

3. What blame can be ascribed to workers in applied linguistics for limited general knowledge of the field?

4. How can linguistics contribute to the preparation of teaching materials:

   (a) in highlighting learners' difficulties?
   (b) in grammatical description?
   (c) in distinguishing **language** from **writing**?

5. What contributions has linguistics made to classroom practice:

   (a) in differentiating language behavior from description?
   (b) in selecting and arranging items for drill?

6. What contribution can historical (diachronic) linguistics make to language teaching?

7. What sort of problems can linguistics make no pretense of solving?

CHAPTER II: A LINGUISTIC TEACHING METHOD?

1. How does a linguist define language?

2. What of the concept that there is a "right" or divinely granted meaning for each symbol?

3. What is important about the concept of **system** in the definition?

4. Why do the "building stones" of the native language fail the learner as a basis for learning the foreign tongue?

5. Why does the existence of parallel structures in two languages actually handicap the learner in many situations?

6. Why are dictionaries termed a "necessary evil"?

7. What are the differences in the linguistic point of view toward grammar and the common traditional view:

(a) in the definition of the grammar of a language?

(b) in the role of grammatical awareness in learning?

(c) in the comparison of the native and the target language?

8. What is the concept of a universal grammar?

9. Even though two languages like Spanish and English are very much alike in much of their grammar, the linguist objects to a grammar–translation approach. Why?

10. What elements of method seem imposed by a linguistic approach?

11. What, then, is the role of *rules*?

12. Does this all apply if the objective is a reading knowledge only?

13. What about the "direct method" and its variants?

14. The "direct method-ist" wants to organize the teaching with reference to _____ . The linguist, with reference to _____ .

CHAPTER III: PSYCHOLOGICAL ASSUMPTIONS

1. What concrete (experimental) evidence do we have of the superiority of modern theories of learning or of "new key" methods?

2. How does behaviorist psychology define learning?

3. Differentiate between

(a) classical conditioning (associational shift)

(b) "instrumental" learning or reinforcement

4. Differentiate between the concepts of

(a) reflex or stimulus–response learning

(b) *Gestalt* or pattern perception

5. Discuss the interrelated roles of

(a) native language interference

(b) language as habit

(c) language as a system

6. How does linguistic teaching methodology support the pedagogical principal of producing correct responses rather than correcting errors?

7. What implications for language teaching does the concept of **intricate systems** have?

(8) In what way are **pattern-perception** and **stimulus–response** (habit formation) concepts in potential conflict? What can be done to resolve this conflict?

9. What are basic ways to combat the interference of mother-tongue habits?

10. What arguments support the idea of eliminating **lexical** or **content** meanings from initial instruction? What are the objections?

11. At present writing, how feasible does a course based on the provisional exclusion of lexical meanings appear to be?

12. What is the position of serious linguists, psychologists, and methodologists toward the often repeated claim that new key methods have the adolescent or adult learn a second language "just as the child learns his own language?"

CHAPTER IV: LINGUISTIC AND NON-LINGUISTIC TEACHING PROCEDURES

1. State some possible values in a controlled use of the native tongue in second language teaching.

2. Which of the above do you think is the principal value?

3 What are the arguments in favor of

(a) use of normal, colloquial English rather than formal?

(b) contrasting rather than parallel construction when both exist?

4. What are the dangers of use of the mother tongue?

5. What is meant by **structural meaning**?

6. What does the linguist mean by provisional exclusion of lexical meanings as basic to his analysis?

7. Does this mean that the learner should not be aware of the meaning of utterances?

8. Give examples of

(a) simple substitution drill.

(b) transformation drill.

9. Differentiate between a **teaching drill** and a **testing drill**.

10. What are the drawbacks of an old fashioned translation drill?

11. What are the drawbacks of blank-filling exercises?

12. Discuss briefly the following types of lesson organization;

(a) presentation of rules and vocabulary items and translation and blank-filling exercises.

(b) organization of a lesson around a grammatical concept, such as negative, the imperfect.

(c) organization around:

(1) a basic unit of experience, or topic

(2) grammatic–semantic concept, such as "the idea of obliga-tion" or "the immediate past."

13. What would be the linguistic approach to the organization of a teaching unit?

14. Discuss the use of picture-type visual aids for:

(a) teaching vocabulary only.

(b) eliciting descriptions as oral or written composition.

(c) learning of fixed sentences or phrases.

(d) general cultural reinforcement.

(e) dramatizing semantic–grammatical contrasts.

(f) signaling substitution items in pattern drill.

(g) signaling basic patterns as cues for transformation or expansion drills.

CHAPTER V: GENERAL PHONETICS AND PHONEMICS

1. Differentiate between **acoustic** and **articulatory** phonetics.

2. Define **vowel**; **consonant**; **semivowel**.

3. What are the three main elements involved in the classification of consonants?

4. List the major **manners of articulation** of consonants.

5. Name the **lower articulators**; the **upper articulators**.

6. Give an English word in which each of the following sounds occurs, and in each case underline the letters which represent the sound: ð; θ; ʒ; ʃ; dʒ; ŋ; ɹ.

7. What is meant by the "cardinal vowels"? What are they?

8. Using as examples the sounds represented by the letters which are in bold type, discuss the difference between the **phonetic** and the **phonemic** description of the sounds of a language.

(a) (Engl.) kin, can, cone, sack
(Span.) *quina, capa, cuña, frac*
(b) (Engl.) feel, fill, fail, fell
(Span.) *fila, disciplina, pena, perder*

9. What do you understand to be the importance of the principle of contrast as a basis for analysis and description of a language?

10. What is a **minimal pair**? How are minimal pairs used in the analysis of a language? What use can minimal pairs have in teaching a foreign language?

11. What are the implications of the following statement: ". . . certain nearly similar sounds are heard as the same in one language, but as different in another."

12. If the learner's "foreign accent" does not lie primarily in his inability to move his jaw muscles or tongue in the foreign language way, wherein does it lie?

13. What linguistic argument supports the statement that the learner must be able to hear and comprehend before he can be made to imitate and to speak?

14. Arrange the English words given as a series in phonemic contrast. Give the transcription used in the text for these vowel phonemes, and construct the corresponding triangle of English vowels: take, took, tuck, teak, toot, tech, toc, talk, tick, toque, tack.

CHAPTER VI: TEACHING PRONUNCIATION

1. List the Spanish consonant phonemes in the groups named, and give an example of each in a word; account for **major allophones**:

(a) voiceless stops
(b) voiced stop-fricatives
(c) fricatives (identify Castilian phonemes as such)
(d) affricates
(e) laterals
(f) nasals
(g) tap
(h) trill
(i) semiconsonants

2. Which of the above phonemes are absent from standard American English—or are so different from the related English phonemes as to cause a major learning problem? Discuss briefly.

3. Identify three Spanish **allophones** which correspond approximately to three separate phonemes in English, and a fourth which has no English counterpart. Discuss the corresponding learning problem.

4. Why are sounds of a foreign language, which seem roughly similar to sounds in the native language, sometimes quite difficult to learn?

5. What is meant by **auditory discrimination**?

6. Discuss (pro and con) the value of **bilingual contrastive pairs** such as Sp. *pico*—Engl. peak, *tono*—tone (for consonants) or *le*—lay, *voy*—boy, *ti*—tea (for vowels) in demonstrating differences between Spanish and English phonemes.

7. What is the point of drills arranged as follows?

> *vez/la vez*   *el día/ese día*
> *boca/la boca*   *!Bueno!/!Sé bueno!*
> *un bus/este bus*

8. Describe briefly some devices for helping English speakers to learn Spanish intervocalic [r].

9. What is the order of difficulty of articulation of [r] in various positions? What devices can be used to help learners master the most difficult of these articulations?

10. What are the main differences between [r] and [rr] (= [r̄])? What help can you give a beginner in acquiring [rr]?

11. List the English vowel phonemes and those of Spanish. What groups of English phonemes correspond, roughly, to each Spanish phoneme?

12. Name three major sources of interference from English in the mastery of Spanish vowels.

13. Describe (with examples) the effect of "linking" in Spanish when

(a) final consonant is followed by initial vowel.

(b) final vowel is followed by initial /b/, /d/, /g/.

(c) final vowel is followed by initial vowel.

14. Discuss the arguments against the use of an exaggerated clarity of pronunciation by the teacher.

15. Of what significance in helping the beginner to learn Spanish phrase or sentence rhythm is the fact that English uses four degrees of stress?

16. In particular, what effect does the typical alternation of a stronger stress with weak stress often have on the learner's pronunciation of Spanish vowels?

17. What is the main pitfall in carrying English intonation into Spanish?

18. Do Spanish and English use sentence stress and/or pitch in the same way to indicate changing emphasis or contrast?

19. Name some specific pronunciation difficulties associated with learning Spanish spelling:

(a) arising from within the Spanish system itself;

(b) arising from the learner's prior acquaintance with the spelling of English.

20. Discuss the matter of word boundaries in relation to Spanish speech and its written representation.

21. What of the often heard claim that reading and writing on the one hand, speaking and hearing on the other, reinforce each other when used in the initial stages of learning a foreign language?

CHAPTER VII: MORPHOLOGY

1. In French, the spoken form /kur/ may be 1st, 2nd or 3rd person singular, or 3rd person plural, in the present indicative. In English, "run" may be any person–number except 3rd person singular. What implication do these morphological facts have for the system of person–number indication in these languages, in comparison with Spanish?

2. What do the linguist and the beginner in foreign language have in common when it comes to identifying "parts of speech" (or "form classes") of words?

3. Why are such "words" as *que, me, lo, se, me, para* classed as "bound" morphemes (or, perhaps, semibound)?

4. In each of the lexical items listed below, determine whether one morpheme or more than one is involved. Mark off and number the morphemes, and identify them by type or function, as in the example.

$$\overset{1\quad 2\ 3}{}$$
Example: *cant/aba/s* (1: lexical; 2: tense–mood; 3: person–number.)

blancas	*desigual*
yegua	*persona*
hermanas	*artista*
comieron	*totalmente*

5. What is meant by saying that "gender in the noun is not a matter of inflection but of vocabulary?"

6. What are noun **markers**? Which ones show only singular/plural contrast, not masculine/feminine contrast?

7. Point out a most noticeable area of interference from native English in learning Spanish noun markers.

8. What formal criteria can be applied to distinguish Spanish adjectives from nouns?

9. All plural adjectives end in s. Does the plural morpheme for Spanish adjectives have one allomorph, two, or three? State what it is/ they are, with example(s).

10. Describe (with examples) a single-step transformation drill which can be used after a minimal-step presentation by substitution, to teach verb morphology with minimum dependence on the paradigmatic type of learning.

11. Where in the scale of devices for presentation and drilling of verb morphology would you place a drill calling for responses to *nosotros*; *tú*; *ellos Vd.*; *ella*; and so forth, in rapid sequence?

12. How would a patterned, audio-lingual, minimal-contrast treatment of verb morphology recognize or use paradigmatic arrangements?

13. What justification is there for considering the Spanish regular verbs as falling into two conjugation classes, with one subclass, rather than the traditional three?

14. Describe briefly the concept of tense–mood markers and person–number markers as a simplification of the regular verb system.

15. What is the argument for eliminating numbers, letters, person–number identifications, or images such as "shoes" or "boots," from the visual scheme for mastery of "stem-vowel changing" verbs?

16. (a) Give the "key forms" of *poner*.

(b) What should the learner be trained to associate automatically with the pair *digo–dices*, for example?

(c) Why must the additional reminder *trajeron* be included with the key forms of *traer*?

17. Besides roots, or **lexical** (vocabulary) **morphemes,** and grammatical or **structural morphemes**, what other type of morpheme can we recognize? Give examples.

CHAPTER VIII: TEACHING SYNTACTICAL PATTERNS

1. What is the difference between morphology and syntax?

2. Are the dividing lines entirely clear between morphology and syntax?

3. Describe the concept of "alternation in a slot" or substitution within a frame as a basis for analysis of syntactic items.

4. How does alternation in a slot relate to certain types of language drill?

5. Give an example of transformation as a basis for analyzing or classifying a group of structures.

6. Describe a pedagogical or drill application of the principle of transformation.

7. What importance for the understanding of syntax does the concept of **bound forms** or "satellites" have?

8. Name some forms inescapably bound to nouns; some bound to verbs; some ambiguous forms.

9. Wherein lie the larger number of syntactical difficulties for the English-speaking learner of Spanish—within the larger basic structure of the sentence, or within the formation of the basic clusters themselves? Elucidate with some examples.

10. What is the shortcoming of a solely analytical understanding of the structure of a noun or verb cluster?

11. What relation is there between pattern drill and the concept of automaticity as fundamental in the manipulation of noun and verb clusters?

12. What is meant by the statement that *se* (in the cluster *no se la he leído*) means one thing in response to one utterance and something else in response to another?

13. What is the place of a drill such as the one here outlined in the series of drills intended to teach a **cluster**:

Cue: *Ha leído Vd. la carta a su amigo?*
 Response: *No, señor, no se la he leído.*
 Ha leído Vd. los ejercicios a sus padres?
 Response: *No, señor, no se los he leído.*

14. Describe the steps which should precede a drill of the sort outlined in the preceding question.

15. Name the devices used by English and Spanish to signal grammatical meanings, or the relationships of words,

16. In which language, English or Spanish, is word order more extensively used as a basic grammatical devise? Give examples.

17. Which language makes the more extensive use of inflection? (Examples) Of agreement? (Examples)

18. What is meant by the statement that "the system of agreements is often more a matter of custom than of necessity?"

19. Discuss the role of **function words** in the English verb as compared with Spanish.

20. How can stress and intonation be said to be grammatical signals?

21. What implications for exercise writing and for successful teaching lie in the understanding of the several "media" or types of grammatical signal, and of their different distribution in different languages?

22. Give an example of each difference:

Spanish	*English*
(a) Inflection and agreement	No corresponding inflection or agreement
(b) Inflection	No inflection
(c) Inflection	Function word
(d) Function word	Inflection
(e) Function word and inflection	Word order
(f) Word order and/or intonation	Function words
(g) Intonation different from that of English	
(h) Word order, function word, etc., in Spanish corresponding to mere change of stress position in English.	

23. Describe a technique for teaching use and non-use of Spanish subject pronouns in contrast with English stress patterns; extend to teaching of use and non-use of "redundant" or emphatic constructions of object pronouns and possessives.

CHAPTER IX: TEACHING VOCABULARY

1. What is the danger of an excessive concern for the learning of large amounts of vocabulary early in the study of a foreign language?

2. To what level of language do we assign "words" such as of, for, although, and; or *para, conque, pero, como*?

3. Why are all words such as *él, su, algo, antes, más,* regarded as presenting more a grammatical problem than a lexical one to the learner?

4. What kinds of words are meant when we speak of **lexical items**?

5. What is the learner's basic problem when Spanish and English content words have similar use or meaning in one context but not in another?

6. Develop the statement, "a group of partly corresponding Spanish and English words may 'cut up' the same semantic area, but do so somewhat differently?"

7. Give an example of **structural difference** involved in the use of corresponding vocabulary.

8. Give an example of **conceptual difference** in vocabulary equivalences; discuss remedial measures for a specifically observed student confusion in this area.

9. Why, apparently, does an English speaker seldom confuse the following:

> get money   *conseguir dinero*
> get up   *levantarse*

while he may confuse other divergent equivalents? For example:

> leave town   *salir del pueblo* (or *de la ciudad*)
> leave money   *dejar dinero*

10. What can structural linguistics contribute to the clarification of a vocabulary problem which involves a confusion of concept, such as that between *conocer* and *saber*?

11. What can be done when purely structural devices fail?

12. Discuss the problems that arise in the area of cognate vocabulary. Use the following pairs (and others as needed) to illustrate your discussion.

> *English*   *Spanish*
> doctor   *doctor*
> editor   *editor*
> pan   *pan*
> conference   *conferencia*
> faculty   *facultad*

13. Illustrate an exercise type which can be constructed to resolve conflicts of the sort pointed out in Question 12.

14. Discuss idioms in terms of

  (a) contrasts between native and "target" languages

  (b) their place within a given language.

15. Differentiate the pedagogical problems involved in teaching cognate words for active use as opposed to preparing for recognition or inferential guessing of cognates met in reading.

16. Discuss some of the form correspondences among suffixes and prefixes which may be exploited to help expand recognition vocabulary.

17. Discuss the matter of relative frequency as a basis for the selection of words to be learned in the two main areas of function or grammatical words, and content or lexical words.

18. Discuss the concept of essential vocabulary as a basis for selecting words to be taught. How does this idea differ from the "basic" idea of *Basic English*, et cetera.

19. What has been observed of late about the proportion of new words which can be expected to occur on a page of ordinary prose?

20. Discuss ideas for the learning and expansion of content vocabulary to which the linguist would subscribe.

CHAPTER X: CULTURE AND READING

1. How does an anthropologist define culture? How does this definition differ from what we ordinarily mean by Culture in "polite society"?

2. Which definition does the linguist have first in mind when he considers language as an element of a culture? Why?

3. Discuss possible interrelations of the contradictory ideas of

(a) approaching Culture through culture
(b) approaching culture through Culture.

4. What lies behind the statement that "there are great dangers in using the fruits of virtuosity . . . as the vehicle for the learning of a language by beginners?"

5. What relationship does the linguist, with all his concern for audio–lingual methods in the manipulation of patterns, see between these methods and the development of reading skills?

6. Why is it proposed that reading should be limited at first to materials already mastered by audio-lingual methods, and that in the early stages no new vocabulary should be presented in written form?

7. What devices can be used for the development of reading skills—including the solution by inference (guessing) of many unfamiliar words—after the beginner has become completely skilled at recognizing the visual symbols of basic patterns?

8. Comment on the statement, "Vocabulary is a function of life experience."

9. Comment on the selection of vocabulary for learning on the basis of frequency lists.

10. Comment on the "basic" vocabulary idea, as presented in such forms as *Basic English*.

Bibliography

This bibliography docs not claim to be exhaustive. The books listed present in greater detail some of the material dealt with in this book. Many matters of great importance have been dealt with in journals rather than in books, but we have not listed articles in general for the reason that there are so very many of them.

The symbol (R) before a reference means that it is particularly recommended because it contains documentation or additional reading supplementing chapters of the text. Items preceded by an asterisk aim at imparting a technical knowledge beyond the minimum needed for the application of linguistic principles in the classroom. Those marked with two asterisks presuppose some prior knowledge of linguistics and are likely to be of use only to the reader with special technical interests.

Theoretical Foundations (General Linguistics, Phonetics, Psychology)

    **BACH, EMMON. *An Introduction to Transformational Grammar*. New York: Holt, Rinehart and Winston, Inc., 1964.
    *BLOCH, BERNARD, and TRAGER, GEORGE. *Outline of Linguistic Analysis*. Baltimore, Md.: Linguistic Society of America, 1942. Reprinted in 1950.
    *BLOOMFIELD, LEONARD. *Language*. New York: Holt, 1945.
(R) CARROLL, JOHN B. *The Study of Language*. Cambridge, Mass.: Harvard University Press, 1953.
    CARROLL, JOHN B. "Research on Teaching Foreign Languages," in GAGE, NATHANIEL L., *Handbook of Research on Teaching*. Chicago: Rand McNally Co., 1963.
    **CHOMSKY, NOAM. *Syntactic Structures*. Leiden: Moton and Company, 1957.

*EISENSON, JON. *The Psychology of Speech.* New York: Appleton-Century-Crofts, 1946.

FERGUSON, CHARLES E. (Supervisor). *Teaching a Second Language* (Series of 5 films on: (1) Nature of Language, (2) The Sounds of Language, (3) Organization of Language, (4) Words and Their Meanings, (5) Modern Techniques in Language Teaching), Teaching Manual to accompany film. Washington, D.C.: Center for Applied Linguistics, 1963; Teaching Film Custodians, New York, 1963.

*GLEASON, H. A., JR. *An Introduction to Descriptive Linguistics.* New York: Holt, 1955.

*HAAS, WILLIAM, UITTI, KARL D., and WELLS, RULON. *Linguistics.* Englewood Cliffs, N.J.: Prentice-Hall, Inc., 1964.

(R)HALL, ROBERT A., JR. *Linguistics and Your Language.* New York: Doubleday and Company, 1960.

**HARRIS, ZELLIG S. *Structural Linguistics.* Chicago: University of Chicago Press, Phoenix Books 1963.

*HEFFNER, R. M. S. *General Phonetics.* Madison, Wis.: University of Wisconsin Press, 1949.

*HILL, ARCHIBALD A. *Introduction to Linguistic Structures.* New York: Harcourt, Brace, 1958.

*HOCKETT, CHARLES F. *A Course in Modern Linguistics.* New York: Macmillan, 1958.

*HOIJER, HARRY, Editor. *Language and Culture.* Conference on the Interrelations of Language and other Aspects of Culture. Chicago: University of Chicago Press, 1954.

*HUGHES, JOHN P. *The Science of Language. An Introduction to Linguistics.* New York: Random House, 1962.

*INTERNATIONAL PHONETIC ASSOCIATION. *The Principles of the International Phonetic Association, Being a Description of the International Phonetic Alphabet and the Manner of Using it.* London: International Phonetic Association, 1953.

JOOS, MARTIN, Editor. *Readings in Linguistics; the development of descriptive linguistics in America since 1925.* New York: American Council of Learned Societies, Columbia University Press, 1958.

*MARTINET, ANDRÉ. *La Description Phonologique.* Paris-Genève: Société de publications romanes et françaises; Librairie Droz, 1956.

———. *Eléments de linguistique générale.* Paris: Collection Armand Colin, 1960.

**OGDEN, C. K., and RICHARDS, I. A. *The Meaning of Meaning.* New York: Harcourt, Brace, 1923.

*OSGOOD, CHARLES, and SEBEOK, THOMAS, Editors. *Psycho-linguistics, a Survey of Theory and Research Problems.* Supplement to International Journal of American Linguistics. Baltimore, Md.: Waverley Press, 1954.

**PIKE, KENNETH. *Language, in Relation to a Unified Theory of the Structure of Human Behavior.* Glendale, Calif.: Summer Institute of Linguistics, Part I, 1954; Part II, 1955; Part III, 1960.

**———. *Phonemics: A Technique of Reducing Languages to Writing.* Ann Arbor, Mich.: University of Michigan Press, 1947.

*————. *Phonetics: A Critical Analysis of Phonetic Theory and a Technique for the Practical Description of Sounds.* Ann Arbor, Mich.: University of Michigan Press, 1943.

*POTTER, SIMEON. *Modern Linguistics.* New York: W. W. Norton and Co., 1964.

RIVERS, WILGA M. *The Psychologist and the Foreign-Language Teacher.* Chicago: The University of Chicago Press, 1964.

SAPIR, EDWARD. *Language: An Introduction to the Study of Speech.* New York: Harcourt, Brace, 1921.

*SAPORTA, SOL, Editor. *Psycholinguistics: A Book of Readings.* New York: Holt, Rinehart and Winston, 1961.

*SAUSSURE, FERDINAND DE. *Cours de Linguistique Générale.* Paris: Payot, 1955.

*————. *Course in General Linguistics* (translation of the *Cours de linguistique générale*, Wade Baskin, translator). New York: Philosophical Library, 1959.

*SKINNER, B. F. *Verbal Behavior.* New York: Appleton-Century-Crofts, 1957.

*WEINREICH, URIEL. *Languages in Contact.* New York: Publications of the Linguistic Circle of New York, No. 1, 1953.

*WHATMOUGH, JOSHUA. *Language, a Modern Synthesis.* London: Secker & Warburg, 1956.

Applied Linguistics (general)

ALLEN, HAROLD B. *Readings in Applied English Linguistics.* New York: Appleton-Century-Crofts, 1958.

BELASCO, SIMON, Editor, *Anthology for Use with a Guide for Teachers in NDEA Language Institutes.* Boston: D. C. Heath and Co., 1961.

————. Editor. "Introduction" to Cárdenas, *Applied Linguistics: Spanish,* q.v.

*BLOOMFIELD, LEONARD. *Outline Guide for the Practical Study of Foreign Languages.* Baltimore, Md.: Linguistic Society of America, 1942.

CÁRDENAS, DANIEL. *Applied Linguistics: Spanish; A Guide for Teachers.* Boston: D. C. Heath and Co., 1961. Introduction by Simon Belasco, General Editor.

CORNELIUS, EDWIN T., JR. *Language Teaching (A Guide for Teachers of Foreign Languages).* New York. Crowell, 1953.

(R) FELDMAN, DAVID M. *The Modern Teaching of Spanish* (independent study). Boulder, Colo.: University Extension Division, University of Colorado, 1963.

FRIES, CHARLES C. *Teaching and Learning English as a Foreign Language.* Ann Arbor, Mich.: University of Michigan Press, 1945.

(R) LADO, ROBERT. *Linguistics Across Cultures, Applied Linguistics for Language Teachers.* Ann Arbor, Mich.; University of Michigan Press, 1957.

(R) ————. *Language Teaching: A Scientific Approach.* New York: McGraw-Hill Book Co., 1964.

MOULTON, WILLIAM G. "Linguistics and Language Teaching in the United States, 1940–1960," in *Trends in European and American Linguistics*. Utrecht: Spectrum, 1962, pp. 82–109.

UNESCO. *The Teaching of Modern Languages*. A Volume of Studies Deriving from the International Seminar Organized for the Secretariat of UNESCO in Ceylon in 1953. Paris, 1955.

General Methodology, Classroom and Laboratory Techniques; Materials

(R) BROOKS, NELSON. *Language and Language Learning; Theory and Practice*. New York: Harcourt, Brace, 1960.

CAPRETZ, PIERRE J., Project Director. *Audio-Lingual Techniques for Teaching Foreign Languages*. (Includes a 60-minute film on the teaching of French.) Washington, D.C.: Norwood Films, 1963.

COCHRAN, ANNE. *Modern Methods of Teaching English as a Foreign Language: a guide to modern materials with particular reference to the Far East*. Washington, D.C.: Educational Service, 1954.

CONNECTICUT STATE DEPARTMENT OF EDUCATION. *Foreign Languages, grades 7–12*. Curriculum Bulletin Series, No. 5, tentative. Hartford, Conn.: State Department of Education, 1958.

COUNCIL OF CHIEF STATE SCHOOL OFFICERS. *Purchase Guide*. For Programs in Science, Mathematics, Foreign Languages. Boston: Ginn, 1959.

EASTON, ESTHER M., and NORTON, LYNN L. *Source Materials for Secondary School Teachers of Foreign Languages*. U.S. Department of Health, Education and Welfare, Office of Education, Circular 1962, No. 681. Washington, D.C.: Superintendent of Documents, 1962.

FINN, JAMES D., and PERRIN, DONALD G. *Teaching Machines and Programmed Learning, A Survey of the Industry—1962*. Washington, D.C.: U.S. Department of Health, Education and Welfare, Office of Education, OE–34019, 1962.

HIRSCH, RUTH. *Audio-Visual Aids in Language Teaching*. Monograph Series on Languages and Linguistics, No. 5. Washington D.C.: The Institute of Language and Linguistics, School of Foreign Service, Georgetown University, 1954.

HOLTON, JAMES S., KING, PAUL E., GUSTAVE, MATHIEU, and POND, KARL S. *Sound Language Teaching, the state of the art today*. New York: University Publishers, 1961.

HUEBENER, THEODORE, *Audio-Visual Techniques in Teaching Foreign Languages, a Practical Handbook*. New York: New York University Press, 1960.

———. *How to Teach Foreign Languages Effectively*. New York: New York University Press, 1959.

HUTCHINSON, JOSEPH C. *Modern Foreign Languages in High School: The Language Laboratory*. Washington, D.C.: Office of Education, 1961.

JESPERSEN, OTTO. *How to Teach a Foreign Language*. New York: Macmillan, 1904.

JODICO, DON R. *Guidelines to Language Teaching in Classroom and Laboratory*. Washington, D.C.: Electronic Teaching Laboratories, 1961.

JOHNSTON, MARJORIE C., and SEERLEY, CATHERINE C. *Foreign Language Laboratories in Schools and Colleges*. Washington, D.C.: U.S. Department of Health, Education and Welfare, Bulletin 1959, No. 3.

KONE, ELLIOT H., Editor. *Language Laboratories—Modern Techniques in Teaching Foreign Languages*. New York Bulletin of the Connecticut Audio-Visual Education Association, Vol. 19, 1959–60.

(R) LADO, ROBERT. *Language Testing*, The Construction and Use of Foreign Language Tests. London: Longmans, Green and Co., Ltd., 1961.

———. See also under *Applied Linguistics*, above.

LÉON, P. R. *Laboratoire de langues et correction phonétique, Essai méthodologique*. Paris: Didier, 1962.

(R) LOUISIANA FOREIGN LANGUAGE TEACHERS' ASSOCIATION, Editor. *Foreign Language Laboratory Techniques* (supplement of *LFLTA News Letter*). Baton Rouge, La., 1956.

(R) MARTY, FERNAND L. *Language Laboratory Learning*. Wellesley, Mass.: Audio-Visual Publications, 1960.

———. *Programming a Basic Foreign Language Course: Prospects for Self-Instruction*. Hollins, Va.: Audio–Visual Publications, 1962.

(R) MÉRAS, EDMOND A. *A Language Teacher's Guide*. New York: Harper, 1954.

MORTON, F. RAND. "The Language Laboratory as a Teaching Machine," *International Journal of American Linguistics*, XXVI (1960), 113–166.

NEWMARK, MAXIM, Editor. *Twentieth Century Modern Language Teaching*. New York: Philosophical Library, 1948.

NOSTRAND, HOWARD LEE, et al. *Research on Language Teaching: an Annotated International Bibliography for 1945–1961*. Seattle: University of Washington Press, 1962.

(R) O'CONNOR, PATRICIA. *Modern Foreign Languages in High School: Pre-reading Instruction*. OE-2700, Bulletin 1960, No. 9, Washington, D.C.

OINAS, FELIX J., Editor. *Language Teaching Today*. Report of the Language Laboratory Conference Held at Indiana University, January 22–23, 1960. Research Center in Anthropology, Folklore and Linguistics, Publication Fourteen, Indiana University, Bloomington, Ind., October, 1960.

(R) OLLMAN, MARY J., Editor. *Selective List of Materials*. New York: Modern Language Association, 1962.

PLEASANTS, JEANNE VARNEY, et al. *Audio-Visual Aids and Techniques in the Teaching of Foreign Languages*. A Report of the Committee on Teaching Aids and Techniques of the 1955 Northeast Conference on the Teaching of Foreign Languages, 1956.

(R) STACK, EDWARD M. *The Language Laboratory and Modern Language Teaching*. New York: Oxford University Press, 1960.

WALSH, DONALD D. *What's What. A List of Useful Terms for the Teacher of Modern Languages*. New York: The Modern Language Association of America, 1963.

Spanish Phonetics, Teaching of Spanish Phonetics

ALARCOS LLORACH, EMILIO. *Fonología española (según el método de la Escuela de Praga)*. Madrid: Gredos, 1950. 160 pp.

(R) BOWEN, J. DONALD, and STOCKWELL, ROBERT P. *Patterns of Spanish Pronunciation, a Drillbook*. Chicago: The University of Chicago Press, 1960.

CÁRDENAS, DANIEL. *Introducción a una comparación fonológica del español y del inglés*. Washington, D.C: Center for Applied Linguistics, 1960.

Entrambasaguas, Joaquín de. *Síntesis de pronunciación española*. Madrid: Consejo Superior de Investigaciones Científicas, 1952. 156 pp.

(R) HADEN, ERNEST F. *How to Pronounce Spanish*. New York: Holt, 1953.
Analyzes Spanish pronunciation, with illustrations. Provides drill exercises. Accompanied by a 10" LP record.

NAVARRO TOMÁS, TOMÁS. *Manual de entonación española*, 2nd. ed. New York: Hispanic Institute, 1948. 306 pp. With four phonograph records.

(R) ————. *Manual de pronunciación española*. Publicaciones de la Revista de filología española, Madrid, 1932. Lithoprinted reprint, cuarta edición corregida y aumentada. New York: Hafner, no date.

————. *Spanish Pronunciation and Intonation Exercises*. Linguaphone Institute, New York, no date. Five double-sided 10" records with textbook.

————, and ESPINOSA, AURELIO M. *A Primer of Spanish Pronunciation*. Boston Sanborn, 1926.

General Works on Spanish Structure (Morphology, Syntax)

ALARCOS LLORACH, EMILIO. *Gramática estructural (según la escuela de Copenhague y con especial atención a la lengua española)*. Madrid: Editorial Gredos, 1951. 129 pp.

ALONSO, AMADO, and HENRÍQUEZ UREÑA, PEDRO. *Gramática castellana*, 3rd ed. Buenos Aires: Editorial Losada, 1943. Primer curso, 238 pp. Segundo curso, 239 pp.

BELLO, ANDRÉS. *Gramática de la lengua castellana*, 23rd ed., with notes by D. Rufino José Cuervo. Paris: Andrés Blot, Editor, 1928. 366 pp. (+ 160 pp. Notas).

KENISTON, HAYWARD. *Spanish Syntax List*. Publications of the Committee on Modern Languages. New York: Holt, 1937. 278 pp.

LENZ, RODOLFO. *La oración y sus partes*, 3rd ed. Madrid: Tip. y Enc. de Senén Martín, 1935. 571 pp.

RAMSEY, MARATHON MONTROSE (rev. by Robert K. Spaulding). *A Textbook of Modern Spanish*. New York: Holt, 1956.

REAL ACADEMIA ESPAÑOLA. *Gramática de la lengua española* (new corrected ed.). Madrid: Espasa-Calpe, S.A., 1931. 534 pp.

SILVA-FUENZALIDA, ISMAEL. *Spanish, Manual and Anthology of Applied Linguistics*, pp. S, 1–S,58. See Section (B) above, Simón Belasco *et al.*

Spanish Vocabulary (Synonyms, Cognates, Frequency)

BUCHANAN, MILTON A. *A Graded Spanish Word Book.* Publications of the American and Canadian Committee on Modern Languages, Vol. III. Toronto: Toronto University Press, 1927. Reprinted in 1941.

GARCÍA HOZ, VICTOR. *Vocabulario usual, vocabulario común y vocabulario fundamental; determinación y analysis de sus factores.* Madrid: Consejo Superior de Investigaciones Científicas, Instituto San José de Calasanz, 1953.

GILI GAYA, SAMUEL. *Diccionario de sinónimos.* Barcelona: Spes, 1958.

IRÍZAR Y AVILÉS, PEDRO DE. *Sinónimos: repertorio de palabras usuales castellanas de sentido análogo, semejante o approximado.* Quinta edición aumentada por Homero Serís. Barcelona; Seix y Barral, 1932.

KALVERAM, CARLOS. *Diccionario de ideas y expresiones afines.* Madrid: Aguilar, 1956.

(R) KENISTON, HAYWARD. *A Basic List of Spanish Words and Idioms.* Chicago: University of Chicago Press, 1933.

————. *A Spanish Idiom List, Selected on the Basis of Range and Frequency of Occurrence.* Publications of the American and Canadian Committees on Modern Languages, Vol. XI, New York, 1937.

(R) LAROUSSE. *Pequeño Larousse Ilustrado.* Paris: Librairie Larousse, 1951.

NUNN, MARSHALL E., and VAN SCOY, HERBERT A. *Glossary of Related Spanish-English Words.* University of Alabama Studies, Number 5. University, Ala.: University of Alabama Press, 1949.

REAL ACADEMIA ESPAÑOLA. *Diccionario de la lengua española.* Madrid: Espasa-Calpe, S.A., 1936.

RODRÍGUEZ BOU, ISMAEL, Director. *Recuento de vocabulario espanol.* Río Piedras, Puerto Rico: University of Puerto Rico, 1952. 2 vols. in 3 parts.

————. *A Study of the Parallelism of English and Spanish Vocabularies.* Río Piedras, Puerto Rico: Superior Educational Council of Puerto Rico, University of Puerto Rico, Rico, 1950.

RUIZ CÁRDENAS, ALBERTO. *Nuevo diccionario de sinónimos y palabras afines . . .* México: Publicaciones Indoamérica, 1956

SAINZ DE ROBLES, FEDERICO CARLOS. *Ensayo de un diccionario español de sinónimos.* Madrid: Aguilar, 1946.

ZAMORA, ANTONIO. *Diccionario de sinónimos españoles.* Buenos Aires: Editorial Claridad, 1954.

Spanish Textbooks

The books listed here are intended for use in secondary schools, except where otherwise indicated. The list is limited to programs avowedly based on linguistic attitudes and to certain multiple-objective series for which important supplementary materials which are in tune with new-key methodologies have been provided.

AGARD, FREDERICK B., WILLIS, R. S., JR., and PARATORE, ANGELA. *Speaking and Writing Spanish.* New York: Holt, 1951. 2 vols.

An early and partial application of pattern drills; comparative and nontraditional grammatical descriptions. Dialogues, etc., for oral practice. Intended for college use primarily.

BOLINGER, DWIGHT, *et al*. *Modern Spanish*. A project of the Modern Language Association. New York: Harcourt, Brace, 1960.

Detailed treatment of phonetics, intonation, et cetera; new vocabulary taught in context of dialogues to be memorized; grammar taught by exposition and paradigm, often new and ingenious. Very extensive use of pattern drills, mostly of the transformation types; cultural readings extensive in latter part of the book. Intended primarily for use in colleges.

BRENES, EDIN, ADEY, MARGARET, and SMITH, GEORGE E. *Learning Spanish the Modern Way*. New York: McGraw-Hill Text–Film Division, 1961.

Texts, 14 reels of sound films and tapes. Total program is for full high school course.

BULL, WILLIAM E. (Originator and Director). *A Visual Grammar of Spanish*. Los Angeles: University of California, 1961.

A set of over 400 colorful posters systematically organized to portray significant contrasts in Spanish syntax, morphology, idiom and vocabulary, through pictures suggestive of the contrasts in objective reality to which linguistic contrasts correspond. Manual of instructions. Intended to accompany or supplement any basic text.

DA SILVA, ZENIA SACKS. *Beginning Spanish, A Concept Approach*. New York: Harper & Row, 1963.

Active use of Spanish, understanding of concepts, provision for reading as well as conversation. Correlated with laboratory work; tapes.

GINSBURG, RUTH R., and NASSI, ROBERT. (1) *Speaking Spanish*. (2) *Primera Vista*. (3) *Segunda Vista*. Rockleigh, N.J: Allyn & Bacon.

Audio-lingual plus features of the multiple-objective text. The first title is introductory or for the junior high school level.

GOWLAND, MARIANO E. *Español, Primer Curso*. Milwaukee: Bruce Publ. Co., 1963.

Pattern drills, fold-out picture aids, dialogues; occasionally uses explicit contrastive analyses of English and Spanish.

HANSEN, TERRENCE L. and WILKINS, ERNEST J. *Español a lo vivo*. New York: Blaisdell Publishing Co., 1964.

Pattern drill teaching, with dialogues of manageable length and expositions brief and intelligible to the traditional teacher. Appears good for audio-lingual teaching in typical college situation.

JARRETT, EDITH MOORE, and MCMANUS, BERYL J. M. *El Camino Real*. 3rd ed. Boston: Houghton Mifflin, 1960.

Dialogues and other materials for oral drills, including a pre-reading program, have been added to this widely used book. Tapes and records available.

LA GRONE, GREGORY G., MCHENRY, ANDREA SENDÓN, and O'CONNOR, PATRICIA. *Español. Entender y Hablar*. New York: Holt, Rinehart and Winston, 1961.

Second level: *Español: Hablar y Leer*, 1962.

Third level, by Elizabeth Keesee, La Grone, and O'Connor, 1963.

MUELLER, KLAUS A., VARGAS, LUIS, FRANCO, ROBERTO B., and WOODWARD, DAVID. *Spanish for Secondary Schools* (first level, Parts One and Two). Boston: D. C. Heath & Co., 1963.

This text features the use of visual cues for much of its pattern drill. An interesting and challenging addition to the field.

O'CONNOR, PATRICIA, and HADEN, ERNEST F. *Oral Drill in Spanish*, 2nd. ed. New York: Houghton Mifflin, 1963.

An extensive collection of pattern drills covering the whole range of Spanish syntax and many idiomatic structures. Section on phonetics. No grammatical expositions. A useful supplementary item.

OLLER, JOHN W., in collaboration with the Department of Education of the Republic of Mexico. *La Familia* Fernández. Wilmette, Ill.: Encyclopedia Britannica Films, Inc., 1964.

An elaborate complex of 54 sound films, coordinated with equal number of taped exercises and drills, test tapes, film strips; student's text for reading and writing, and visually cued text. Based on concept of language in units of experience.

Pathéscope–Berlitz Audio-Visual Spanish Language Series. Pathéscope Educational Films, New Rochelle, N.Y., 1959.

One of the first large scale attempts to integrate film strips, discs or tapes, and scripts in a full course.

RICHARDS, J. P., METCALF, RUTH C., and GIBSON, CHRISTINE. *Spanish Self-Taught through Pictures*. New York: Pocket Books, 1950.

Application of the *Basic English* idea and of the conceptual approach with the aid of stick figures.

STARR, WILMARTH H., PELLEGRINO, ALFRED G., and CASAVANT, HENRI A. *Functional Spanish*. New York: American Book, 1955.

Applies the *minimal step* concept to some degree, and uses pattern drills which are mainly triggered by English.

STAUBACH, CHARLES N., and WALSH, JOHN W. *First-Year Spanish, Revised*. Boston: Ginn, 1961.

A new revision of a well known high school book, with pattern drills and other oral–aural exercises increased and accompanied by a new and extensive set of tape-recorded drills, including a pre-reading program.

STAUBACH, CHARLES N., ELDON, JANE R., and WALSH, JOHN W. *Second-Year Spanish, Revised*. Boston: Ginn, 1962.

Continuation of *First-Year Spanish, Revised*, with the same increased emphasis on pattern drills.

THOMPSON, MARY T., Coordinator. *A-LM. Audio–Lingual Materials: Listening, Speaking, Reading, Writing. Spanish Level One*. New York: Harcourt, Brace, and World, Inc., 1961; *Spanish Level Two* (Harcourt, Brace, and World, Inc., 1962); *Spanish Level Threee* (Harcourt, Brace, and World, 1963).

Complete series of audio-lingual materials for junior high school and high school utilizing conversations, structural recomposition of essential elements, pattern practice. Tapes, records for the pupils, tests, teacher editions, teachers manual, etc., are available.

TREVIÑO, SOLOMON N. *Spoken Spanish*. Boston: Heath, 1945.

The first linguistically oriented Spanish text generally available; dialogues, use and re-use of basic sentences, but lacks substitution and transformation type pattern drills.

TURK, LAUREL H., and ALLEN, EDITH M. *El español al dia*. 3rd ed. Boston: Heath, 1963.

A new revision utilizing audio-lingual principles; retains much of original multiple-objective material, but tapes and pattern drills increase usefulness.

WOLFE, DAVID L., HADLICH, ROGER L., and INMAN, JOHN G. *A Structural Course in Spanish*. New York: Macmillan, 1963.

Unusual in the care with which it teaches through pattern drills, with careful differentiation from testing drills. Also unusual in taking the student through most sentence structure types before completing study of all persons and types of verbs.

Journals dealing with pedagogical problems

Hispania. American Association of Teachers of Spanish and Portuguese, University of Connecticut, Stores, Conn.

International Review of Applied Linguistics in Language Teaching, Julius Groos Verlag, Heidelberg, Germany.

Language Learning: A Journal of Applied Linguistics. English Language Institute, The University of Michigan, Ann Arbor, Mich.

The Linguistic Reporter. Center for Applied Linguistics, 1346 Connecticut Ave., N.W., Washington, D.C.

ML Abstracts. Department of Foreign Languages and Literatures, California State College, Fullerton, Calif. (Summaries of pedagogical research, methodological articles.)

BCDEFGHIJ   706987

ABOUT THE AUTHORS

Robert L. Politzer received his B.A. from Washington University in 1941, and his M.A. in 1942 from the same institution; in 1947 he earned a Ph.D. in French and Romance Philology from Columbia University, and in 1950 the degree of Doctor of Social Science from the New School of Social Research. He has taught at the University of Michigan, Harvard University, the University of Washington, and Columbia University, and held a Guggenheim Fellowship for the study of Italian linguistics. He is now a professor at Stanford University, responsible for the education and training of foreign language teachers.

The author of *The Language of the Eighth Century Lombardic Documents, Romance Trends in Late Latin Documents from Italy, Active Review of French*, and of the companion to this volume, *Teaching French: An Introduction to Applied Linguistics*, Dr. Politzer has also published many articles in the fields of Vulgar Latin, French and Italian Linguistics, French Literature, and Methodology and Problems of Language Teaching and Learning. He has served as chairman for several of the committees that formulated the widely used Proficiency Tests for Foreign Language Teachers.

Charles N. Staubach is Professor of Spanish at the University of Arizona. He received the degrees of A.B., M.A., and Ph.D. from the University of Michigan, and joined its teaching staff as Instructor in Spanish in 1930. For many years Dr. Staubach was in charge of basic instruction in Spanish at Michigan, and he was Chairman of the Department of Romance Languages from 1951 to 1959.

The author's activities outside these positions have been varied. He pursued researches in France and Spain in 1933 and 1934. Under the sponsorship of the United States Department of State he was a visiting professor of English in Bogotá, Colombia, from 1944 to 1945. He was technical adviser to a Language Institutes film project under the NDEA in the summer of 1959, has been visiting professor in NDEA Summer Language Institutes at the University of Missouri and Iona College, and in the Spanish Institute at the University of New Mexico (1963–1965). He served as an evaluator of NDEA Institutes in Mexico in the summer of 1964. Publications by Dr. Staubach include a number of articles on Spanish language and literature and on language pedagogy; two books concerning English as a foreign language; two anthologies of Spanish-American magazine articles; and a high school Spanish series, *First-Year Spanish* and *Second-Year Spanish* (Ginn and Company).

THIS BOOK WAS SET IN

TIMES ROMAN AND PERPETUA TYPES

BY J. W. ARROWSMITH.

IT WAS DESIGNED BY THE STAFF OF

BLAISDELL PUBLISHING COMPANY.